Never Stop on a Hill

Never Stop on a Hill

. . .

Chris D. Lewis

Author photograph by Vincenzo Sergi

ISBN: 1535154462
ISBN 13: 9781535154468

Table of Contents

Dedication · vii
Introduction ·ix

"Never Stop on a Hill" · 1
The Study · 7
Why Leadership? · 12
What Is Leadership? · 28
Management, Leadership...or Both? · 37
Leaders: Born This Way? · 47
We Are Nothing without Trust· 59
Communication Is Key · 71
People and the Need to Connect with Them · · · · · · · · · · · · · · 86
Emotional Common Sense · 103
Ethical Behavior and Acting with Integrity · · · · · · · · · · · · · 112
Fair Is Fair! · 126
Only the Resilient Will Survive · 131
Just Make a Decision! · 142
Other Vital Leadership Qualities · 163
    Encouraging Innovation · 163
    Being Accountable in All We Do · · · · · · · · · · · · · · · · · 169
    Supporting and Caring · 175
    Setting the Right Example · 176
Change Leadership · 181

The Good, the Bad, and the Ugly · 194
It's a "Me, My, I" World · 217
Forging and Maintaining Relationships · 224
Personal Attacks: Survival of the Fittest · · · · · · · · · · · · · · · · · · · 236
Development and Selection · 246
Police Associations: "Can't Live with Them…" · · · · · · · · · · · · · · · 257
Media: Problem or Solution? · 273
What Are Our People Saying about Leadership? · · · · · · · · · · · · · · · 288
The Leaders on Leadership · 304
We Can Never Forget Our Veterans · 312

Final Thoughts · 319
Afterword · 323
References · 325
About the Author · 343

Dedication

• • •

This book and the many months that I have spent writing it over a two-year period are dedicated entirely to Ontario's Special Olympics athletes. All personal profits will be gratefully donated to them. The Special Olympics Athlete Oath across the entire world is a mere fourteen simple words that we could all learn from: "Let me win. But if I cannot win, let me be brave in the attempt." The Special Olympics movement is international in scope, including every state of the United States, every province of Canada, and many other countries around the world. From a personal perspective, I am particularly enamored with the Ontario folks, given my continuing involvement with them. The commitment of thousands of people from all walks of life to bring joy to the lives of many people with intellectual disabilities, young and old, through year-round involvement in sport brings a tear to my eye every time I see their poetry in motion. They do all they can to promote respect, acceptance, inclusion, and human dignity for people with intellectual disabilities through organized sports.

If you have never been to the Opening Ceremonies for a Special Olympics event, try to go sometime. It will change your life forever. The excitement, joy, nervous energy, and, for some athletes, tears are overwhelmingly infectious. Then there are the beaming parents in the crowd, so proud to see their sons and daughters capitalizing on years of commitment and dedicated training, and likely reflecting on how Special Olympics has been such a positive factor in their lives. I always struggle emotionally and inevitably choke up when I see the parents clapping and cheering for their loved ones. I immediately think of my wonderful parents and the positive impact they had on my brother Robbie's development. He quite easily could have lived his life in an Ontario hospital if my parents had listened to his doctor in 1971. But they would have none of that. Of course, he ended up graduating from high school and taking some courses at a community college. A number of my childhood friends didn't make it that far. I barely did myself.

Within this wonderful organization, there are coaches, sponsors, volunteers, board members at various levels, and fund raisers (in Ontario these are largely the men and women of the Ontario Law Enforcement Torch Run for Special Olympics, of which I am quite proud). They do it all, day after day, raising funds and public awareness for the most important members of the movement: the Special Olympics athletes themselves. It's all about the athletes. They are my heroes, and they will *never* stop on a hill. Please visit the Special Olympics Ontario website at www.specialolympicsontario.com.

Introduction

• • •

Surround yourself with great people. Have beliefs and communicate
them. See things for yourself. Set an example. Stand up to bullies. Deal
with first things first. Loyalty is the vital virtue. Prepare relentlessly.
Under-promise and over-deliver. Don't assume a damn thing.

—Rudolph Giuliani speaking of the leadership
principles he learned within hours of the
attack on the World Trade Center

This book is not about me, but it is about leadership. Although I relate my beliefs, my experiences, and some of my personal journey as a leader, it is not a story about all of the wonderful things I've done or arrests I've made or lives I've saved, if any. That is not who I am as a person.

I am a student of leadership and have been for most of my life. The great leaders have held me in awe, and the poor ones have disappointed me, but I've always been fascinated by leaders of all types.

Sadly, I think as an advanced society, we have lost it on the leadership front in a number of respects. Too many people, albeit many of them capable and intelligent, are so focused on their own careers, therefore making every decision with a view toward what is in it for them; actually *leading* people is the least of their concerns. Their clawing and clambering for promotion far outweighs their desire to build morale, support their people, and encourage them to be the best they can be. In that process, they spend an inordinate amount of time assessing their perceived competitors and plotting their demise, deserved or not, as opposed to simply being honest and committed employees. Much of that is a learned behavior, —learned from piss-poor leaders that they have watched succeed through tyranny, oppression, and backstabbing.

Would it not be more personally fulfilling and less stressful for the career motivated to focus on the lessons they can learn from good leaders and to fashion their own styles accordingly?

We can all remember watching natural leaders as we were growing up. They were the captains of the football and hockey teams, the presidents of the school clubs, the Prom kings, and more. They weren't always the cutest, the smartest, the most academically or athletically gifted, but they just had a certain charisma or je ne sais quoi that made people want to be around them. They possessed a spark of sorts that drew more attractive, intelligent, and capable people to them without fail.

There were others that we'd follow anywhere as well, but more out of a sick sense of curiosity as we waited to see what stupid thing they would do next. Perhaps that's why some people followed me!

On the other hand, as kids we all knew who the very gifted athletes, the best-looking teens, and the smartest or most talented young people all were. A number of them couldn't buy a friend if they tried. Some were shunned, many were not accepted into the "group," and many didn't surface as leaders among their peers.

As I got older and began working, even part time and on summer breaks, I similarly saw leaders emerge in the workplace. I worked with the best mechanics in various garages as a teen. The most talented ones were often introverts and wouldn't waste the oxygen to say even "Good morning" to the young gas jockeys like me. We weren't worthy. Everything we did was blatantly wrong or stupid, in their expert opinions, no matter how trivial. They looked for things to be critical of. But people drove from miles around to have those guys work on their cars and trucks because of their technical ability, not because of their people skills. They turned me off so much, however, that I wouldn't let them so much as change the oil in my lawn mower.

Conversely, there were other mechanics I worked with who took the time to teach me things. They would point out ways I could have done some tasks better, but they made me feel good about myself in the process. They encouraged me to be the very best that I could be and made me enjoy going to work. I couldn't tell you how proficient they were at their trade, and I didn't care. I was just proud to work alongside them. They simply inspired me to try hard—and so I did.

Football and wrestling coaches were much the same for me. There were the good, and there were the bad. The good coaches had the ability to make you feel better about yourself when you erred; they possessed the innate ability to make you feel like a superstar whether you made a mediocre play or won a match.

People often feel bad for the coach that is fired from a sports team because his or her players aren't pulling it altogether. As multimillion-dollar athletes, aren't the players perhaps the ones who should be fired for not earning their exorbitant salaries? But the great coaches can and do get the best out of their players; they know their strengths and weaknesses, know when they need a pat on the back or a kick in the rear, and can motivate them to work as an effective team. The most talented players in the world won't excel without the right coach pulling them and their talents together. Unfortunately, in some cases, the team just needs a new coach.

When I finished school, I began to work on the Great Lakes as a sailor. As a young man working as part of a fourteen-man crew on a 140-foot tugboat in the middle of Lake Superior, I experienced the best and the worst in people, coworkers and bosses alike. I definitely saw the good, the bad, and the ugly, but I learned from them all. The true leaders made themselves known and respected quickly. They could bark orders as we were coming into the dock in rough weather, and I knew that what they said was gospel, so I'd follow their orders blindly and with total confidence. I trusted them completely. I knew they always had my safety and best interests in mind, and what was best for the ship itself. In the sailing world, what is best for the ship usually dovetails well with the safety of the crew. I'd have jumped overboard for those guys; fortunately, though, it never came to that!

One such individual was a first mate named Bob Hupman. He was an East Coaster, came from a family of fishermen, and was as comfortable in the ship's wheelhouse in a November gale on Lake Michigan as I was while lying on the couch watching football on television on a winter day. Nothing fazed him.

I spent countless hours in the wheelhouse with Bob, all hours of the night and day. Like the mechanics I had enjoyed working with earlier, he made me feel as if I were the captain of the ship when I was at the helm. If I made a mistake, he turned it into a positive experience that I could learn from. He told me stories that taught me valuable lessons about sailing and about life in general. He wanted me to do well and encouraged me in all that I did. Did he know as much about navigation as the cantankerous old captain did? I don't have the foggiest idea. Could he hook the tug up to a ship we were towing in rough seas with the precision of the ship's captain? I didn't know or care. But if the ship had begun to sink and I could have saved only one person, him or the captain, my decision would have come easily.

This is when I started to put it all together. It's all about people—not things, technical skills, or ability.

As Canadian general Rick Hillier said in his book entitled *Leadership*, "Never forget, it's all about people."

It was the people skills those popular high school kids were blessed with that carried the day, not their athletic prowess or academic talent. Other kids wanted to be around them because of how they felt when they were. The mentoring and support and friendship from the mechanics I worked with as a kid and then received from Bob Hupman on that ship in the worst of weather on the Great Lakes made me want to succeed. It made me want to be the very best that I could be.

That very lesson learned is firmly ingrained in me to this day. From my year as a rookie cop in northern Ontario, through every rank I've held and every position in which I've served, the true leaders I have worked for, worked with, and at times supervised made me want to excel. If I erred, they told me, but they didn't do so in a way that made me feel like a failure or that destroyed my morale. When I did something good, they didn't hug me and give me a cash bonus, but through a few words and a smile, I wanted to go right out and do it again.

Those individuals that shaped me as a police officer and as a leader may or may not have been the best police officers in the Ontario Provincial Police (OPP), the best investigators, managers, tacticians, or traffic cops, but once again I didn't care. They earned my trust, and I'd walk through broken glass for them all, till this very day.

Similarly, within various service clubs, associations, boards, and other groups that I was a member of, natural leaders seemed to rise to the fore. They generally held the groups together, unified our vision, set direction, and got us through the difficult times.

Yet we've all worked for the opposite—those autocratic people who survive on positional power and by striking fear in the hearts of all those around them. I'll have more to say about them later, but we can learn from them as well. As I've said publicly on many occasions, there are leaders that you'd gladly take a bullet for and those that you would love to put a bullet in. Just remember everything they did to make your life a living hell, and never do any of it to anyone you lead. It's not rocket science.

I don't profess to be an expert on leadership. I know what has worked for me and what hasn't. I've watched others succeed and fail based on specific approaches, and I've learned from them all. Although I was a noncommissioned officer (NCO) or a commissioned officer (CO) for twenty-eight years of my career, I'm still learning every day. What worked with the baby boomers like me in the 1970s likely won't work with generation X or Y of the new millennium, let alone the emerging "next-gen" folks who are graduating from colleges and universities as we speak. But regardless of one's occupation, successful leadership still comes down to some very basic principles in my view and in the view of other police leaders who have provided valuable input for this book.

When I started writing this book, I struggled somewhat with whether I should focus simply on leadership as a skill and stay away from the focus on policing. But it is what it is, and I am who I am.

Fortune 500 sales and marketing executive and author Dana Manciagli says: "When it comes to successful leadership, attributes like vision, communication, integrity, and curiosity never go out of style. Today, executives also must be able to build strong teams in the face of recruiting and retention challenges, keep up with the latest technology, and demonstrate strong business acumen.

Those at the helm of their organizations need these skills, among others, to navigate the business environment, which recent research suggests is increasingly difficult to do."

All of the skills and leadership qualities that I speak of are transferable. It doesn't matter whether you're leading police professionals, private sector employees, volunteers, girls, boys, tinkers, tailors, soldiers, or sailors; leadership is leadership. Whether in government, industry, not-for-profit organizations, or the policing or military sectors, our leaders of today and tomorrow will face new, unprecedented, and unpredictable threats and challenges—or "hills" of sorts. These skills are a must for leaders of all kinds, in both private and public sector organizations. The company or agency goals and the client groups may well differ, but employees are human beings and people are people, so the people skills required remain the same.

Join me in a walk through my thoughts and experience, my research, and the personal views and experiences of a variety of police leaders, academics, political figures, coaches, private sector CEOs, historical and modern-day military leaders, and more. You are bound to end up a more effective leader than you were before you picked up this book.

"Never Stop on a Hill"

• • •

So why the title *Never Stop on a Hill*?

Leadership, like life, involves a series of peaks and valleys. The true leader knows when to push and when to pull his or her people up or down those hills or mountains, or sometimes steep cliffs. My theory is that strength of the real leader will be more evident to followers on the steepness of a hill than on the downslope. The old adage "When the going gets tough, the tough get going" is very true in policing, probably more so than in any other profession, I'd suggest, short of the military when engaged in combat. Unfortunately, we have all seen leaders get going when things got tough, all right—sometimes home to bed and other times as far away from the action as they could possibly get.

> *Remember the difference between a boss and a leader;*
> *a boss says "Go!"—a leader says "Let's go!"*
>
> —E. M. Kelly

This is a risky business that we in policing have chosen as our calling. If you're not predisposed to taking risks, you've probably chosen the wrong profession. Similarly, if you're not willing to take risks and bear the consequences if things get ugly, you will not survive as a leader. Although your people are going to watch you closely on the quiet and tranquil days as you either earn their trust in you or not, when the proverbial poop hits the fan, there is definitely nowhere to hide. That's what separates the leaders from the followers: The hills. The mountains. The peaks. The challenges that block our path to our organizational goals. Leaders have to be able to tackle them and know which hills are worth dying on and, alternatively, when to take the path of least resistance.

The people you lead will also watch you more keenly in the failures than in the successes. Ontario's former chief coroner Dr. Jim Young once called me at a time when I was particularly disappointed in the outcome of a promotional process. His sage advice was "Keep your powder dry. They're watching you. People will judge you much more harshly when you react to a failure versus a success." Truer words were never spoken, and I've offered that exact same advice many times since that day.

I don't measure a man's success by how high he climbs
but how high he bounces when he hits bottom.

—GEN. GEORGE S. PATTON

Many years ago, when my eldest daughter, Melissa, was six or seven years old, she started jogging with me at the cottage and at home. She remains a stubborn lady to this day and was pretty strong willed already as a child. However, in those days of her youth, she lacked the confidence at times to take on any challenge that she thought was beyond her, no matter how simple, starting with little hills along the jogging path. She'd constantly want to stop at the bottom of the hill and walk up it.

My standard line was "Never stop on a hill, honey. If you have to, stop at the top so that the hill doesn't beat you. We can walk down the other side." Then, of course, once we got to the top of the hill, running down the slope was a cakewalk, and on we'd go, to the next hill. My theory always was and always will be "Anyone can stop when he or she hits a roadblock. If I'm going to rest at all, it will be when I reach the other side of the hill."

Shortly thereafter, Melissa got into gymnastics. She mastered cart-wheels before any child her age, even performing on picnic tables in front of horrified crowds at family gatherings. She then climbed on the balance beam and excelled for her age.

That same headstrong little girl received her junior black belt in jujitsu by age fourteen. She's since tackled rock-climbing and a variety of sports and hobbies, was a competitive cheerleader, and obtained her degree in aeronautical engineering in Sydney, Australia. She never did martial arts again, however, because she had already conquered that hill and wanted to try something else. An interesting and refreshing mind-set, to say the least.

Now an officer in the Royal Canadian Air Force, Melissa reminds me of those words to this day whenever we walk, run, or talk about it. When we get to a hill, she'll turn and look at me with a smile, milliseconds before she bolts and beats me to the top.

In any police service, fire department, military branch, business, company, organization, or group, there are challenging hills to face. Some of them are tremendous and seemingly invincible. But to fail may mean the loss of life in the public-safety realm, a fall from power for a sitting government, total financial ruin in the private sector, and the loss of public confidence in any organization.

I used to be a proponent of never giving up against any challenge, no matter how daunting. But as I matured and developed as a leader, I began to change that philosophy. One day I found myself saying, "Is this really a hill we want to die on?" I began to realize that some things aren't worth fighting for or over, and that if you fight every little thing in your way, then when a real critical issue that *is* worth the fight comes along, people will think, "Here he/she goes again." It's much like the story of the little boy who cried wolf. Eventually, no one will feel the impact of your argument when it's truly important, and you also need to save your energy for the hills that count.

In 2012, I had the pleasure of meeting an interesting speaker at the FBI National Executive Institute, in Quantico, Virginia. Ed Viesturs is a renowned mountain climber and has climbed to the top of the world's fourteen highest peaks.

Ed talked mostly of his quest to reach the top of Mount Everest. He said that if you don't plan and execute well or if you take any shortcuts along the way, failure may mean death. He added, "Mountain climbing should be a round trip!" He also explained that some people get too tempted by the summit and break the rules and end up losing it all. Ed had to stop one hundred meters from the summit of Everest on one occasion because the weather conditions made it unsafe. He knew that his team didn't have the energy or the oxygen to make it the rest of the way and then all the way back down in the weather they were being confronted with. As the leader, he made the decision to turn around rather than risk some members dying. Can you imagine being so close to your lifelong goal and having the fortitude to turn back, knowing that you may not ever get that close again? But he did it for the team. That is true leadership. Of course, he eventually did get to the top of Everest, on a number of future occasions.

Ed said that one needs to "listen to the mountain." In other words, evaluate the conditions and follow your instincts because if it "feels wrong, it is wrong." He added that "there is no pot of gold at the top...so you need to be personally motivated."

I could draw so many parallels between Ed Viesturs's presentation and my own thoughts and feelings about leadership. Certainly most or all of what he said about his experiences in leading mountain-climbing expeditions can be applied to police leadership, and largely to leadership in most fields.

Collaboration, meeting opponents halfway, win-win scenarios, negotiated outcomes—all these usually make good business sense. But when the inevitable mountain comes along, one that must be beaten because there is no other option, it's time to pull out all of the stops. If you haven't been fighting everything in your way, people will know that you mean business, rather than consider it just another fight that you've started over nothing.

The challenges that a career as a leader brings come and go. Some of those hurdles are worth the risk—"hills worth dying on"—and others are not. The decision can't be personal. It has to be for the client and the team, not for leaders and their own agendas. The personal motivation Ed Viesturs speaks of in terms of climbing mountains is somewhat different than that of organizational leaders who have clients that come first—in police services, the client being the public they serve. Consequently, if the goal isn't in the clients' best interests, the climb should stop there. If it is, then the well-being of the men and women of the team has to be considered as the climb progresses. The decision to turn around and climb back down the hill if required needs to be made for the betterment of the team.

So as much as I profess that leaders should "never stop on a hill," I completely agree with Ed Viesturs's approach. Whenever humanly possible, the journey to meet the challenge should always be a round trip.

If you've ever been in a fistfight for any duration—not a wrestling match but a toe-to-toe brawl—you'll know that eventually your arms start to tire. But you cannot let them fall. That's when you'll take one on the chin, and the fight will be nothing but a history lesson.

Facing challenges is much the same. You may want to back off from the hill for the betterment of the team and because of the principle "Discretion is the better part of valor." You owe it to your team to live to fight another day, so you can never completely drop those arms (your guard) when you do.

My personal view is that when you're down and out, mentally or physically exhausted, and it feels as if the weight of the world were on your shoulders, you have only two choices. It's much like fighting cancer: you either fold your tent, give up, and suck your thumb while you cry yourself to sleep, or you get up and fight again and again. You can't let those personal challenges beat you, or you will never be there for the team you lead.

In the 2006 movie *Rocky Balboa*, the hero, Rocky (Sylvester Stallone), gives his son a lecture at a bad time in the boy's life. The words, although not necessarily Shakespearean in terms of grammar, should be a lesson to us all as we face the dark days of life:

Let me tell you something you already know. The world ain't all sunshine and rainbows. It's a very mean and nasty place, and I don't care how tough you are, it will beat you to your knees and keep you there permanently if you let it. You, me, or nobody is gonna hit as hard as life. But it ain't about how hard you hit. It's about how hard you can get hit and keep moving forward; how much you can take and keep moving forward. That's how winning is done! Now, if you know what you're worth, then go out and get what you're worth. But you gotta be willing to take the hits, and not pointing fingers saying you ain't where you wanna be because of him, or her, or anybody. Cowards do that and that ain't you. You're better than that!

The Study

• • •

I HAVE HAD A VARIETY of personal experiences in various leadership roles throughout my life and career. Some were positive, some clearly negative, but they were learning experiences all. I also have strong opinions as to what works and what doesn't work for me and where I see many police leaders floundering or outright failing as leaders as they let their egos govern their decision-making and communication styles. However, I certainly do not profess to know it all, not by a long shot. I dare say that nobody truly does.

That personal experience, combined with studying the terabytes of leadership literature available on the Internet, reading countless books, articles, and studies, and attending numerous lectures delivered by true leaders as well as so-called experts, became the foundation for this book. That wasn't enough, however, so I decided to go the extra mile.

In 2012, I sent out a survey to twenty-four currently serving or retired police chiefs from across Canada. I surveyed chiefs from small, midsized, and large police services from coast to coast. I really wanted to ensure that all regions of Canada were represented in my work. To achieve a balanced perspective, I included a number of female chiefs among the recipients.

The survey was structured as follows:

1. What years were you police chief (or commissioner/director) and of what police service(s)?
2. What does "leadership" mean to you?

3. Why is leadership vital to the success of a police service? If you don't feel it is, please explain why.
4. What is the most important quality that the great leaders possess?
5. Are leaders born to be leaders, or can people be made or developed into effective leaders?
6. Describe the best police leader you ever worked for and what he or she did that made him or her great. (Feel free to name the individual if you like, but it is not required.)
7. Without naming names, describe the worst police leader you ever worked for and what he or she did that made that person a poor leader.
8. What was your greatest challenge as a police leader?
9. Describe your greatest success in a leadership role.
10. Describe your greatest failure as a leader and what you learned from it.
11. What is the key to developing a positive relationship with a police association or union, in your view?
12. What do you think is the realistic time frame that a police chief can or should survive in his or her role?
13. Please provide me with a personal quote on leadership in general that I can attribute to you as appropriate in terms of chapter content.
14. Any additional comments would be appreciated, please.

I was pleased to receive responses from the following chiefs:

* Chief Bill Blair was chief of the Toronto Police Service from April 2005 to his retirement in April 2015. He is currently a member of Parliament in Canada's Liberal government.
* Chief Jim Chu was the chief constable of the Vancouver Police Department, having been appointed in 2007. He retired in May 2015.

* Ian Davidson is deputy minister with the Ontario Ministry of Community Safety and Correctional Services. Following a career in the Ottawa Police Service, Ian was the chief of the Greater Sudbury Police Service from 2002 to 2009. He was then commissioner of community safety for the province until being appointed deputy minister in 2010. He retired in early 2014.
* Chief Richard Deering (Ret.) was the chief of the Royal Newfoundland Constabulary (RNC) from 2001 to 2006, following his retirement as a chief superintendent in the OPP.
* Chief Frank Elsner is currently the chief of the Victoria Police Department, having assumed that role in January 2014. Prior to that, Frank was chief of the Greater Sudbury Police Service from 2009 to 2013.
* Chief Jennifer Evans is the chief of the Peel Regional Police and has been since October 2012.
* The Honorable Julian Fantino, PC, MP, held various roles including minister of veteran's affairs in the federal government. Fantino served as chief of the London Police Service, 1991–98; chief of the York Regional Police Service, 1998–2000; chief of the Toronto Police Service, 2000–2005; and commissioner of the OPP, 2006–10.
* Chief Leanne Fitch of the Fredericton Police Force, New Brunswick, was deputy chief from 2005 to 2012 and acting chief 2012–13 and has been chief since.
* Chief Kimberley Greenwood was appointed the chief of the Barrie Police Service in March 2013 following a lengthy career with the Toronto Police Service.
* Chief Laurie Hayman has been chief of the Strathroy-Caradoc Police Service since 2012. She previously served there as deputy chief, following many years with the London Police Service.
* Chief Barry King (Ret.) was the chief of the Sault Sainte Marie Police Service from 1987 to 1995 and then was chief of the

Brockville Police Service from 1995 to 2007. Prior to that, he was a member of several Ontario police services and the military.

* Chief Rod Knecht has been chief of the Edmonton Police Service (Alberta) since 2011 and was a member of the Royal Canadian Mounted Police (RCMP) from 1977 to 2011, where he rose to the rank of senior deputy commissioner.

* Chief Robert F. Lunney (Ret.) was chief of the Edmonton Police Service, 1974–87; commissioner of Protection, Parks, and Culture, Winnipeg, 1987–90; and chief of the Peel Regional Police, 1990–97. Bob also served for many years with the RCMP prior to 1974.

* Chief Edgar MacLeod (Ret.) was chief of Shelburne Police Department (NS) in 1976; New Waterford Police Department (NS), 1993–95; and Cape Breton Regional Police Service (NS), 1995–2008. Edgar is currently the executive director of the Atlantic Police Academy and has been since 2008.

* Chief Dan Maluta (Ret.) was chief of the Nelson Police Department (BC) from 2001 until his retirement in 2011.

* Chief Dale McFee (Ret.) was chief prince of the Albert Police Service (Saskatchewan), 2003–12. He is currently deputy minister of corrections and policing, Ministry of Justice, Province of Saskatchewan.

* Chief William McCormack (Ret.) was chief of the Toronto Police Service from 1989 to 1995. Sadly "The Chief" passed away on September 8, 2016.

* Commissioner Emeritus Thomas B. O'Grady (Ret.) was commissioner of the OPP from 1988 to 1998.

* Commissioner Robert Paulson is commissioner of the RCMP. He was appointed in November 2011.

* Chief Paul Shrive (Ret.) was chief constable of the Port Moody Police Department in British Columbia from 1999 to 2007. Prior to that, he served in the OPP, retiring in 1999 at the rank of chief superintendent.

- Chief Clive Weighill is chief of the Saskatoon Police Service. Immediately prior to that, he was deputy chief of the Regina Police Service from 1997 to 2006. He served as president of the Canadian Association of Chiefs of Police (CACP) from 2014 to 2016.
- Senator Vernon White retired from the RCMP at the rank of assistant commissioner in 2005. He then served as chief of the Durham Regional Police Service from 2005 to 2007 and subsequently as chief of the Ottawa Police Service from 2007 to 2012.
- Commissioner Giuliano "Zack" Zaccardelli (Ret.) was commissioner of the RCMP from 2000 to 2006.

The feedback I received was greatly appreciated. I understand how busy these folks all are, whether serving or retired, and also how some retirees (in the words of Tom O'Grady) are "pretty busy, and very slow."

I did note a bit of difference in the responses I received from some of the older and retired chiefs versus those received from some of the younger and currently serving leaders, but many of the comments, experiences, and opinions were, surprisingly, fairly consistent. You will see that the assorted quotes I document truly demonstrate the importance of people skills over the much less critical job-knowledge and technical-ability attributes that we have traditionally based promotional processes on.

Duc, sequere, aut de via decede. ("Lead, follow, or get out of the way.")

—LATIN PROVERB

Why Leadership?

• • •

*Leadership is the motive force for achievement of organizational
objectives and goals. Lack of leadership leads to slack
performance, directionless activity, and lapses in integrity.*

—CHIEF ROBERT F. LUNNEY

I AM A FIRM BELIEVER that in this era of twenty-four-hour live news coverage
supported by members of a society that all carry cellular phones equipped
with cameras and video recorders, a social media–driven culture, increasing
oversight and demands for transparency and public accountability, a global
economic crisis, rising labor and technology costs and shrinking budgets,
increasing bargaining-group pressure, the threat of international and domestic terrorism, ongoing volatile and potentially economically crippling
public protests, the severe and dangerous impacts of climatic change, a new
generation of potential employees, and more, no organization, company, or
agency can survive without strong leadership from top to bottom.

But why do I say this? If an organization offers high-quality products and competitive pricing; has high ethical standards, strong managers,
educated and capable employees, and a robust mission, vision, corporate
value statement, and business plan; and is supported by the very best of
enabling technology, why wouldn't it be successful?

The answer is simple: it's because it takes *people* to bring all of that together into an effective, sufficient, and sustainable package that delivers the goods and services consistently, professionally, and with a strong customer-oriented focus. When all else fails, it is *people* that make or break any organization, and it takes *leadership*, not *management*, to keep that team focused, engaged, healthy, and strong.

In an article entitled, *Businesses don't fail, leaders do*, regular Forbes' Magazine contributor Mike Myatt stated, "Why do businesses fail? If you're willing to strip away all the excuses, explanations, rationalizations, and justifications for business failures, and be really honest in your analysis, you'll find only one plausible reason -poor leadership."

He went on to say, "It doesn't matter what your title is, if you don't do the right things for the right reasons you will fail. Leaders who don't display character won't attract it or retain it in others. Leaders who fail to demonstrate a constancy of character won't create trust, won't engender confidence and won't create loyalty."

Business leaders, consultants, and academics that study the successes and failures of major corporations and government organizations around the world speak relentlessly about the need for effective leadership in this rapidly and constantly changing world.

Author Ray Williams has this to say about leadership:

Leadership must be important—more than 20,000 books and thousands of articles have been written about the critical elements of and the impact it has on people, organizations and countries, if not the world. Yet despite the fact leadership training programs abound, they have failed to produce good leaders.

Despite the collective wisdom of centuries on this topic, confidence in our leaders is low and continues to decline. In a 2012 survey by the National Leadership Index (NLI), released by the Center for Public Leadership at Harvard Kennedy School and Merriman River Group, 77% of respondents said the United States now has a crisis in leadership and confidence levels have fallen to the lowest levels in recent times.

Shell Corporation, a worldwide energy and petrochemical company with more than ninety thousand employees spanning all continents, clearly recognizes the critical need for effective leadership, as evidenced in its 2012 announcement "Shell's Leadership Develops the Best People to Secure Global Future Energy." The media release stated,

> As the world becomes more uncertain with significant emerging economies, future leaders will need to equip themselves with a number of leadership competencies and skills to enable them to deliver their vision.
> The new Shell Leadership model provides a focus on the leadership qualities needed for the future. The qualities are defined by four key attributes starting with "Authenticity"..."Growth"... "Collaboration"...and "Performance."

Is there anything in Shell's announcement that doesn't apply equally to government agencies? To police organizations? To the private and not-for-profit sectors?

Police agencies around the world undoubtedly share the same needs and concerns as they face the world's economic realities, new and unique operational pressures, and more.

During a presentation to the Ontario Association of Chiefs of Police in Niagara Falls, Ontario, in June 2008, former police officer, lecturer, and author Jack E. Enter presented the following points:

- Law enforcement is in a leadership crisis.
- Ninety percent of US law-enforcement managers are rated as inconsistent and ineffective as leaders.
- Leadership failings are rated as one of the primary sources of law-enforcement stress.
- It (a lack of leadership) is the most serious organizational problem.

His comments were fascinating to me. Not because they were a shock but because he was validating what I had always believed: that leadership either makes us or breaks us. Not civilian oversight, the media, guns, gangs, or shrinking budgets, but leadership.

What is morale?

> *Morale is the state of mind. It is steadfastness and*
> *courage and hope. It is confidence and zeal and loyalty.*
> *It is élan, esprit de corps and determination.*

> —GEN. GEORGE CATLETT MARSHALL

Morale is difficult to define, but it's quickly apparent when it falters. It's a positive, confident feeling, energy, an enthusiasm, a spirit, or a committed and united will to succeed. Former US president Gen. Dwight David Eisenhower once said, "Morale is the greatest single factor in successful wars."

So what impact does the level of employee morale have on a police service, or on any company or organization, for that matter?

If you think back on your own career, I'm sure that there were times when you felt better about yourself, the job, and your organization than during others. Most of us have had weeks, months, or even years when we considered changing organizations or starting a new career. We all have had peaks and valleys in our careers and personal lives. Unfortunately for some, personal life challenges can't help but have an impact on careers, and vice versa. That is the reality until we start hiring robots instead of human beings. Even more concerning is when an individual doesn't have a good work life to escape to when his or her home life isn't stable or, conversely, a solid personal life to help balance out his or her existence in a positive way when the career isn't what it should be. When one's personal life and job are both at extreme lows, times can be really tough.

That aside, when we were in one of those work-life "valleys," so to speak, were we working for supervisors that inspired us? Did they give us the confidence and support to be the best that we could be? Did they really care about what motivated us as individuals or what our strengths and weaknesses were? Did they do and say the right things and provide us with the right mentoring and encouragement to be successful? Likely not. It's more probable that they provided little or none of that; in some cases, they were even guilty of deliberately trying to make our lives a living hell. They may well have been the sole cause of the valley.

In 2001, I was transferred into the OPP's Eastern Region as its commander. Having come out of many years at General Headquarters (GHQ), I, like a number of GHQ colleagues, thought that I had a good grip on what was going on out in our frontline operations. How wrong I was. I really had no idea and was about to have my mind opened on numerous fronts.

One of the many misconceptions I had was that morale was deplorable in our frontline detachments, particularly in the Eastern Region. Morale is an elusive beast in my experience: it's next to impossible to measure, but where it's poor, the impacts can be profound. Over the several years prior, I'd commanded tactical and investigative units composed largely of handpicked people. I was pretty spoiled in terms of being able to simply move the few poor performers back to uniform without hesitation, when necessary, and never having to make the best out of less-than-stellar-and-committed staff.

What I actually found after months of visiting detachments and talking to people from all ranks—some being members that I knew and trusted, others simply seeing an opportunity to vent to a regional commander that opened the door—was that in fact morale was not at rock bottom. It was very poor in some locations but extremely high in a few stations, and there were pockets of high morale and low morale in others.

I wrote a comprehensive paper on the issue and forwarded it to my then deputy commissioner. I've included only pieces of the report in the interests of brevity, but I'm sure that in terms of morale issues, parallels can be drawn between my comments then and any police service or company anywhere, to this very day:

Since my arrival in the Eastern Region, I have been very conscious of the morale of our employees, as I had been led to believe that within the field, morale was low across the province. As a result, I have spoken personally to hundreds of staff of all ranks, in every detachment and unit across the region, in an effort to examine the state of morale, as well as cause and effect where applicable.

I have found that although there are definite peaks and valleys in terms of employee morale, generally speaking, morale is not as bad as I had been told. As you and I have discussed this issue a number of times, I felt it important to share my observations with you and the other regional commanders. Although I do outline some of the attempts to improve morale we have made in the Eastern Region, I do not have all of the answers. I raise the identified issues only for information purposes and discussion.

Where morale is low, it can almost always be attributed to one or more of the following causes:

1. staffing issues,
2. leadership deficiencies, and/or
3. facilities deficiencies.

Leadership Deficiencies:

Leadership is a very critical issue as far as morale is concerned. Our frontline staff expect their leaders, at all levels, to lead by example, be accountable, be ethical, give credit where credit is due, treat all employees equally and fairly, be decisive (not all-knowing but able to make decisions), deal with issues as they arise (including problem employees), and communicate with them. Anything less can lead to employees losing faith in their supervisors and managers. This holds true right up to and including the regional commander.

The "Team Leader" designation that came out of our OPP reorganization in the 1990s had a negative effect on the mind-set of some uniformed sergeants. They put too much emphasis on the "team" portion of the title and not enough emphasis on the "leader" side. Some of these sergeants view themselves as team members with signing authority and do not take on issues, make decisions, set the example, and so on. When this same attitude is prevalent in the detachment commander, regardless of his or her rank, the detachment members feel they have no one to turn to for leadership, and it can have a tremendous effect on morale.

Sergeants and detachment commanders can lead to a further deterioration of employee morale by fueling the staffing concerns, sometimes making mountains out of molehills, and other times stating the truth but in front of their subordinates. They are also at times guilty of bad-mouthing regional command staff or GHQ decisions or direction. Young officers can be easily influenced into falsely believing that RHQ and GHQ are determined to make their lives difficult.

From a regional-leadership perspective, the front line feels disconnected from regional command in some cases. Members have complained they don't know their regional command staff, "wouldn't know them to see them," and never hear anything from them. This creates a difficult challenge for regional command staff in terms of their ability to be visible and ensure appropriate lines of communication, given their other responsibilities and commitments.

In one example, a large, busy detachment had a number of sergeants who did not take their jobs seriously and were guilty of many of the faults identified above. They reported to an inspector who was often absent and downloaded many of his responsibilities onto his operations manager (staffs). That individual was capable operationally, but his interpersonal skills were not what they should have been. This resulted in tremendous morale issues as frustrated constables reported to sergeants who were often not doing their jobs and were overseen by a staff sergeant who didn't effectively deal with any of it. Morale suffered accordingly.

This leadership issue is being addressed within the Eastern Region to some extent. All commissioned officers are committed to getting out to detachment events, doing ride-alongs, conducting detachment visits, and doing their best to open up the lines of communication. Operational and other exigencies often hamper those attempts, unfortunately.

Detachment commanders and sergeants have all been spoken to at meetings and workshops about this issue, including my observations and direction, lectures on leadership, and presentations on dealing with problem employees. Corrective action has been taken in areas that have come to light as being problematic, and subsequently employees felt some comfort when they witnessed management's response.

In summary, when you combine a few or all of the above influencing factors in some OPP locations, it should not be a surprise that morale would be adversely affected.

However, when those environmental issues are combined with ineffective or negative leadership, aging facilities, or staffing shortcomings, or in some cases all of the above, it can be a recipe for disaster in terms of staff morale. I am confident that a more detailed study of this issue would reveal that there is a direct link between performance and the level of employee morale, so it is an important issue for OPP managers.

In my view, strong leadership is the key to overcoming this. Effective leaders can positively affect morale despite the challenges our members face. I have seen examples where despite the many hurdles our members face, they do so in a more optimistic way as a direct result of the encouragement and leadership of their supervisors and managers. Knowing and appreciating the reality of the challenges our people face, openly communicating with personnel in a positive way, and striving to make their working environment as safe and efficient as possible can all go a long way to keeping morale high among staff members.

Chris D. Lewis
Chief Superintendent
Commander—Eastern Region

It was abundantly clear to me even then, as it is now, that leadership was key to employee morale. The good leaders kept morale high, and the weak, poor, or nonexistent leaders dragged it down. I still fully believe that premise holds true.

There were detachments that were in deplorable physical condition there, as the deteriorating 1960s-era buildings had been built for a detachment complement that was half of the current staffing level. In one detachment, when the constables sat around the two computers in the main office at shift change, they could smell the toilets from the cell block. Their police cruisers were miled out, and there weren't enough personnel to properly maintain a duty roster with adequate uniformed coverage. But surprisingly, morale was high.

There was a similar detachment that was so old and run down that there was an infestation of rats in the building. Then the rats started disappearing, and the dreaded "brown snakes" began to appear. As the rats went away, the snakes got fatter and started to shed their skins on the detachment floor. I told the concerned staff that it was a "good news, bad news" scenario: fewer rats but fatter snakes. Some didn't find the humor in that. Nor did they see the humor in the ceiling tiles shimmering as the snakes slithered across them. But the bottom line was that despite the conditions and poor staffing levels, again, morale was high. Coincidentally, both of those detachments had strong leaders in command.

Conversely, there was a detachment that had a swanky new building and newer cruisers, and the staffing level was pretty good for their workload. The morale there was rock bottom. Other detachments had high morale on some platoons, low on others. Almost without fail, the detachments or platoons having low morale—other impacting factors being relatively equal—suffered from weak leadership on some or all of the platoons or in charge of the detachment.

In her article "The Leading Edge," Nicole Fink describes the potential impacts morale can have on health care workers as follows: "Morale can be the fuel that drives an organization forward or the fuel that feeds the fires of employee discontent, poor performance, and absenteeism (Ewton, 2007). With low morale comes a high price tag. The Gallup Organization estimates that there are 22 million actively disengaged employees costing the American economy as much as $350 billion dollars per year in lost productivity including absenteeism, illness, and other problems that result when employees are unhappy at work."

She continued: "Unchallenging environments with little or no opportunities for professional growth and advancement often lead to low employee morale (Workforce, 2006). In addition, other leadership related competencies that contribute to low morale in healthcare workers include poor communication, lack of empowerment, lack of energizing staff, distrust of management, poor interpersonal relations, and inflexible working conditions."

In addition to the negative impacts that low morale can have on the day-to-day performance and professionalism of police officers—for example, attitude, public interaction, and motivation—further challenges can arise when leaders aren't properly engaged.

What are the impacts of poor morale on professionalism and productivity?

If you closely examine any major scandal in policing in North America, from the criminal activity of the Los Angeles Police Department (LAPD) Rampart Division's CRASH Unit in the mid-1990s, to allegations of corruption by a segment of the Toronto Police Service Drug Squad in the early 2000s, to the improper use of the Internet by on-duty OPP officers in northeastern Ontario around the same time, or the so-called Mafia Cops fiasco in the New York Police Department (NYPD) a decade earlier, there has always been a leadership failing at some point in the chain of events. Generally not at the chief or commissioner level, but somewhere along the timeline, a supervisor or manager dropped the ball, deliberately or because the person just wasn't taking obvious issues head on or doing what he or she was being paid to do.

Not that poor leadership will turn subordinate police officers into thugs or make them shake down drug dealers or commit murders for the mob, but in the majority of these cases, when things become public, officers are heard to say, "I knew something was going on" or "It doesn't surprise me, knowing those guys."

Why didn't sergeants, staff sergeants, inspectors, or lieutenants and captains see it coming and take proper action when allegations of impropriety surfaced or when they knew certain officers were living well above their means financially? Why didn't supervisors take action when they saw that some officers seldom left the office and rarely laid a charge because they were spending ten hours a shift on the Internet? Where were supervisors and managers when the paperwork didn't match the expenditures or when officers couldn't account for their time?

I'm not suggesting willful blindness here, although at times that has been the case. Some of the officers involved in some of the better-known scandals were in fact NCOs or higher. We've all been guilty of trusting some subordinates more than we should. But most often, when these calamities arise and cause no end of embarrassment for a police service, some supervisors or managers, leaders in the organizations, neglected to do something along the path that could have mitigated or totally prevented the public shame.

A number of years ago, the OPP's twelve-man Tactics and Rescue Unit (TRU) in Barrie was completely decimated following an incident on a First Nations territory. A single team member did something totally stupid and inappropriate, which inevitably brought down a whole team. That publicly embarrassing fiasco could have been prevented but for a failure in leadership.

While legally in a residence on a reserve in southwestern Ontario, the team members saw a newspaper clipping that showed a photo of a native protestor from the 1990 standoff at Oka, Quebec. One of the officers took a pen and drew an X over the face of the protestor. He also in some way defaced a Unity flag (commonly known as the Mohawk Warrior flag) at the residence. It was completely wrong and potentially harmful to the fragile relationship that existed between the police and the First Nations people, particularly as it was a TRU member that did it. Following the tragic shooting of Dudley George by the TRU at Ipperwash in 1995 and the emotional criminal and civil trials and inquiry that followed, tensions between the TRU and First Nations people ran high. TRU members felt that they and the Ipperwash events had been wrongly portrayed in the media, and they lost a friend and teammate in Acting Sgt. Ken Deane, who was subsequently killed in a traffic collision after he left the OPP. Conversely, many people from the broader First Nations community believed that the OPP had killed an unarmed man. There were and still are a variety of versions and perspectives of what occurred that night, but the bottom line is that the Supreme Court of Canada ruled that Ken's conviction for criminal negligence causing death stood. Regardless of one's particular perspective, during the melee that occurred on September 5, 1995, a life was lost, citizens and OPP members were injured, and lives were forever altered within the communities and within the OPP.

Ken was a friend of mine. I miss him to this very day. He accepted his fate following the many years of onerous legal processes and appeals, and moved on with a less bitter mind-set than many of his teammates and colleagues had.

So fast-forward to 2004 and this event with the defacing of the flag and newspaper clipping by OPP TRU members. Had the officer who did it bellied up to the bar and taken ownership like a man, he would have been appropriately punished under the Police Services Act. Organizational apologies would have been made, and business would have resumed for Barrie TRU. Its reputation would have been blemished, undoubtedly, but it would have continued doing what it did so well. Sadly, that was not the case.

When this incident became known, the team members feared that this would result in the disbandment of the entire team. They held secret meetings and implemented a cover-up plan to lie and deny any knowledge of what had occurred. The acting staff sergeant and team leader, also a friend of mine, wrongly condoned this action. He admittedly should have dragged the constable responsible in to his superiors by the ear and dealt with him as per the discipline process. It was clearly a failure in leadership, and the acting staff, who has since left the OPP, would be the first to admit that. However, his rationale for supporting the cover-up was that his own superior officer had previously warned him that he was tired of having to deal with prior issues with the Barrie TRU and that one more incident would result in the disbandment of the entire team. Whether it was his perception or reality, he felt unsupported by his leader and thought the team was going to be dismantled either way, so it was worth the risk. I'm not saying that was right, but that was his perspective.

Unfortunately, team members who hadn't been on the operation and had nothing to do with the incident whatsoever participated in the cover-up scheme and lost their positions on the TRU as well. It was truly an embarrassing mess all around. Members were disciplined, some were charged under the Police Services Act, all were reassigned, and several quit the OPP. All of this occurred owing to the silly actions of one constable and was then unnecessarily exacerbated by the failing of leaders above him.

We have all done things in our careers that may not have been at the high professional standard that we usually function at. It may have been a case where we were rude to a customer, bad-mouthed a coworker, or were not totally honest with a supervisor. Hopefully, it was an isolated instance, or perhaps several isolated situations over a long career. When these behaviors occurred, they were likely related to our moods or attitudes on those days, and I suggest that some external factor was often an influence.

In her article "Why Engaged Employees Can Make or Break Your Business," author, marketer and Dale Carnegie trainer Piera Palazzolo said this:

According to a recent Dale Carnegie Training white paper, employees who are disengaged don't just cost your company money over time. They can actually be dangerous to those around them due to workplace accidents. Also, chronic absenteeism due to un-engagement can put a serious strain on co-workers who do show up regularly to work. Eventually, these employees may start to suffer from unengagement as well.

Satisfied, committed and engaged employees are the only employees worth having. They will not only go the extra mile for you, but they'll go above and beyond for customers, their co-workers and your organization.

As I have said, we are all human beings, as are those we lead, and as such, we have emotions that often impact what we say and what we do. At times this impact is a negative one.

At any given time in any organization, there are many people who are hurting in their personal lives—financial difficulties, marital problems, personal or family health challenges, aging parents, substance abuse issues, and sadly, much more, perhaps even a number of them occurring all at one time. As we deal with these problems, it undoubtedly effects our work-life demeanor—including our professionalism and productivity—in some way. You can't always walk into work, turn all of those other pressures off, and put on a smiley face.

What happens when an employee that is dealing with one of more of those troubling matters, or perhaps is simply physically tired or fighting a cold or the flu, goes to work and has to deal with a supervisor who has no personality? Who doesn't care about anyone but himself or herself? Who treats people like crap, doesn't set realistic expectations, never listens to the thoughts or suggestions of the members he or she supervises, and so on? It's tough to impossible for the vast majority of people to then smile and go about their business with gusto.

Quite often, life is totally wonderful at home—financially stable and completely healthy and happy—yet we still react negatively to a supervisor that is void of personality and therefore without any discernible leadership skills. We likely are still not totally productive and consummate professionals at work. Throw in the off-duty challenges of life that we all face at times, and you may have a train wreck in the making.

I'm confident that if we had the ability to survey a thousand officers anonymously, they had full confidence that they could be 100 percent open and honest, and we asked them to detail something completely inappropriate and unprofessional they did on duty in their career with total impunity and to describe two things: what was going on in their personal life and what kind of supervisor they were working for, it would be abundantly clear that the leadership piece is the common denominator.

In the Canadian Association of Chiefs of Police (CACP) study *CACP Professionalism in Policing Research Project*, the authors stated, "Generally, management practices had the most significant impact on integrity and commitment followed by work environment variables and finally agency programs. Across all three—management practices, work environment variables and agency programs—the variables that had the largest impact on integrity were supportive supervision and perceived organizational support."

Author Sidney Madwed said, "The motivation for all personal behavior is to produce a sense of 'FEEL GOOD,' a sense of inner peace and well-being. People will do things which seem contrary to this concept, but the bottom line is they perceive some kind of payoff which will make them feel good. And the payoff is almost always emotional."

In an *HR Future* article, "Catch the High Tide to Productivity," Des Squire said, "Increasing productivity requires a commitment by all to self, to the company and to the management of the company. Unfortunately this is sadly lacking, and many employees at various levels are committed to nothing but their own personal objectives. Loyalty and commitment to companies and management is sadly lacking. Why is this?"

He went on to identify some of the influencing factors:

* Lack of trust
* Poor or little communication
* Lack of understanding of business principles

* Lack of understanding of self and others
* Poor, inexperienced, or untrained managers and leaders

Most, or sometimes all, of those levers are influenced mostly by the leader(s) of the affected employees.

As one proposed solution, he added, "Strong managers and leaders will ensure a good return on what has been invested in employee development and loyalty. Bad leaders will destroy what you want to achieve."

You'll read in further chapters that I believe the trust of the public in its police force can be significantly impacted by the conduct (professionalism) of its members. Similarly, client confidence can be shattered in any ineffective organization.

So bearing that in mind and accepting the premise that morale can make us or break us as an organization, if the quality of leadership directly impacts the level of employee morale, professionalism, and productivity, does it not stand to reason that effective leadership is the lynch-pin to success?

> *Strong leadership is the backbone of an organization. Leaders create
> the vision, support the strategies, and are the catalyst for developing
> the individual bench strength to move the organization forward.*

> —Ken Blanchard

What Is Leadership?

• • •

Leadership is about an activity. It's not about a rank or position. It is the ability to lead by example—by creating an environment of respect and appreciation for value/worth of people. Leaders can emerge at all levels of an organization.

—JULIAN FANTINO, ASSOCIATE MINISTER

THERE ARE A MILLION DEFINITIONS for leadership out there, and many leaders themselves aren't really sure what the word means. A commonly accepted definition of leadership is basically "to get things done by influencing others." *Merriam-Webster's Dictionary* defines a leader as "a person who leads: a guide or conductor…a person who has commanding authority or influence."

That can mean a lot of things.

Saddam Hussein had commanding authority. He ruled through the fear of torture and death. You did things his way or had your head cut off and your torso dragged through the streets behind a car. That doesn't work particularly well in modern police forces or companies.

Osama Bin Laden influenced a number of intelligent grown men to fly airplanes full of innocent people into the World Trade Center, the Pentagon, and a Pennsylvanian field to their certain death, killing thousands of innocent people in the process. He certainly was a leader.

A truly evil one. I, on the other hand, couldn't convince adult men and women who made almost $100,000 a year to wear their uniform hats outside the car while on duty. So much for my commanding authority and influence.

Author Howard E. Gardner says that a leader is "an individual who significantly affects the thoughts, feelings and/or behaviours of a significant number of individuals."

We have all worked for people like this at different times in our careers. Their impacts on our thoughts and feelings weren't always positive. Some of them made us consider quitting the job. Others made us fantasize about strangling them, and certainly that didn't have a positive effect on our behavior and professionalism!

A quote I read from an old text on the Cheyenne people said, "A chief is brave, generous, liberal, deliberate, shows good judgment, gives his whole heart and whole mind to work of helping his people, is simple, honest, generous, tenderhearted, often merry, but can be stern, severe, and inflexible of purpose. Successful chiefs make good use of consensus" (source unknown).

That may have been written four hundred or more years ago, but it is valid to this day. It speaks of people skills, not job knowledge. Although a small piece of it flies in the face of much of what I say about leadership, there are a time and a place for "stern, severe, and inflexible of purpose," depending on the circumstances and skill level of the people being led.

Although a Scotsman, John Paul Jones is considered the father of the American navy. He once said, "Leaders should be the soul of tact, justice, firmness and charity. No meritorious act of a subordinate should escape his attention or be left to pass without its reward, even if the reward is only a word of approval. Conversely, he should not be blind to a single fault in any subordinate, though at the same time, he should be quick and unfailing to distinguish error from malice, thoughtlessness from in competency, and well meant shortcomings from heedless or stupid blunder." Apparently there weren't a lot of female leaders in John Paul Jones's era, judging from his use of solely masculine pronouns!

Few if any words in this famous quote do not apply to my view of leadership. Leaders should know their people and what makes them tick, including their strengths and weaknesses. The true leader will always acknowledge good work, even if it is with merely a smile, a pat on the back, or a simple word of thanks. It doesn't normally require a ceremony or a parade.

John Paul Jones died in France in the late 1700s at age forty-five, and his body was returned to the United States over a hundred years later, escorted by ten US Navy ships. If you ever visit Jones's tomb at the US Naval Academy in Annapolis, Maryland, you'll see that a military vigil is proudly in place every hour that the crypt is open to the public. The commitment of military resources for all of those years clearly demonstrates the high esteem in which he is held, over two hundred years following his death. The US government doesn't do that because Admiral Jones was an amazing manager. He was obviously an extraordinary leader, whose words ring true so many decades after they were stated.

We in policing, with our traditional paramilitary environment, are often hard on our people when they err. I truly believe that some leaders want to make examples out of personnel that have made an honest mistake, just to show that they "hold people accountable" to make themselves look good in the eyes of their bosses. I recall OPP bosses who would all but drag a subordinate's bloody corpse through the street, like a scene from Somalia, simply to prove a point. No one in the organization would ever forget that erring employee's name as a result of the public flogging that was meted out. I also worked with and for leaders that had the total opposite approach, dealing with the indiscretion quietly but effectively. The individual at fault learned a lesson, those around him or her knew that the issue was dealt with and the behavior wouldn't be tolerated, but the punished officer wasn't in the penalty box for life. Many such people went on to wonderful careers, promotions, and fulfilling opportunities.

In his best-selling book *Lincoln on Leadership*, author Donald T. Phillips states, "In general, a lack of malice on the part of a leader— genuine caring—inspires trust among subordinates and fosters innovative thinking. It also keeps followers from being terrified, allowing them to be themselves. Contemporary leaders should adopt Lincoln's style and 'pardon' mistakes as opposed to chewing out subordinates."

When people err, we can't throw the towel in and cast them aside like an empty chicken bucket. We should always differentiate error from ill will and maliciousness when doling out punishment, or we are dissuading our people from taking any risks in their daily duties.

I love this quote from former US president John Quincy Adams: "If your actions inspire others to dream more, learn more, do more and become more, you are a leader." The leaders that have had the most positive impact in my life have done just that. They made me want to learn, develop, and be the very best that I could be.

Chief Jennifer Evans said, "Leadership is the art of inspiring others to do things and go places that they would not necessarily believe they could. Leaders inspire others to work harder and improve conditions because it is the right thing to do and not necessarily because people are watching. Leaders act ethically and set the example for others to follow. Leadership is not easy to define but can be easily identified by actions more than words."

I love her use of the word "inspire," as when used by John Quincy Adams in his famous quote on leadership above. I was inspired by the best, and voided of all incentive to be productive by the worst, over my thirty-six years in policing. I strongly believe that inspiring people to be their best should be the primary goal of all leaders.

> *The best way to inspire people to superior performance is to*
> *convince them by everything you do and by your everyday*
> *attitude that you are wholeheartedly supporting them.*
>
> —HAROLD S. GENEEN

That's not always easy, but nobody ever said that leadership was.

When speaking publicly, I often refer to two very different OPP leaders that I had the pleasure of working for as having a tremendous impact on my career.

The first one was Chief Superintendent Howard Williams (retired). We jokingly called him "Howard the Heartless" owing to his outwardly matter-of-fact, direct, and seemingly uncaring façade. His children allegedly referred to him as "Captain Tense," so we often threw that into conversations Howard was engaged in for no other reason than to elicit a colorful response, usually ending with his famous "It's out of control."

A tremendous investigator in his own right, Howard spent most of his career within the then Investigation Division of the OPP as he progressed through the ranks from corporal until he retired as chief superintendent. He had the rare capacity to both lead and manage the areas he commanded quite effectively. He also had the ability to put the fear of God into those he led with little effort.

As my boss off and on from the late 1980s to the mid-1990s, Howard would often point out things I had done—or more often, had said—as not meeting his expectation or perhaps as being blatantly wrong or inappropriate. He'd be quick to mention it if I had overindulged at an event or was too strongly opinionated in a discussion. In one case he voiced his concerns about my association with a group of colleagues that were well known to party hard at times. Although I didn't always agree with him, I grew to appreciate and value his advice. Compliments weren't always front and center with Howard, but he would give the occasional smile or brief words of approval when warranted. You certainly always knew where you stood with him.

I didn't always heed his advice as to whom I should pick as friends or imbibe with, but his comments were a wake-up call that perhaps I needed to slow things down just a tad. It was sound advice. I knew in my heart that he had immense responsibilities in his command role and could have easily let me self-destruct, but he saw something in me that was worth his investment, so he put the effort into saving me from myself. I needed that at the time and will always appreciate it.

Wayne Frechette was also my boss in various ranks for many of those same years. I think he just about drove poor Howard to complete insanity with his sense of humor, particularly when Wayne spoke publicly as a presenter or as a sought-after emcee at one of literally hundreds of OPP functions. He retired as a chief superintendent in the OPP and went on to serve as chief of the Barrie Police Service for ten years, a period in which the Barrie Police doubled in size owing to their rapid business and residential growth. I'll have more to say about Wayne in later chapters, but he had a very positive impact on me as a leader. He inspired me to be my best.

When I was going through a difficult time in my personal life, many years ago, Wayne came into my office, closed the door, sat down, and put his feet on my desk. He asked, "What's going on with you?" When I asked why, he said, "You're not yourself lately. I can see something is bothering you." When I explained that my first marriage was in shambles, he offered advice and a pledge of support and then followed through by checking up with me every few days just to see how I was doing. Wayne knew his people. He knew which Criminal Investigation Branch (CIB) inspector was best suited for which assignment. He knew who faced personal or professional challenges, whose paperwork required closer inspection than others, whom he could count on when the chips were down, and in my case, when I simply wasn't myself. How many bosses know their people well enough to see subtle personality changes in them? How many supervisors or managers will then take it one step further, close the door, and have the conversation to see whether they can help?

Oddly, when Tom O'Grady retired and Wayne, who was a leading contender to replace Tom as OPP commissioner, did not get the job, another high-ranking OPP officer pulled me aside one day and offered what he thought was sage advice. I'll never forget it. He said, "You have to distance yourself from Frechette. You're viewed as one of his boys, and that might hurt you with the new commissioner. Wayne didn't get the job, so you should pull away from him."

I replied, "Where were you when I was eating day-old egg-salad sandwiches out of my desk drawer?" He didn't have clue what I meant and looked at me as if I had just grown a horn out of my forehead. I explained, "When I split with my wife, didn't have two nickels to rub together, and couldn't afford to buy myself lunch, where were you? Wayne was there for me, helped me through a tough time in my life, when many so-called friends like you distanced themselves from me because they didn't want their wives to know they hung around with a separated guy. Not Wayne. I will never distance myself from Wayne Frechette, and I don't care who has a problem with that."

That's because Wayne Frechette was a true leader. He knew his people and cared about them. I'd take a bullet for Wayne to this very day.

Commissioner Thomas B. O'Grady said about leadership that "it means influencing and enabling others both within and outside your organization through various means, including personal involvement, to accomplish certain goals, with the ultimate objective of improving the organization and its service."

I agree emphatically. Leadership shouldn't be about fulfilling your own personal agenda or building your own résumés. True leaders work for the betterment of the client group they serve first and foremost, closely followed by the betterment of the people (or organization) they are honored to lead.

When I made that statement while lecturing some years ago, one police-association leader told me, "Our people come first, not the public." I disagreed and pointed out that we send our people out in police cars, fully armed, into very dangerous situations twenty-four hours a day to protect the public. How can we say our people come first? They go into homes and face armed individuals. They run into burning buildings and jump into lakes and rivers to save lives. They continuously place themselves in harm's way to prevent the victimization of vulnerable people. They are spit on, assaulted, and threatened. The people they serve obviously come first, or they wouldn't do any of that.

However, I truly believe that the good of the people we lead comes a close second. We must do all we can to ensure their safety and security, their health and wellness, and their professionalism and morale and to ensure they are properly equipped and trained to do what they are sworn to do.

I don't remember where or when I read it, or whom to attribute it to, but I recall several years ago a new commander somewhere within the US military saying words to the effect of "My personal goal is to ensure that the men and women under my command are the best trained and equipped and led to face the dangers and challenges they will confront across the world." That was in response to an interview question about his personal aspirations. He didn't say that he wanted to obtain his doctorate degree, run a marathon, or solve world hunger; he spoke only of his commitment to the people he was so honored to command. It was beautiful. I love it! I've used similar lines in interviews myself since then.

Robert Jarvik, scientist, researcher, and inventor of the artificial heart, once said, "Leaders are visionaries with a poorly developed sense of fear and no concept of the odds against them."

True leaders are not afraid to take risks, and in the world of policing, risk is the business we are in. I've seen so many leaders that are so afraid to make a decision—because to err or fail might adversely impact their chances at promotion—that they never make a decision. Or they make decisions based on what will make them look good, regardless of the impact their decisions will have on the community and their people. When the decision goes bad, they'll be the first to point the finger at someone else and not accept one iota of responsibility. The lack of decision making, or the fatal flaw of making decisions for the wrong reasons, will be their demise. How did we ever promote these people?

Former US Speaker of the House Newt Gingrich said, "We're all human, and we all goof. So you've got to be able to take risks. And when you make mistakes, you have to be willing to say, 'Yeah, that proves I'm a leader.' Do things that may be wrong, but do something." Although I am reluctant to use a quote from Gingrich after watching him perform in the US election primary debates in 2012, it is a great quote!

To *not* take risks as a leader is risky business in itself. In policing, whether responding to a barricaded-person call or a domestic disturbance, tracking a killer, conducting an investigation, or directing traffic, our people take tremendous risks. As their leader, if you are viewed as afraid to take risks or incapable of making a decision, the people you lead are undoubtedly going to wonder why they are taking such enormous risks if you won't, and may not ever, truly have their backs if things go bad. We can never forget that things *will* go bad at some point.

Motivational speaker and author Brian Tracy says, "Leaders think and talk about the solutions. Followers think and talk about the problems."

How true. How many so-called leaders who occupy the seats of senior managers do nothing or contribute very little to the organization, as they merely sit back and throw snowballs at every decision made above them? That is not an easy ship to turn around as a leader.

Now, no one ever said that leadership was easy. Striving to continually do the right things for the right reasons can be challenging, but true leaders have to stick to the script. It's all about the people we serve and the people we lead. It is not about us as individuals. Many managers don't get that, but the true leaders do.

I have my own definition of leadership. Like the many above, it's not perfect, but it sums up leadership from my perspective. This was communicated OPP-wide as part of our renewed focus on leadership within the force:

> Leaders build trust through their actions and words; they inspire and support others to be the very best that they can be, as they work together to achieve results that are in the best interests of the people they serve.

That was my expectation of the supervisors and managers in the OPP. In my view, that is leadership. It is also my expectation of myself. I refuse to be anything less.

Management, Leadership...or Both?

$$\bullet\ \bullet\ \bullet$$

*Leadership in itself doesn't carry a positive or negative connotation.
It really means the management, guidance, discipline, and control of
the workforce but can be inspiring or impoverished. Through common
usage, "leadership" has become synonymous with good management,
but this is a bit of a misnomer. Great leadership is the hard-sought and
rarely attained quality that causes organizations to thrive, businesses to
prosper, governments to rule justly, and all of humankind to benefit.*

—Chief Dan Maluta

In 2005, I was having a debate with my direct supervisor about a policy issue. The manager smugly stated, "It's a leadership issue, Chris." I wholeheartedly disagreed and argued that it was a management issue, clearly not one of leadership, but I then received the hateful glare that usually accompanies an individual's displeasure with my actually having an opinion and, God forbid, possessing the gall to express it. What truly terrified me was that a person in such a very senior position didn't begin to understand the difference.

Management is your day job; leadership is your career.

—JOHN BALDONI

I often ask classes I'm addressing, "Is there a difference between management and leadership?" There's generally an agreement that a difference exists, but very few can actually define it. One answer that really caught my attention was that "leadership is hard." I'm sure most managers would be offended by that, but dealing with real people that have emotions, agendas, personalities, egos, motivators, and so much more, as opposed to manuals and ledgers, is without a doubt more demanding to the real leaders—the ones who truly care.

Author Dan McCarthy says, "Really, it's not as easy as it looks, or as easy as the books tell you it is. Leadership roles are chock full of dilemmas with no clear cut answers. These are highly visible positions, which magnify every mistake. I also think managers are often held to an unrealistic standard when it comes to leadership, standards set by all of those leadership books out there that describe the 72 things a leader has to be great at."

Here is Chief Frank Elsner's slant: "Leadership is art, management is science; leadership is pull, management is push."

In my view—and I probably read this somewhere years ago, so I apologize to whoever inspired my thoughts—leaders are more visionary and motivating, actually caring about substance while seeing a bigger picture, whereas managers focus more on planning, efficiency, form and process, and ensuring policy is followed.

There is no doubt that many leaders are good managers and many managers have the ability to lead. People aren't exclusively one or the other, thank God.

Author Dorie Clark said this while quoting Annmarie Neal in the article "Why Great Leaders Make Bad Managers—and That's OK": "'A leader is somebody who sees opportunity and puts change in motion. A manager is somebody who follows that leader and sees how to structure things to create value for the company,' she says. 'I've found that the best leaders weren't really good managers. Yes, they understood the discipline, but they weren't the best accountant, or the best technical person, or the best brand manager. They can do it, but they have a way of [thinking about the issues] at another level.'"

There is so much to be learned from books, articles, and quotes.

Leadership guru Warren Bennis is one of the best. His slant is this (source unknown):

A manager...	A leader...
Administers	Innovates
Is a copy	Is an original
Maintains	Develops
Focuses on systems and structure	Focuses on people
Relies on control	Inspires trust
Has short-range view	Has long-range perspective
Asks how and when	Asks what and why
Always has eye on the bottom line	Has eye on the horizon
Imitates	Originates
Accepts the status quo	Challenges the status quo
Is the classic good soldier	Is his or her own person
Does things right	Does the right things

Most of the greatly admired military leaders in history are probably not well known and respected for their management ability.

I recorded this quote about legendary US marine lieutenant general Lewis B. "Chesty" Puller a number of years back and apologize that I cannot find the source: "Although Puller was well known for his bravery and medals it was his reputation as a Leader that made him a legend. He was always out in front with his men in the thick of the fight, whether it was the enemy or the bureaucracy. He made the welfare of his men his greatest interest and he always inspired them to follow his example and give everything they had."

There's not one iota of that statement about Puller that speaks of management. In fact, I've yet to meet a great manager whom men and women would follow anywhere. I've met a few whom I'd undoubtedly follow, but simply out of morbid curiosity because I knew they would self-destruct at some point and it would be fun to watch.

Author John Kotter said, "Some people still argue that we must replace management with leadership. This is obviously not so: they serve different, yet essential, functions. We need superb management. And we need more superb leadership. We need to be able to make our complex organizations reliable and efficient. We need them to jump into the future—the right future—at an accelerated pace, no matter the size of the changes required to make that happen."

My friend, Chief Wayne Frechette (retired), was a leader, and although he was not an incapable manager, management was not his forte and he was proud of it. When it came to knowing policy, budgeting, and administration, Wayne's favorite saying was, "We've got people for that."

Wayne once caught the ire of his deputy while he was still a chief superintendent in the OPP, when he ordered an inspector to drive to Toronto and purchase a few dozen laptop computers from an electronic wholesaler. We needed the laptops, we had the money in the CIB budget, and Wayne was tired of waiting for proper government procurement processes to kick in, which we all knew would cost us two or three times as much money. But that was the policy.

The men and women in the CIB loved Wayne's un-manager-like decision, but the deputy ended up with a bleeding ulcer over it, I'm sure. Was that a good management decision by Wayne? Not at all. Did the world come crashing to an end over it? No. It actually met our dire operational needs and saved tax dollars, and Wayne won the hearts and souls of his people in the process.

There's a lot that can be learned about leadership from various military entities, but when it comes to the whole debate around management versus leadership, I love the following points from "Why Marines Never Use the 'M Word.'" I've added my own commentary after each point:

* Managers push their people.
* Leaders pull theirs by sheer force of personal example.

True leaders don't have to push; they make the people they lead want to be the better than the best. They continually demonstrate their expectations of others in their own actions.

* Managers order their personnel to get the job done.
* Leaders inspire their personnel to get the job done.

Haven't we all worked for those that we'd walk through broken glass for? Were they managers or leaders? Do we recall how well they managed a budget?

* Managers build a fire under your butt.
* Leaders build a fire in your belly.

What else can I say? Building that fire in our people should be foundational to us.

* "Hands-on" managers cultivate obedience.
* "Hands-off" leaders cultivate independence and resourcefulness.

Micromanagers can take away people's self-confidence and force them to second-guess all they do. Those being led start to question every decision they make, wondering how the boss will react to it.

* Managers consider themselves part of an exclusive club.
* Leaders maintain the respect and fellowship of the rank and file.

Maintaining that respect isn't easy—but it is quite possible. Some will say, "Oh, he or she has changed since being promoted." That is an unfair statement, given that the role of the individual has changed. If you and I work side by side as colleagues, it's not my job to deal with the fact that you're late for your shift or sneak away early, although as a friend I'd probably say something to you eventually. It is my responsibility, however, if I become your supervisor.

Being "one of the boys," so to speak, as a leader is a challenging balancing act at times. For the most part, however, it is simply common sense. When to socialize and when not to, when is the best time to leave an event, the appropriateness of comments or actions—none of that is akin to splitting an atom. We're smart people—we can pull it off!

When Julian Fantino was announced as the new OPP commissioner in 2006, the then president of the Ontario Provincial Police Association (OPPA) called me and told me that the membership was disappointed that I wasn't chosen. Although Julian was the right man at the right time and place for us, I was disappointed as well! But I thanked the president, saying, "You know I'd much rather not get the job and still have the respect of the members than get the job and have you all think that I'm a goof." I truly meant that.

- Managers accept credit for the success of their subordinates.
- Leaders turn away from the spotlight, letting it shine upon those they have the honor to lead.

Simple logic, but how often have we seen the exact opposite? We more often see those who clamor to accept undeserved credit.

- When a project turns sour, the manager asks, "Who is responsible?"
- Leaders say, "I am."

I'll have more to say about that key point. Bellying up to the bar when things go bad is a true sign of a leader.

- You work overtime for a manager.
- You work all the time for a leader.

The leaders out there easily tap the best of the best in their people, whereas the managers nickel and dime and micromanage their subordinates to the point that they won't give an extra inch.

* Managers need to constantly make their presence known.
* Leaders inspire from afar—even from the grave.

No kidding. We still admire the great leaders, even centuries after they are gone.

No one can read those *"m-word"* points about managers and leaders without conjuring up a face for every point made. We *all* know someone who fits the manager descriptors and someone who fits the leader descriptors, and it's never the same person. We all remember those who want to take the credit when they didn't do a single thing to earn it, and similarly we all know people who rise up and take the fall when things go wrong, even when they aren't wholly responsible.

Case in point: In the summer of 2007, when I was still deputy commissioner, I was travelling to Ottawa at a time when all police services in Canada were on the lookout for a killer named Jesse Imeson. He had brutally killed a Windsor man, then savagely murdered an elderly couple in southwestern Ontario. He was on the run in a stolen pickup truck, which was eventually located in a rural area north of Ottawa, very near the Quebec border. The regional commander of the day, Larry Beechey, was keeping me apprised as our officers scoured the surrounding area. The OPP had scads of resources there, including tactical officers, investigators, a helicopter, canine units, and every other thing we had that could run, bite, and shit, as this killer was a tremendous threat to public safety.

Following a lengthy search and coming up with nothing, all of our officers met and decided to send the majority of resources home. The Sûreté du Québec (SQ) was kept apprised throughout, and it was believed Imeson was now traversing its turf.

That night, Larry called and updated me that our officers had arrested Imeson without incident on the Quebec side. We had at the time—and frankly we still do, for the most part—legal issues with the timely carriage of firearms from province to province. The issue had yet to be even partially solved at that time. Larry and I discussed the fact that our officers went into Quebec armed, without authority, but based on the fact that when the SQ called, they had only a single officer in the area and no tactical resources and Imeson had been spotted running from a cottage in a populated recreation area while carrying a rifle, our people made the made the right call "in the interests of public safety." I learned that when the SQ notified them, our officers huddled and discussed the pros and cons of going into Quebec, then decided to do what they had to do. They caught Imeson, and no one, including Imeson, was injured. It was a huge success story and national news.

The following morning, I dropped by the regional headquarters and met a group of staff that were still high-fiving each other for this great capture. One said, "Hey, Deputy, did you hear that we caught Imeson?"

I put on my game face and said, "Yes I did. And who made the decision to send our people into Quebec armed, without authority?" You could have heard a pin drop. It was as if they realized, "Damn. He figured it out. He's not as stupid as he looks." People were nervously glancing at each other, the walls, and the floor, but no one would make eye contact with me.

Then a young, newly minted inspector stepped forward, and said, "I did, sir." I simply smiled and said, "Good decision."

My point here is that this shiny new inspector, who was the incident commander at the scene the night before, was willing to take the hit for what they all collectively thought I was ticked off about. Of course, I wasn't upset at all and couldn't have been prouder, but he didn't know that. Regardless, he stood up and accepted responsibility for the perceived error. I wish we had a zillion more just like him. That is leadership. The true manager would have followed policy to the letter, and God only knows what might have occurred as a result.

Many of the leaders that we study to this day are long gone: Washington, Lincoln, Roosevelt, Sir John A. MacDonald, Gandhi, Churchill, and many more. But we still remember what they did to lead people and entire nations.

Have you ever gone into a town square somewhere and seen a majestic stone monument of a man standing tall or riding the back of a sculptured horse while brandishing a sword? I'm sure if you did that you also took the time to read the inscription on the plaque that accompanied the statue. Did it ever, even once, call him a great manager? I think not.

In his article "The Difference between Managing and Leading," author Steve Keating says:

> Believing that managing and leading are one in the same is very, very outdated thinking. You manage "stuff." You lead people.
> Every organization needs both managers and leaders. Sometimes those two very different skill sets can belong to the same person. It should however never be assumed that because someone is a skilled manager that they are or will become a skilled leader.

I do truly believe that organizations, whether they are police services or not, need strong managers. Someone needs to know policy, manage a budget, ensure diary dates are kept, oversee the business-planning cycle, administer procurement processes, ensure records are properly kept, and much more. Those are all vital matters for any organization, private or public sector. However, the leaders therein will get us through the tough times, supported by strong managers.

Author Russell H. Ewing says the following:

> A boss creates fear, a leader confidence.
> A boss fixes blame, a leader corrects mistakes.
> A boss knows all, a leader asks questions.
> A boss makes work drudgery, a leader makes it interesting.
> A boss is interested in himself or herself, a leader is interested in the group.

In a perfect world, all police leaders would have the right mix of leadership and management skills. In the real world, I'll take the leaders any day of the week and ensure they are supported by good managers to ensure the i's are dotted and the t's crossed. I'll make sure they are bolstered by managers who provide solid advice on policy, systems, and process matters, but I want and need leadership.

Leaders: Born This Way?

• • •

Leaders are made, not born. Leadership is forged in times
of crisis. It's easy to sit there with your feet up on the desk
and talk theory. Or send someone else's kids off to war
when you've never seen a battlefield yourself. It's another
thing to lead when your world comes tumbling down.

—Lee Iacocca

Are leaders born, or are they made? The question is as old as "What came first: the chicken or the egg?"

Here is Senator Vern White's perspective: "Some things are inherent; many things can be developed for sure. Every great leader I have worked with and around, I have seen positive growth and changes in their skills."

This age-old debate regarding leadership traits being learned or intrinsic will never be concretely decided. I am convinced, however, that many of the greatest leaders—whether in sport, military, policing, or the private sector—were born with natural leadership ability but then significantly developed the key skills over time.

There is no doubt that some individuals are "born leaders," and
they will be easy to identify for any police manager. They may face
hurdles as well but intrinsically possess the key qualities that compel

their peers to follow them, and thus the battle is at least half-won.
For others, attaining and giving credibility to a leadership position
may be daunting, despite their genuine efforts and altruistic
motives. Then there are those among the ranks that will surprise
you, when it's observed that "sometimes the position makes the man
(or woman)." People with core competency that were never leaders
do rise to the occasion and the challenge put in front of them.

—CHIEF DAN MALUTA

A few days following the Denver Broncos' playoff loss to the New England Patriots in January 2012, a football analyst on the Headline News Network was talking about Tim Tebow, the Broncos' young religious quarterback, about whom there had been considerable controversy prior to the playoffs and after. Some said that he "doesn't look like a quarterback," and others that "he's too tall and heavy…he's built more like a lineman." His forward passes were allegedly unorthodox. But the young man led his team to the American Football Conference West Championship, with some impressive victories.

Amid the calls and e-mails denouncing Tebow, the analyst defended him, saying something like this: "He may be unorthodox. He may not look like most quarterbacks or throw the perfect spiral, but he makes great things happen. If you're a true leader, they respond to your way, not your play."

This young man, just twenty-four years old at the time, captured the hearts and souls of a team, a city, and a state, at minimum. Despite the fact that his football skill level is thought to have declined in the years since, he was born to lead.

However, many great leaders are not born with all of the requisite skills. They develop themselves into strong leaders by watching and listening to others, learning what works and what doesn't, and working hard to better their proficiency at certain skills.

Internationally known author and speaker Meghan M. Biro says:

So, can this ability to touch and inspire people be learned? No and yes. The truth is that not everyone can lead, and there is no substitute for natural talent. Honestly, I'm more convinced of this now—I'm in reality about the world of work and employee engagement. But for those who fall somewhat short of being a natural born star (which is pretty much MANY of us), leadership skills can be acquired, honed and perfected.

Lecturer and author Jonathan Byrnes stated in his article "The Essence of Leadership,"

> Natural leaders have important core abilities, but they often need careful training in the more practical aspects of converting a creative vision into a concrete program of action.
> Most people, however, can develop their leadership skills by working at it.
> Once you decide to become a leader, you can develop the characteristics you'll need by being thoughtful about the accomplishments that you want on your résumé, and deciding to devote the time and attention needed to achieve them. Like anything else, practice makes perfect.

Here is author and regular Forbes' Magazine contributor Erika Anderson's opinion as stated in "Are Leaders Born or Made?":

> People tend to ask me a few questions over and over. By far the most common…is "Are leaders born or made?"
> What I've learned by observing thousands of people in business over the past 30 years, though, is that—like most things—leadership capability falls along a bell curve. Some people are, indeed, born leaders. These folks at the top of the leadership bell curve start out very good, and tend to get even better as they go along. Then there are the folks at the bottom of the curve: that bottom

10–15% of people who, no matter how hard they try, simply aren't ever going to be very good leaders. They just don't have the innate wiring.

Then there's the big middle of the curve, where the vast majority of us live. And that's where the real potential for "made" leaders lies.

Chief Paul Shrive agrees: "In my opinion, the ability to lead is not a gene but a developed skill."

So does Julian Fantino, associate minister:

Leadership is an acquired—learned—ability.

Some people are better suited to become good leaders; however, I believe that wholesome leaders are developed through a process of practical and theoretical learning and experience where they can still develop and refine their skills.

Julian once told me that when he was interviewed by a provincial-government panel for the position of OPP commissioner, they asked him the standard panel question, "Why should you be the commissioner of the OPP?" Julian's reply was simple: "Why not?" You've got to love it.

People can certainly learn from other leaders and as well from their own successes and failures. They can also learn from the feedback of those they lead, if they are open to hear and accept criticism. That ability in itself is a critical element of effective leadership but is not necessarily inherent in all who lead. We should recognize our own faults as well as know our strengths. We don't hesitate to utilize our strengths to our advantage, so we should do all we can to develop our weaknesses, or at minimum do what we can to control, minimize, or completely avoid exhibiting them.

Quite often, we can learn more from failures than we do from successes. They are usually more impactful, either on the people we lead or the people we serve and therefore on us as individuals.

"We need to understand and conquer failure if we are ever to master success," Australian leadership coach Siimon Reynolds writes in "Why People Fail." But if we can learn from our own failures, it's also possible that we might learn from the failure of others, and through that, avoid making the same mistakes ourselves.

—HARVEY SCHACHTER

As a young constable in my second northern posting, I worked for a corporal detachment commander who shall remain nameless. Julian Fantino told me years ago, "Never speak poorly of the dead," so I won't.

This corporal was a bitter, grumpy man. Nothing pleased him. You could solve a rape case, and he'd give you hell for not using the radar that day. He never saw the good in anything. He'd come into the small office each morning, grunt, fart, scratch himself, and go into his office for the entire day as if he had the weight of the entire world on his shoulders. He had six constables and one civilian admin person to supervise, and they were all good workers. He lived in a government house fifteen feet from the detachment. He kept an unmarked cruiser in his driveway for his exclusive use. Life wasn't all that bad, in my view. In fairness, the man had lost a young son to drowning some years prior and was in the police boat that recovered the body, so his life had not been easy. But as I told a colleague that was defending him one time, "My father buried a son as well, but he didn't start treating people like shit afterward."

One day the sergeant detachment commander from the neighboring Kapuskasing Detachment stopped into our office as he was driving by. He asked me how my corporal, who was absent, was doing. Feeling rather cocky as the grizzled three-year veteran that I was and being in a foul mood to begin with, I answered, "He's a useless prick."

The sergeant, a man named Ed Clinton, stopped dead in his tracks as he walked toward the door. His head spun toward me, and without so much as a smile, he made a clear statement that I will never forget. He said,

"He is not useless. He's a perfectly good bad example. Watch everything that moron does, and never do any of it. You'll then be a success on this job."

I figured I was heading even further north when his head spun, but in fact Ed taught me a valuable lesson. You can learn as much or more from the bad leaders. Simply watch everything they do, remember how they made you feel when they did, and never do any of it to anyone else.

Ed Clinton, whom I respectfully call "Dad" whenever I see him, is long retired now. He was and is a colorful character and a good leader. When he was an inspector at our old General Headquarters in Toronto, one day a superintendent from our Audit Branch was interviewing him as part of an audit process. He asked Ed, "So tell me in layman's terms exactly what you do here day after day." Ed replied as only Ed could: "Well, to be honest with you, most of the time I just sit and look out that fucking window right there." Ed reported to his new job in the Audit Branch a day or two later. I love the man.

Commissioner Bob Paulson said,

I think some people are born with qualities that make it easier or more natural for them to become good leaders, but I absolutely believe that a person, no matter what qualities they naturally possess, must be developed through experience, learning, and mentoring in order to become a truly effective leader. Leadership is not a trait that turns on charisma, charm, or good looks. It requires the thoughtful, deliberate application of principled behavior, which can be understood and therefore learned. The challenge, of course, is in the execution: you know how to take the reservation, but you need to learn how to keep the reservation! Which is not to say that everyone can develop into an effective leader. It seems to be clear that a small number of people are born impervious to acquiring the skills, abilities, knowledge, and discipline required of an effective leader.

I totally agree with Bob. There are many people out there in all types of workplaces that will never, ever become good or even mediocre leaders. This is a hard concept to accept for those seeking promotion but don't have it and never will. They just don't have any innate leadership skills and are incapable of learning. Sadly, some of them are already in leadership positions and erode away at the morale within their organizations. But they think they know what they are doing, which can be even more damaging to the fabric of the organization.

> *Here's the problem: many people who call themselves leaders are only posing. They're wearing the label or accepting the title without putting their skin in the game. So I'm asking you—assuming that you really do aspire to lead—to approach the act of leadership as you'd approach an extreme sport: learn to love the fear and exhilaration that naturally comes with the territory. And that takes a personal commitment and a significant, personal choice. As my friend and colleague, Terry Pearce, said in an article in the* San Francisco Examiner*: "There are many people who think they want to be matadors, only to find themselves in the ring with two thousand pounds of bull bearing down on them, and then discover that what they really wanted was to wear tight pants and hear the crowd roar."*

—Steve Farber

As a young and new corporal in January 1986, I was the team leader of the OPP's Tactics and Rescue Unit (TRU) in London. I'd been a member of the team since 1982, was very close friends with the team members that I served alongside as a constable, and had been to hell and back with some of them, both on duty and off. Any of us would have put our lives on the line for any other team member, day or night, and that actually came close to happening on many occasions.

My closest friend was a member of that team. I am godfather to his eldest son. He was and is the greatest guy in the world. When he is in a room, he is almost always the nicest guy in it. I won't name him, but he knows that I anonymously speak of him in leadership lectures, and he's OK with that.

Now retired into a successful private sector career, he was a dedicated officer and is a good husband and a wonderful father. He was a superb member of the TRU. But at the same time, he was a walking disaster. He lost almost everything he had, on duty and off, then broke the few things that he didn't lose. He would show up for work late, driving into the police station in a personal car with one headlight and an expired license plate, and would be missing pieces of his uniform, sometimes his coat or his hat or, God forbid, both. He drove a motorcycle that he wasn't licensed for. He'd seize weapons and license plates and other items from people and throw them in his locker along with half-completed property reports.

The staff sergeant had to go into his locker looking for something at a time when my friend was away and found thirty bottles of liquid Wite-Out therein. He came to me and said, "What's wrong with that man? Does he have some kind of a Wite-Out fetish?" Actually, I think he did.

It was always kind of funny to us all, and he took the kidding from his teammates jovially. Then suddenly, I wasn't his teammate; I was the team leader and his supervisor. I wasn't finding it quite as humorous as I once did.

Within weeks of my promotion, my friend told me he was going to compete for promotion himself and asked whether I would support him. I muttered an agreement of some sort and then began to lose sleep over it. How could I support him? How could I tell my best friend that he was not ready to be a corporal and why? I had yet to discuss any of his short-comings with him. Not a good start to corporalhood for me, and it was entirely my own fault.

I made a list of all the things that he did wrong that showed me he wasn't ready for promotion and that he needed to fix. It was extensive, and I sat on it. I didn't have the parts to disappoint my best friend by sharing it with him. My wife said, "You're losing sleep over this, but he's not. He doesn't even know he's done anything wrong." She was totally right. I was failing as a leader. I did not possess the fortitude to take on my best friend.

So we had a meeting. I went over many of the issues on my list, and he looked very sad. I had hit him with way too much at once. I said, "Why don't you make a list of all the things that you do that show you're ready for promotion, and we'll compare lists?" He replied, "I don't know what I'd put on mine." He went on to tell me how hard it was to hear all of that from me, as his friend, but that all I had said was true. He agreed not to compete in the promotional process.

I don't know who was more hurt by the conversation, he or I, but I learned some valuable lessons throughout.

We grow up together in policing and in a variety of other careers. We generally start young and go through the best of times and the worst of times together, on duty and off. Weddings, the birth of children, separations, new homes, incredible times, and unfortunately the occasional tragedies. We put our lives in each other's hands day after day. In smaller agencies we work side by side for decades, and even in larger ones, where we transfer around, we remain in contact and often end up posted somewhere together again. Sometimes we are of equal rank, and other times one has to supervise the other. Those roles can end up reversed at different junctures, but we remain connected like family.

I didn't do my friend any favors by letting things slide, never raising an issue with him, and then hitting him with a laundry list of items all at once. From that point on, if an issue was worthy of a discussion with a person, friend or not, I would have it immediately or soon thereafter at the right time and place. That early issue taught me lessons and skills that I was not born with.

When I transferred away from the team some time later, my friend spoke at my farewell party. I'll never forget his words. He said, "You're weren't always easy to work for. In fact, at times you were hard on us. But we always knew that when you were, you were never trying to make yourself look good. You were trying to make us and the team better."

He went on to have a tremendously successful career and retired as a chief superintendent. Although I like to think that I had a positive impact on his career, it certainly wasn't because of my strength and wisdom as his new corporal back in 1986. I learned more from that early leadership failing on my part than from any other situation in my career. I know in my heart that he did as well.

Chief Leanne Fitch said, "I believe that certain inherent characteristics can set people up to be more likely leaders than others. Those natural characteristics or personality traits are only part of the equation. Life is a journey, and great leaders never stop learning life lessons along the way and apply those lessons accordingly. Sometimes the meek will emerge over their lifetimes to become very effective and well-respected leaders in their own right. The right social conditioning, experience, and learning can certainly play a significant role in shaping leadership skills."

In his book *Leadership*, Canadian general Rick Hillier (retired), a man whom I have a ton of respect for, stated his beliefs in terms of the question of whether leaders are born or developed:

> My view of leadership is that it is a combination of art and science that, when practised, gets people to do more as a group than they thought humanly possible. And, I believe, it can be taught. At the very least, budding leaders will always have the opportunity to learn from the mistakes of others. We can and must teach people to become leaders. I'm not certain that leaders such as Churchill, Gandhi and King can ever be developed through a leadership program, but if people are born with at least some of the right DNA, they can learn enough to effect enormous change.

My personal belief is that some people are born with natural human skills that are harder to learn than others and will contribute greatly to their leadership ability. At the same time, those and other skills can be further developed or improved in those people, as well as in some (not all) people that they don't come naturally to.

The key skill is the ability to communicate. Some people climb out of the womb ready to talk and listen. They are gifted that way, and that gives them an advantage from the start. You can learn to talk—both one-on-one and publicly to groups—but it's never quite as effective if it's forced.

My youngest daughter, Stephanie, was very shy as a child and was probably close to twenty years old before she would freely talk to people that she didn't know. She is in a supervisory role now with the Ontario government, and I'm very proud of how she's developed herself, including her ability to talk to people. She's a wonderful young woman, personally and professionally.

Some years back, Steph and I were talking about communicating, and I said something to the effect that she needed to try to be more open with people and have more dialogue with colleagues, people working in stores, and neighbors.

Her reply was, "Words don't fly out of my ass like they do out of yours." She was indeed coming out of her shell. She must have gotten that smart mouth from her mother!

I am very blessed. I have the ability to remember names and faces and often things about people. I've never been shy and enjoy talking to almost everyone and anyone. Although I also have the ability to say the wrong thing at times and can even be a bit inappropriate when my brain is not in full gear before my lips are, truly liking people and being able to talk to anyone have undoubtedly worked for me. This comes naturally to me and, combined with an ability to remember faces and things about those faces, has helped me to really get to know people in a different way. It was a skill that I was fortunate to have been born with, not one I had to learn, but I still had to hone it and use it appropriately to my advantage.

Wally Bock is a leadership consultant, author and blogger. He makes an excellent point regarding the 'born or made' argument when he states:

Leaders Are Always Made
Leadership can be learned by anyone with the basics. But an awful lot of leadership cannot be taught.

That's because leadership is an apprentice trade. Leaders learn about 80 percent of their craft on the job.
They learn from watching other leaders and emulating their behavior. They choose role models and seek out mentors. They ask other leaders about how to handle situations.
Leaders improve by getting feedback and using it. The best leaders seek feedback from their boss, their peers and their subordinates. Then they modify their behavior so that they get better results.
Leaders learn by trying things out and then critiquing their performance. The only failure they recognize is the failure to learn from experience.
Effective leaders take control of their own development. They seek out training opportunities that will make a difference that will make a difference in their performance."

Chief Rick Deering said this about leadership:

It is my firm belief that leaders are both born and developed. The great leaders are individuals who demonstrated certain personality traits from an early age that enabled them to gravitate to positions of leadership. These are the people who rose to prominent positions in school, in the sports that they participated in, and in the social activities and organizations they were part of.
From a policing perspective, most of those who became leaders were afforded the opportunity, through demonstrated merit, skill, and ability, to develop and progress through the ranks.
Conversely, there are those who were not born to be leaders but were able to manipulate the system and become what I'll describe as faux leaders. Fortunately, through their own undoing, their lack of leadership qualities is usually exposed over time.

So what is your answer to this centuries-old debate? You decide.

We Are Nothing without Trust

• • •

*I don't trust easily. So when I tell you "I trust
you," please don't make me regret it.*

—J. Cole

LEADERS NEED TO TRUST THEIR people. Their people need to trust them.
Trust in the leaders of an organization is paramount to its success.

> *The growing tensions between leaders and their employees are
> creating productivity challenges as uncertainty becomes the new
> normal in the workplace. Furthermore, leaders are beginning to lose
> control of their own identities and effectiveness as their employees
> begin to lose trust in their intentions because of hidden agendas and
> political maneuvering—casting clouds of doubt over their futures.
> Employees just want the truth. They have learned that the old
> ways of doing things just don't apply (as much) anymore and
> more than ever they need their leaders to have their backs.*

—GLENN LOPIS

Although trust is earned only through effective leadership and not because of rank or position, if the men and women don't trust the daily decision making of their leaders, they can't be expected to trust them in dire situations.

> *Trust is a tremendous asset and distrust an enormous liability yet time and time again our corporate and political leaders forfeit their claim to trust and the critical benefits of credibility by dishonest or misleading statements or by doing things in secret that, if found out, will be considered a betrayal by those who trusted them.*

—MICHAEL JOSEPHSON

In *A Leadership Primer*, Gen. Colin Powell says, "The day soldiers stop bringing you their problems is the day you have stopped leading them. They have either lost confidence that you can help them or concluded that you do not care. Either case is a failure of leadership."

It is my belief that effective leadership can positively influence the morale of the workforce in any public sector organization or private enterprise. Morale, although difficult to define, ultimately impacts the productivity or performance of the workforce, as well as their behavior, in terms of professionalism. In a police service, performance and professionalism weigh heavily in the development and sustainability of the trust of the public the agency serves. Public trust is vital and must be sustained.

It is critical to note that effective leadership and the morale of the organization are invariably linked, that morale impacts the professionalism and productivity of the organization's members, and finally that productivity and trust can greatly influence public opinion and therefore the trust a community has in its police service.

The world of policing is a competitive business. If the police service doesn't have the trust of the community it serves, community leaders have the option of going to a police service that they do trust for service. Officers and staff are faced with the challenge of serving their community well and professionally or losing the policing contract and having to move to another community to continue their careers.

Leadership is the critical nexus to police services ultimately earning and retaining public trust.

According to author Joe Costantino, Jim Burke, former CEO of Johnson & Johnson said, "You can't have success without trust. The word trust embodies almost everything you can strive for that will help you succeed. You tell me any human relationship that works without trust, whether it is a marriage or a friendship or a social interaction; in the long run, the same thing is true about business, especially businesses that deal with the public."

Trust impacts policing in at least two ways. Firstly, the officers and personnel within the service earn and sustain a level of public trust by their actions, on duty and off. As I have said a million times, there is a high expectation from the public that the police will be the "good guys," and incidents that portray the police in a negative light, deserved or not, totally shake public confidence in the police as individuals and in police organizations. Unproductive and unprofessional police officers undoubtedly hurt public trust. The loss of public trust in a police service may well result in witnesses not coming forward and victims being reluctant to report crimes they've endured, and the negative focus of the media on a police organization is only one trust-impacting incident away.

Author Margaret Thorsborne said and I completely agree,

Trust is an incredibly precious commodity, and is always the first casualty when relationships in the workplace are damaged...what is common is the deterioration of relationships and the decrease of trust in management.

Goleman, Boyatzis and McKee...conclude that transparency—an authentic openness to others about one's feelings, beliefs and actions—engenders integrity, or the sense that a leader can be trusted; that he (or she) lives by his values and is genuine. They also stress that integrity is a leadership virtue and an organisational strength.

The International Association of Chiefs of Police (IACP) "Model Policy on Standards and Conduct" states, "Actions of officers that are inconsistent, incompatible, or in conflict with the values established by this agency negatively affect its reputation and that of its officers. Such actions and inactions thereby detract from the agency's overall ability to effectively and efficiently protect the public, maintain peace and order, and conduct other essential business."

In 2011, I visited the Trinidad and Tobago Police Service and met with a number of senior officers there. They were and continue to be in a state of rebuilding and rebranding that force. Following a number of scandals involving police corruption, they faced a tremendous uphill battle in earning public trust. One senior officer told me that the average citizen had this attitude: "If you call the police, they won't come, but if they do, they'll be corrupt anyway." What a sad situation to recover from.

In a message from the director general entitled *Management of the RCMP Disciplinary Process 2009–2010 Annual Report*, Chief Superintendent Richard Evans said, "The Royal Canadian Mounted Police (RCMP) and indeed all law enforcement agencies in Canada depend on public trust to do their job well. When citizens start to question the actions of the police and that public trust is shaken, police work becomes immeasurably more difficult. Law enforcement agencies depend on the willingness of the public to share information and provide assistance; neither will be forthcoming when citizens do not trust the police. Earning public trust may take years while its loss can take seconds."

That statement applies to all police departments across the world.

During a panel discussion at the 2012 International Conference for Police and Law Enforcement Executives in Seattle, Washington, in which I participated, my friend Chief A. C. Roper of the Birmingham, Alabama, Police Department said, "Community trust can be fragile. It is difficult to build and difficult to maintain. It requires a constant effort."

Leaders come in all shapes and sizes, and more than one leadership
style can be successful, from high profile to quiet effectiveness.

Envisioning goals, affirming values, motivating, explaining,
representing, and serving as a symbol are all part of the chief's role,
but the chief must also foster the process of organizational renewal.
A leader who demonstrates moral courage—one who is steady,
reliable, and fair—will consistently attract loyalty and trust.

—Chief Robert Lunney

Secondly, the issue of trust also impacts the ability of leaders to effectively lead and to ensure morale, and thus professionalism and productivity, remain high.

Trust in a leader isn't earned overnight. For the most part, people don't develop trust for their leaders in crisis situations but through their day-to-day interactions. Even when the level of trust is high, it can be altered in the blink of an eye when leaders let their people down when things go bad, particularly if they try to pass the blame or don't step up to the plate at the right time and in the proper way.

It's not human nature to develop the level of trust we require as police leaders without a personal connection of some degree with the people we lead. Those leaders who sit in their offices, are seldom seen outside the building, are rarely seen or heard in the media, and don't say so much as "Good morning" to staff members in the hallways are destined for failure. On the other hand, those leaders that take the time to chat with people, get to know them as much as possible by name and role, endeavor to understand what makes them tick, learn a little bit about them, and actually interact with their folks at public events or even in operational situations will develop that necessary connection.

In her article "Four Lessons from the Best Bosses I Ever Had," author Deborah Mills-Scofield says, "What else did I learn from three incredible manager-mentors? While there were many lessons, this has stood out for me over the past 30 years: Trust trumps everything. And everything flows from trust—learning, credibility, accountability, a sense of purpose and a mission that makes 'work' bigger than oneself."

How many times have employees heard or said the words "We never see him" in regard to a leader? Or "She has never darkened the door of our office." If the people don't know the leader except for the photo on the company's website or its annual report, how are they ever going to develop any level of trust in him or her?

Lincoln knew that true leadership is always realized by exerting quiet and subtle influence on a day-to-day basis, by frequently seeing followers and other people face-to-face. He treated everyone with the same courtesy and respect, whether they were kings or commoners. He lifted people out of their everyday selves and into a higher level of performance, achievement and awareness. He obtained extraordinary results from ordinary people by instilling purpose in their endeavors. He was open, civil, tolerant, and fair, and he maintained a respect for the dignity of people at all times.

—DONALD T. PHILLIPS

From an operational perspective, leaders can't necessarily lead the charge during a raid on a Hells Angels clubhouse, but they can appear at briefings for large events like mass arrests and offer encouragement. They can walk around and support the troops at protests and significant public gatherings. And they must be front and center when the chips are down, such as, God forbid, when an officer is injured or killed and for funerals and memorial parades. They can't simply show up for the accolades and for ribbon cuttings.

I've probably attended more operational events than I should have as a senior officer. That's my style—right or wrong. I realize that it may have confused the chain-of-command issues when I appeared at operational events. Although I always did my best to make it clear that I was not the incident commander and that another person was, I fully understood that there was inherent risk in that. If I was there and things got bad, the world would know that I was there, at an inquiry or inquest. So be it. I accepted that risk as the commissioner. I'd rather be criticized for attending an event with my vest and gun belt proudly displayed than be an absentee landlord when the chips are down.

Let me tell you that when I appeared, it did have an incredible impact on our people and those from other agencies. It was never an attempt on my part to be a hero or to say, "Hey, look at me." That is not who I am. But I was a police officer and the leader of the organization that I proudly served. I am convinced that this has resulted in the development of trust in those that I have led.

When Julian Fantino became our commissioner in the fall of 2006, we were embroiled in the Caledonia land-claim dispute. We had undoubtedly made some mistakes there over several highly volatile months of violent protests and clashes, but I will defend our overall approach to it until my dying breath. Within a day or two of assuming command, Julian went there personally. He was in full uniform, wearing his duty belt. He attended the command post and every one of the surrounding checkpoints. He got out of the car at every stop, put his hand out, and said, "Hi. I'm Julian Fantino," to every OPP member that he met. It was poetry in motion. He swung the vote on his appointment instantaneously. Those who didn't want a commissioner from the outside or had heard of this legendary tough-guy chief from Toronto and feared his expected heavy-handed approach largely changed their opinions on that day.

It wasn't magical, but it was impactful. One big, strong senior sergeant told me afterward that he "almost started crying" when Julian approached him at a checkpoint. It was a challenging and protracted operation, and everyone involved was exhausted, physically and emotionally. But Julian appeared like a phoenix from the ashes and restored the confidence of our people. Although I've always felt that approach is the best course of action for a leader, actually witnessing it happen had a huge impact on me as well. It validated my personal beliefs, and it made me proud of my boss.

In the more relaxed and day-to-day environments of our offices, how we interact with all of our people is critical to our success as leaders as well.

I always did my best to say "Hello," "Good morning," "How are you?" or "Have a nice weekend" to every employee I met in our large headquarters building, regardless of how busy or stressed I was. That was important to me. It included part-time employees, uniforms, cafeteria personnel, civilians, admin staff command personnel, cleaners, contractors, and Michael, "the Dish Nazi," who grumpily scraped plates in the cafeteria day after day but just wanted to be a part of the group. Who they were and what they did made no difference to me—they were all a part of our team and of the OPP family. I wouldn't have had it any other way. I talked to them more about weather, current events, families, and life than I ever did about work. If work came up, it was because they mentioned it.

In the book *Motivating the "What's in It for Me?" Workforce*, author Cam Marston said,

> When interacting with Gen X or New Millennial employees, broaden the topics of conversation and don't focus on work to the exclusion of everything else. If your goal is to get to know your employees, let them talk about the things that are important to them, which may make you realize that work isn't necessarily high on their lists. As a dedicated Boomer, this might seem foreign to you. However, in the long run it pays off to allow your employees to lead the conversation so you can learn about their families, hobbies, and lives.

Good interrogators always take the time to develop a rapport or common bond with suspects before they close in for the confession, in an attempt to at minimum make the suspect feel, "This cop isn't a bad person. If I'm ever going to tell anyone about what happened, it's this cop." Then if the interrogator can lay out the case facts and provide the right stimuli and effective analogies, there just might be a confession in the offing.

When lecturing on interrogation over the years, or even when speaking to recruits about developing rapport with the community at large, I always said, "If you were forced to tell someone the worst thing you ever did in your life, that one thing your mom or wife or husband or kids don't even know, or if you were forced to tell someone something horrendous that happened to you, like being the victim of some awful crime, would you want to tell someone that you kind of think isn't a bad person, isn't afraid to look you in the eye and say hello, listens to you when you speak, and is polite and professional and seems to actually care? Or would you choose to tell someone that you think is a dick? Your job from this point on, as an interrogator (or new police officer), is to become that person that people will feel they can trust."

So if you apply that simplified version of interrogation theory to leadership, are employees likely to trust leaders that they don't know, respect, or even like? Trust doesn't come because a leader has rank or positional power; it has to be earned.

In the 2012 *CACP Professionalism in Policing Research Project* paper, the authors stated, "A number of questions suggest that police officers do not believe that the organization or its senior managers take an interest in their concerns. Lack of support is related to reduced trust and lower commitment to the organization's success. To enhance support, police agencies need to communicate their concern for employees' well-being, solicit employees' input on decisions affecting them and provide support for employees' goals."

Once earned, trust has to be retained for the leader to succeed. Day after day, year after year, the concerted effort on the part of the leader has to be there. Then when the big event occurs, those being led will walk through a bed of hot coals to get the job done, because the leader they trust so much will be there with them The leaders will give them direction that they trust, and if things go badly (and they occasionally will), will stand tall and support them through it. When things go well (and they more often do), he or she will allow the light of success shine on those being led.

Stephen M. R. Covey says in his landmark book *The Speed of Trust,*

Talk straight. Let people know where you stand. Use simple language.
Demonstrate respect. Genuinely care and show it.
Create transparency. Tell the truth in a way that can be verified. Err
on the side of disclosure.
Right wrongs. Apologize quickly. Make restitution where possible.
Show loyalty. Give credit freely. Speak about people as if they were
present.
Keep commitments. Make commitments carefully. Don't break
confidences.
Extend trust. Extend trust abundantly to those who have earned
it. Extend trust conditionally to those who are earning it.

On personal or professional levels, once trust is lost, it is extremely
difficult to attain again. The loss of trust is difficult to recover from.
Many people will agree that they can forgive someone for an error or
omission if the person admits to it, but once they are lied to, it's almost
impossible to trust the person again. German philosopher Friedrich
Nietzsche once said in a now-famous quote, "I'm not upset that you
lied to me; I'm upset that from now on I can't believe you." That axiom
applies to leaders every bit as much as it does spouses, friends, partners,
and children.

That critical element of trust also works in reverse. It's not just about
leaders being trusted by those they lead; the leaders have to trust, and
demonstrate their trust, in employees as well. Author Randy Conley ex-
plains it very well:

Some would argue that trust has to be earned before it is given,
so that places the responsibility on the follower to make the first
move. The follower needs to demonstrate trustworthiness over a
period of time through consistent behavior, and as time goes by,
the leader extends more and more trust to the follower. Makes
sense and is certainly valid.

I would argue it's the leader's responsibility to make the first move. It's incumbent upon the leader to extend, build, and sustain trust with his/her followers.

...Trust is an absolute essential ingredient, and establishing, nurturing, and sustaining it has to be a top leadership priority.

Trusting our people to do the right thing and to do it well—and giving them some freedom and flexibility to sink or swim without micromanaging the heck out of them—resonates powerfully through the masses. That in turn builds even more trust in the leader by his or her team members.

Legendary US general George S. Patton sums the concept up well in two famous quotes:

If you tell people where to go, but not how to get there, you'll be amazed at the results.

Never tell people how to do things. Tell them what to do, and they will surprise you with their ingenuity.

When the entrusted employees fail—and they will on occasion (don't we all?)—the way the leader reacts to the failure ultimately sets the course for the future of the individuals involved and undoubtedly impacts their trust in their leader. Malice versus honest mistakes, honesty in response versus lying to cover the mistake, and learning from the failure and moving on as stronger employees are all factors to consider.

As I've said, leadership style directly affects the trust employees have in their leader. Their level of trust in their leader undoubtedly impacts their morale. Morale profoundly impacts productivity and professionalism, which then impacts public trust. Public trust greatly influences the success of the organization, which in turn further builds the trust of the client and increases the company's likelihood for success. Key to all of this is the leader's ability to build the trust of the employees he or she leads, therefore keeping morale high. I know that is quite a mouthful and is easier said than done, but did anyone say it would all be a cakewalk? It's well worth the effort.

All of these critical issues are inextricably linked, in my opinion, and leadership can make or break an organization when you consider the downstream impacts it can have on the trust variables I've detailed.

> *The ability to gain and hold the trust of subordinates is a sign of a real leader. I believe that trust is the most important factor when examining why people accept the direction of a leader. Earning the trust of subordinates is a critical component to leadership. The ability to develop trust involves a number of components. You best know what you are doing if you expect others to follow. A proven track record is a huge benefit when developing trust. Subordinates must trust that your directions and actions are directly related to the known goals of the organization.*

—CHIEF PAUL SHRIVE

Communication Is Key

• • •

Take advantage of every opportunity to practice your communication skills so that when important occasions arise, you will have the gift, the style, the sharpness, the clarity, and the emotions to affect other people.

—Jim Rohn

In my experience and humble opinion, the most critical aspect of leadership is the ability to communicate up, down, and across, effectively and with authenticity. Three hundred sixty degrees. The good, the bad, and the difficult. A leader doesn't have to be an award-winning orator, the life of the party, or a stand-up comedian, but 99 percent of what leaders do, or should do, involves the many forms of communication. If you can't talk to and listen to people, your odds of success in a leadership role are zilch. Move to the assembly line.

We must communicate to and with our people. We must accept that it's a foundational premise of leadership in this millennium. Our people expect and deserve that level of interaction.

And it's not just about being heard. No one wants to hear drivel from their supervisors. Nor do they want to listen to bragging or things that are either nonsensical or airy-fairy. It's important that you communicate in a way that your message is actually understood, using your own voice. Don't try to be someone else. Be an original, not a carbon copy. Your credibility is at stake if people view you as trying to be someone that you're not.

The *CACP Professionalism in Policing Research Project* points out that communication is critical:

> Demonstrating support for employees and clarifying the basis for decisions both require enhanced two-way communication between managers and employees.
>
> Time spent on communication may, in the short-term, seem less important than time spent on operational demands, but in the longer-term, investments in communications pay significant dividends.

We have so many tools at our fingertips now, all of which allow us the flexibility to communicate effectively through a variety of mediums, as opposed to the paper memoranda and sticky notes of days gone by. The need to utilize all these tools to our communication advantage has never been greater, as have the opportunities available and the expectation that we will.

Available tools we have include E-mail, websites, blogs, text messages, PINs, BBMs, video messaging, teleconferencing, social media, written communiques, and the age-old, tried-and-true face-to-face communication: walking around work locations and operational or social events, talking to people where they feel comfortable. Being visible is a form of communication too. A friendly smile or a nod is much more than many employees are used to getting from their bosses. Actually sitting on the corner of their desks, looking directly into their eyes, talking to them, and listening to them will blow them away. It has an even bigger impact when you talk about things other than work, joke a bit, laugh, and let them see you as a human, as opposed to a photo on a company wall.

We must do it all, talk and listen nonstop and capitalize on the multimedia approach. Sink or swim, folks.

The speed of communications is wondrous to behold.
It is also true that speed can multiply the distribution
of information that we know to be untrue.

—Edward R. Murrow

In her article "The High Cost of Low Morale," author Nicole Fink states,

> Effective communication is another essential leadership competency when it comes to improving low morale in healthcare employees. Communication that lacks clarity, focus, important details, is too infrequent, lacks meaning, and does not allow staff to respond and discuss their concerns can contribute to morale problems in the workplace.
>
> In addition, highly effective leaders will communicate widely and allow their messages to be discussed in person or at staff meetings. Allowing employees the opportunity to respond and ask questions helps to improve morale by making them feel that their thoughts and opinions are important (Dye & Garman, 2006).

As critical issues come and go in any organization, the people want to know what's going on. Most of them want to hear the truth, although there are always the few that would rather believe something ugly and evil is happening. In absence of any communication of facts from someone credible, the rumor mill takes over. The leader is much better off communicating quickly and transparently before that happens, as appropriate, rather than trying to play catch-up to correct the false rumors.

There are extremely difficult times that a leader has to communicate broadly across the organization. People simply need to hear from their leaders, especially when folks are wrought with emotion. This comes easier to some than it does to others, but there's no way around it. The method of delivery can differ, however.

I am not afraid to show my emotions. Some might feel that's one of my many weaknesses, but frankly I really don't care. It is who I am, as a person and as a leader.

Following the death of a young OPP officer named Al Hack in an on-duty collision in 2009, I felt a huge sense of loss as the deputy commissioner, and it hurt me to see so many of our people suffering through the tragic death of yet another member. Although I spoke to Al's fiancée, family, immediate colleagues, command staff, training officer, and platoon mates, I could feel the wave of sadness permeate the entire organization. I felt compelled to say something to the broader membership of the OPP and thought it might be therapeutic, for me personally and for those hurting, for me to say how I was feeling.

So I sent an e-mail out to the entire organization entitled "If You Could See What I Saw." I reflected on Al's death, the impact on his detachment and family, how proud I was to see our people and emergency-services colleagues pool together, the funeral, and the emotional impact that it had on me.

The reaction was instantaneous. I met people in the halls of headquarters that actually cried when they spoke of my e-mail message. People from across the OPP and beyond sent messages to thank me for sending it out. There were comments that indicated it made people feel as if they had actually attended the funeral themselves, although they couldn't, and that they couldn't believe a senior leader could so genuinely tell the story and reflect on his own feelings.

I didn't do it for that reaction, and although I was gratified by it, it told me yet again that our people hunger to know things. They truly appreciate it when we as leaders make the effort to communicate with them candidly and from the heart.

The downside, for lack of a better word, is that once you start communicating full bore like that, it becomes the expectation, and it is difficult to then cut back. In my view, it remains a positive, and we should be doing it regardless. The good in that approach far outweighs the bad.

*Communicate downward to subordinates with at least the same
care and attention as you communicate upward to superiors.*

—L. B. Belker

Communicating is a two-way street. It involves listening as much as it does talking. Our people know when leaders are only talking *to* them and not really listening to what they have to say. It's like the typical coworker who wanders the halls asking people, "How are you doing?" but never hears the response. I'm convinced that the reply could be "I just found out that my whole family was killed by terrorists," and those dudes would simply keep on strolling, not catching a syllable of the reply. Not actually listening is more harmful to leaders in terms of their ability to build trust as not communicating at all. You really have to stop and look people in the eye to show that you are actually listening.

Think about that. Have you seen people's eyes glaze over when you or someone else is speaking to them? What does that say to you?

*The most important good listening habit is to totally
concentrate on what the person is saying.*

—Unknown

Phil Murray was the commissioner of the RCMP for a number of years in the 1990s. A finer man I've never met. He had the amazing ability (albeit rare) to make you feel as if you were the only person in the room when he spoke with you. I didn't know Phil all that well, but at any event that he saw me, he'd come over and say hello. As we spoke, inevitably (especially when he was still serving) someone more important than me would walk by, and although Phil might say hello to the person in reply, he would immediately return his focus to me and finish the conversation. On the other hand, I've said hello to other leaders and watched their eyes searching the room for people of a greater ilk to glom onto before they were even done shaking my hand. There's a huge and impactful difference in those two approaches.

> *I would say the best leader I worked for always took the time*
> *to listen to what everyone in the room had to say.*

—CHIEF JENNIFER EVANS

This doesn't come naturally to everybody. But since leaders can be made as opposed to having to have been born, this is a skill that can be worked on and enhanced.

When employees no longer believe that their manager listens to them, they start looking around for someone who will. That may or not be someone that you would prefer they communicate with or turn to for guidance.

In his article about the collapse of Enron, legendary author Warren Bennis stated,

> When I consulted for the State Department, I quickly learned that junior Foreign Service officers often decided not to tell their bosses what they had learned in the field because they believed the bosses wouldn't like it. In fact, their bosses often felt exactly the same way about telling their own bosses what they knew.
> It is never easy for subordinates to be honest with their superiors.
> …Exemplary leaders reward dissent. They encourage it. They understand that, whatever momentary discomfort they experience as a result of being told they might be wrong, it is more than offset by the fact that the information will help them make better decisions.
> Organizations tend to fail when decision making is based on feedback from yes men.
> But a culture of honesty, like a healthy balance sheet, is an ongoing effort. It requires sustained attention and constant vigilance.

Some of what we hear from those we lead may not be pretty. It may well be critical of us or the organization and its practices and direction. It may in fact be emotional or confrontational. C'est la vie. Once again, it comes with the turf. No one said communication was easy—nor did they say leadership was. Maybe critics are actually right. Perhaps they're offering an opinion that is felt by the vast majority but no one else had the nerve to say. Is this not something you should know so that you can either correct the record and clear the air, or immediately fix it? Perhaps it's a valid suggestion that you should instantly embrace or study further as to its feasibility. Either way, you need to give folks their say and create an environment in which they'll feel comfortable speaking up.

> *It tends to be safer for exploitative and irresponsible leaders to keep their citizens in the dark; in their view less independent thought is better. Independent thought leads to an inquiring mind, a mindset that eventually leads to the questioning of authority figures, and that is the one thing that inadequate leaders do not want. When a leader discourages questioning of his/her leadership style, actions, and motivations, that is a sign that they have something to hide, that they may not be worthy of the public's trust. A responsive leader welcomes and encourages questions from the citizens that have entrusted them with their safety, economic stability, and their confidence that a certain level of civility in society will be constant. Responsive leaders would be appalled, disappointed and disgusted if the public did not question such factors.*

> —TERESA STOVER

As much as it is key to properly communicate with employees, it's just as critical to know when to be quiet. Employees deserve to know that private conversations with their boss will remain confidential. Too many supervisors and managers have violated that premise, often destroying any trust that their subordinates may have had in them. Those that hear their leader say negative things about other employees or betray the confidence of their colleagues are apt to lose total trust in their boss. The degree of harm caused in such scenarios is irreparable. Silence can truly be golden at times.

Nicole Fink also said,

> Improving morale is good for business. The Gallup Organization estimates there are 22 million actively disengaged employees costing the American economy up to $350 billion per year in lost productivity, including absence, illness, and other problems that result when workers are unhappy at work. Leaders who keep their employees involved, engaged, and connected are ultimately improving business performance through their people. Employees want to believe their ideas are being heard and want to feel empowered to make decisions and changes in the workplace. Taking time to build relationships with employees through personal interactions is a key step managers can take to keep morale high.

Natural comfort when speaking in a group setting isn't for everyone either. This doesn't come easy to some people, but it's a reality for leaders, particularly as they attain higher positions in organizations. This is a skill that can be developed and improved upon with some commitment.

Comedian Jerry Seinfeld reportedly once said, "A recent survey showed that people's number one fear is the fear of public speaking. Their number two fear is death. Does that seem right? So for the average guy, if you have to go a funeral, you're better off in the casket than delivering the eulogy."

It may be as simple as briefing a work unit, governance board, community group, or media scrum or addressing an auditorium full of personnel. It comes with the leadership turf. But it always comes down to knowing your audience and fashioning your statements based on having an understanding of their concerns and agendas. To avoid doing it as a leader will undoubtedly put you in a box in terms of your leadership persona and effectiveness.

A senior leader must have public speaking skills. I think few of us are
born with this talent. I personally had to work very hard on this.

—Chief Jim Chu

What we say and how we say it are closely examined by the people we proudly lead. Some are always looking for fly shit in the pepper, but most just want to hear the honest facts. We all say things on occasion that we wish we could take back, or we regret not finding a better word or phrase than the one we used. But some leaders throw gasoline on the fire every time they open their mouths. We all know them well. I'm talking about the people that can say something as innocuous as "good morning" and piss off most of the listeners.

Whenever I speak to leaders in a classroom and say that, several in the group exchange glances because they are all thinking of the same person, whether it is someone in the class, a previous speaker, or somebody they all know and have talked about over coffee. These particular folks give their audiences the ammunition to mistrust and dislike them at every turn. They always sound critical or conceited; they absolutely cannot resist talking about themselves, and no one ever knows more about any subject than they do. They may be beyond help, but we can learn from them as well. Simply remember the things they said that struck the wrong chord with you and never say it yourself.

The leaders who work most effectively, it seems to me, never say
"I." And that's not because they have trained themselves not to say
"I." They don't think "I." They think "we"; they think "team."
They understand their job to be to make the team function. They
accept responsibility and don't sidestep it, but "we" gets the credit...
This is what creates trust, what enables you to get the task done.

—Peter Drucker

I find that the art of storytelling is a tremendous communication tool when we're really trying to drive home a critical point. Not stories about us or how wonderful we are, or all the crimes we single-handedly solved for no other reason than our awe-inspiring brilliance. Save those for the golf course. I'm talking about real-life, true stories that really capture the attention of the audience, big or small. People don't necessarily listen attentively to facts or figures. But combine statistics with a real-life story about something that tugs on the heart strings of the audience, and they'll hear every word of it. They'll retain the key elements of the message forever.

It requires telling the right story to amplify the importance of your key message, including the situation, what happened, and what the lesson in it was. If it's a personal experience or reflection and truly comes from the heart, you've got the audience in the palm of your hand. I have a repertoire of personal experiences that I tell in specific situations, depending on the point I'm trying to make. I know some stories that always make someone in the room cry. That's never my goal, but when it happens, most of the audience won't forget the story or the lesson learned from it.

Some people don't think that they have the ability to tell stories. They just need to listen to those that do and learn from them. Try it. It's well worth the effort.

Abraham Lincoln was a master of storytelling. He would sit for hours wherever he went and tell a number of his many stories and anecdotes to his listeners. Many of those stories are recounted in the many books about him. It is said that he had the ability to convince anybody of anything through his effective use of storytelling. According to his biographer Donald T. Phillips, he once said,

> I believe I have the popular reputation of being a story-teller, but I do not deserve the name in its general sense, for it is not the story itself, but its purpose, or effect, that interests me. I often avoid a long and useless discussion by others or a laborious explanation on my own part by a short story that illustrates my point of view. So, too, the sharpness of a refusal or the edge of a rebuke may be

blunted by an appropriate story, so as to save wounded feeling and yet serve the purpose. No I am not simply a story-teller, but story-telling as an emollient saves me much friction and distress.

Lincoln also believed that the use of humor was a very effective approach, in particular to help alleviate stress. His time as president was never without considerable strain, of course, given the horrendous impacts of the Civil War. Donald T. Phillips said about him, "Laughter gave him a momentary break from his troubles. 'I tell you the truth,' he once related to a friend, 'when I say that a funny story, if it has the element of genuine wit, has the same effect on me that I suppose a good square drink of whisky has on an old toper; it puts new life into me.'"

A communication challenge for some leaders is finding the courage to confront people. Superiors, peers, or subordinates, either privately or in a group dynamic, generally all have something in common: they do not like to hear criticism. As a rule, nobody does. Yet at times it has to be heard.

As leaders, we most often deal with top-notch subordinates and peers. But the world isn't a perfect place, so we have the occasional employee, colleague, or superior who doesn't play by the same rule book that the vast majority of professionals in our midst obey. Unfortunately, less-than-stellar performance levels, inappropriate and unprofessional acts, and, God forbid, even offenses against provincial and federal legislation do occur in many organizations, regardless of size. That activity may be extremely rare, but sadly, it's all a reality that we cannot escape. We cannot close our eyes to such issues, and although it might not be easy to challenge colleagues and friends, we have to do what is right. Willful blindness is not an option.

I'll be the first to admit that there were times in my career when I had difficulty confronting friends over performance issues or inappropriate comments or actions on their part. No profession in the world sees people confronting others more than policing, and I never once hesitated to confront offenders and suspects as appropriate, but telling friends that they had done something wrong or that their performance was substandard was a whole new and challenging world for me. Frankly, at times I totally dropped the ball.

Relationships with colleagues in policing are totally different from work relationships in the private sector, in my view. We go through many good and bad times together, some of which are life threatening. That changes things for us. It's certainly not like many nine-to-five careers, where near-death experiences, experiencing the fear, exhilaration, and tragedies of the job, and sharing the emotional consequences of all of that seldom occur, if ever. Sometimes we're closer to our peers than we are our own families. That is one of the great things about the policing profession, but it doesn't diminish the leaders' responsibility to always deal with issues in a fair, unbiased, and timely way. Anything less is not in the best interests of the employees or the welfare of the team. It is a failure of leadership.

Those leaders who don't address employees who are doing things wrong, doing things they shouldn't, or generally not doing enough are letting down the majority of the employees that *are* doing their best and obeying the rules. Conversely, we can't forget to acknowledge the good. It doesn't matter how old and tired we get; we are still human beings. We owe it to our staff—uniformed, civilian, and volunteers—to pat them on the back for all those good things they do.

For some, it is not easy to hear or accept the truth when it is critical of them. We've all worked with people like that. Real leaders want to know what the members of their team think of their style, decision making, and performance. They encourage debate when the time and place are right. They don't always let the feedback and input completely rule their decision making, but they consider it all as they synthesize it with other information and make their decisions after having considered the entire picture. They continually seek that input as they strive to make decisions in the best interests of those they serve and those they lead.

Throughout all the years I've been in a supervisory or management role, I've read a pile of performance appraisals in various forms. I've been surprised how many employees received "outstanding" performance ratings when in reality they were barely acceptable. In my view, in most of those cases, the supervisor who completed the evaluation simply took the easy way out. It's easy to be the nice guy and give employees good ratings, but it's not fair to anyone, including the member involved, nor is it fair to the organization as a whole. When those employees compete for promotion, they may well be competing against good or above-average officers whose performance was rated honestly. How is that fair to the good employees when the poor performer enters the process with an equal or higher but unearned rating? This can make the entire process fail. All of us have wondered (sometimes aloud), "How was that person ever promoted?" Then, after the fact, the supervisors had tons to say as to why the person shouldn't have ever been promoted, though having never documented a negative observation along the way. They failed as leaders, and we failed as an organization, when the undeserving individual got moved into an even-higher position.

In addition, when poor performers are improperly overrated by weak supervisors, it sets the organization up for failure if/when they have disciplinary issues or a future supervisor appropriately challenges them for their performance. The file will be reviewed, and there won't be a single negative issue documented to support the disciplinary or performance concerns.

No leader should set out to have their people fail, nor should they try to set employees up for failure. However, it's a recipe for disaster when employees don't receive proper feedback and aren't honestly rated along the way.

Similar situations do arise within organizations where people say or do totally inappropriate things. I'm talking not about rumor-mill issues but about things we may see or hear in the workplace, such as discriminatory statements, harassing comments, or totally ignorant remarks. Are they acceptable if someone we like makes them? Are they a blasphemy if they are made by a person we don't particularly like? Are there two sets of rules: one set for the "good guys" and another for the B team? What do we do or say when it occurs? There are no easy answers to these questions, but the real leaders among us won't remain mute. They'll take the issue on in real time without hesitation. Short and sweet, much as if they would challenge a person on the street that said something inappropriate to them.

All problems become smaller if you don't dodge them but confront them.

—William F. Halsey

Several years ago I sat at a meeting with several managers that reported to me, and one said something somewhat inappropriate. Before I could even open my mouth, a subordinate manager very professionally set the individual straight in front of us all. All I had to do was look at the person who made the comment and say, "Do I need to add anything to that?" He indicated that it was quite clear, and the meeting continued. In that case, the individual knew it was wrong and that it wouldn't be tolerated by his friends and colleagues, let alone by me. I then thought the world of the manager who had the courage to speak up and challenge a colleague. Unfortunately, we don't always see this kind of response, but we should.

In summary, we should all encourage those we lead to provide input and not be afraid to offer honest opinions on issues, regardless of whether their opinions are contrary to our own. We should also be open to professional criticism. None of us are perfect, and in reality we are still learning lessons every day that we lead. And as leaders, we must offer straightforward feedback to our people so that they know what they are doing right or wrong, why, and how to do it better. They won't properly perform or develop if we don't. Then all of us need to be open and honest with one another in terms of what acceptable behavior is and isn't. If we can't confront the good guys in a respectful and candid way when required, how will we confront the bad guys in society when called upon?

In her article "The One Thing Every Great Leader Must Do?," leadership and management author Mary Lorenz said, "You must create a culture that welcomes conflict like a special guest to a holiday party. Confronting conflicts and taking on the big elephant on the table can create breakthrough bridges to growth."

There is no way to succeed as a leader without the strong ability to communicate all around yourself, but most importantly to those you lead. It is indeed the most essential quality that the great leaders possess, from Abraham Lincoln to Barak Obama and many around the world prior to and since. It is critical that we communicate in a way that will be understood, using all the modern communication mediums available to us. Although not always feasible, face-to-face communication remains the most effective tool that we possess. That includes delivering the good news, the mediocre news, and the bad news, actually listening to people, choosing our words carefully, and not allowing our emotions to negatively impact our messages.

> *The biggest thing that I have learned in my various leadership*
> *positions is the importance of communication. This is a skill set*
> *that can always be improved upon. I continue to work on ensuring*
> *that all stakeholders are involved in consultation and that the*
> *message I intend to communicate is the one that is received.*
>
> —CHIEF LAURIE HAYMAN

George Bernard Shaw once said, "The single biggest problem in communication is the illusion that it has taken place." Let us be guided by his observation and strive to ensure that we truly are communicating.

People and the Need to Connect with Them

• • •

It's people who make you, and your company, organization or community, successful or not, in good times and in bad.

—Gen. Rick Hillier

THE STEEL COMPANY DOFASCO HAS long publicized its catchy motto: "Our product is steel, our strength is our people." It's beautiful. Many other private and public sector organizations have similar catchphrases when talking about their agencies to capture the value they at least claim to attach to their employees. Whether they actually live up to that claim is another question altogether, and only those who work there would truly know.

I heard an Ontario Ministry of Corrections district manager speak at a conference in the early 1990s, and he had the crowd in stitches when he said that in Ontario's correctional system, the motto was "Our product is people, our strength is our steel."

Most managers and leaders in any organization that is worth its salt say that their employees are their greatest asset. But do they really practice what they preach? Do the employees themselves actually feel valued?

Effective executives build on strengths—their own
strengths, the strengths of their superiors, colleagues, and
subordinates; and on the strengths in the situation, that
on what they can do. They do not build on weaknesses.
They do not start out with the things they cannot do.

—PETER DRUCKER

I once walked down the hall of the OPP's General Headquarters after recently returning from three years in the Eastern Region. I was accompanied by a colleague chief superintendent and saying hello to various people along the way. When a long-serving administrative support person ran out of her office, gave me a hug, and told me it was good to have me back, my colleague asked, "How do you know all of *those* people?" I replied, "That lady works in your bureau. She's been with us for twenty-five years, and she sits seventy-five feet from you. You must walk by her a million times a day." He shrugged his shoulders and said, "I don't know her." I couldn't believe my ears.

Was it just me, or was there something wrong with that picture?

Similarly, a few years later, I met with a superintendent who reported to me, and toured the smaller bureau he had been commanding for at least a year. He struggled to remember the names of many longtime employees that he dealt with daily. They would jump in and tell me their names when they saw him fret; however, I already knew many of them, who their spouses were, where they had worked over the years, and some successes or failures they had throughout, on both personal and professional levels. He was mind-boggled by that. Perhaps I'm luckier than some in terms of my ability to recall faces and names, but I also make the effort to remember them. When I asked him the name of a member that I had seen around the building for years that had walked by, he casually said, "I don't have a clue," despite the fact that she would have walked by his door at least eight times a day for a full year.

Authors and professors Roy E. Alston and George E. Reed are a police lieutenant and retired military officer respectively. In their article *Toxic Police Leadership*, they said,

The last supervisors to get officers to voluntarily sign up for their sectors are often the ones being avoided by police officers because they display toxic tendencies. Patrol officers are not likely to voluntarily select the sector of a supervisor that displays these characteristics:

1. An apparent lack of concern for the well-being of subordinates.
2. A personality or interpersonal technique that negatively affects organizational climate.
3. A conviction by subordinates that the leader is motivated primarily by self-interest.

It is not one specific behavior that deems one toxic; it is the cumulative effect of de-motivational behavior on unit morale and climate over time that tells the tale.

Professor, author and social scientist Author Keith Murnighan wrote:

Research shows you must sincerely care about your staff if you want to be an effective leader...because if you think back to the best leaders you have had over your career, a common trait will be they cared about you as a person. Your team members must know you care about them.
Indifference is a characteristic not well suited to leadership. You simply cannot be a leader if you don't care about those you lead.

Early in the first month that I commanded our Eastern Region in January 2001, I was talking on the phone to an inspector detachment commander about a young constable who had been hit by a car while directing traffic in a snowstorm. He had a broken shoulder or collarbone and was resting at home. I asked, "What's his home phone number? I want to give him a call." The inspector's reply was, "Are we getting all warm and fuzzy here now?" I could have crawled through the phone and choked the inspector into unconsciousness.

I said, "Does this happen often here? I know I've been in headquarters too long, and maybe I'm out of touch, but are our people hit by cars a lot? I thought it sounded like a pretty big thing. If it happens every five minutes, I won't have time to call them all, but if not, I think a call from the chief superintendent would be nice, and I better not be the first commissioned officer to call him." I knew the inspector would call him the minute I hung up, so I waited a few minutes before calling.

I told the young constable, "You don't know me, Marvin, but I'm the new regional commander. I heard what happened to you and just wanted to let you know that I'm thinking about you. I'm glad you're OK. Look after yourself number one, and don't worry about work until you're well." You would have thought that I had called to offer him my job. He was so blown away that he drove in to the detachment, with one arm in a sling, in a snowstorm and told the staff there that the new chief superintendent had called him. Then I started getting calls and e-mails from folks I knew to tell me how much Marvin appreciated the call! I was just as blown away; I was flabbergasted that this call was such a big surprise to everyone and not an expectation. I thought that we must have been doing something wrong as leaders if our people didn't assume the call from the boss would be a given and not a total shock to the system.

Over the coming months, I did more of the same. I told the various commanders across the region that I wanted to be made aware of employees who were hurting in some way or had family members that were, as well as employees that were retiring, so that I could contact them. I travelled the region and visited hurt and ill officers and civilian personnel. I went to funerals for retirees and for family members of serving personnel. I sent handwritten cards and e-mails, as I always had in the smaller bureaus and sections that I previously led. The response was shocking, to say the least.

One day, a superintendent whom I have the world of respect for and who is a personal friend came into my office. He said, "You know this is a big region with a pile of personnel. You are going to have a hard time keeping this up." I said, "Watch me."

> Make a list of the 5 leaders you most admire. They can be from business, social media, politics, technology, the sciences, any field. Now ask yourself why you admire them. The chances are high that your admiration is based on more than their accomplishments, impressive as those may be. I'll bet that everyone on your list reaches you on an emotional level. This ability to reach people in a way that transcends the intellectual and rational is the mark of a great leader. They all have it. They inspire us. It's a simple as that. And when we're inspired we tap into our best selves and deliver amazing work.
>
> --MEGHAN M. BIRO

Chief Rod Knecht similarly says, "Leadership is all about the people. It is about the ability to motivate others toward a common vision or goal. In life and particularly in policing, credibility is everything. It's not about what you say but rather what you do—and that you can be trusted."

Without dwelling on this issue—and I'm not trying to make myself look good here—I'll tell two more quick stories to demonstrate the impact this sort of leadership style can have.

A huge uniformed detachment sergeant then under my command in eastern Ontario was six feet four inches, had arms like tree trunks, was as tough as nails, but suffered from a bout of cancer. He had some difficult surgery, and after some months getting back to health, he was back to work and out on the road. While he was off, I called him at home and had a forty-five-second talk with him, to do nothing more than show that I knew what was happening with him and that I actually cared. That bit of time didn't wreak havoc on my busy schedule that day.

Some years later I was up north, speaking to over a hundred Northeast Region supervisors and senior officers about leadership, and got into the topic of caring for and supporting our people. I specifically spoke of the need to be genuine and not have it look like robotic activity when you do. That same great big sergeant was in the room, as he was by that time serving in the north. In front of his many peers, I asked him, "When you were ill a few years back and I called you at home, did you feel that I actually cared or that I was checking something off my daily to-do list? Please be honest." He said, "It felt totally genuine, and I really appreciated the call." Then his voice cracked, and he got choked up. He added, "But it meant even more to me when I went back to work months later, and when I turned on my computer that morning, there was a short e-mail message from you that said 'Welcome back.'" To this day I do not recall sending that little message, but the impact that it had on this member was obviously significant to all in that room. My point here is that we can never underestimate how much that little human contact, no matter how trivial to us as leaders, can have on our people.

A few years back, I heard that a longtime civilian employee had lost her elderly father. I put on a suit that Saturday and went to the funeral home an hour away to offer my condolences. She looked shocked to see me and said, "I can't believe that you'd be here for me with your crazy schedule." Once again, I had to shake my head and ask myself why this simple gesture would be such a shock to her system. That's not a criticism of her, but it certainly made me sadly wonder what the heck we had been doing as leaders for me to get such a response.

If you don't truly know the people that report to you and those that you interact with regularly (even if they report to another manager), how will you know when they aren't themselves? Are they troubled or upset? Are they hurting in some way over something, whether work related or not? How will you know to reach out and offer a supporting hand? How will you know their strengths and weaknesses or how committed they are, if you never interact with them at work?

Heinz Landau in his article "Knowing Your Employees" said,

> Managers often don't know enough about their employees. Not knowing their employees will have a major impact on the loyalty of the employees, since 43% of the persons surveyed want to leave their company. In the age group 30–39 years, even 53% want to quit.
>
> If you want to have a high employee retention rate, make high employee engagement a priority in your company.
>
> If you will invest enough time in having greater knowledge and understanding of one another, you will surely see the result in form of better employee engagement, higher productivity and higher employee retention.

I suffered from a brain tumor in 2000. It ended up being benign, or you wouldn't be reading my thoughts in a book right now, but the surgery was invasive and, frankly, absolutely terrifying. Nonetheless, I got through it. The reaction of friends and leaders within the organization at the time was an interesting study in itself.

Some friends, colleagues, and leaders above me were totally missing in action. Although surprised, I get that to some extent. Much like walking up to the family member of a deceased person at a funeral home, it's hard to know exactly what to say in some circumstances; it's human nature to be uncomfortable. I was totally disappointed in some folks—including some of my leaders—but that's life.

A number of senior officers below me watched my struggle and recovery with bated breath, hoping that my anticipated passing would create some job opportunities for them. That didn't surprise me at all.

What really did surprise me were those that unexpectedly rose to the fore.

Colleagues and leaders—whom in some cases I didn't really get along with or even like for that matter—made the effort and reached out to me. Others who I knew would in fact be there for me went all out to help and support my wife and me, bringing food over to the house and more.

While I was in surgery for several hours, my direct boss, Deputy Commissioner Moe Pilon (now retired), sat with my wife, parents, closest friends, and brother while they waited to learn my fate. It meant the world to me that he would do that. It is not something that I will ever forget.

A story that is totally unrelated to leadership, but is a great story just the same, involved my wife Angie's first five minutes alone with me in the recovery room. The neurosurgeon had expressed some fear going in that given the proximity of the tumor to the optic nerve for my left eye, I could lose the sight in that eye, depending on whether the tumor had adhered to the nerve. That was the least of my worries, as I simply wanted to live. When the surgeon met with her to tell her I survived the surgery and would likely recover just fine, she asked about the optic nerve issue. Out of an abundance of caution, he stated that he believed it had not been damaged but they would have to wait to find out for sure.

While she was sitting in recovery with me, my eyes started to flutter, and I was whispering incoherently. She leaned in close to try to hear what I was saying, and when my eyes opened, they were totally crossed.

She thought, "Oh my God, the eyes were affected, he's cross-eyed. But at least he's alive, and I'm sure they can fix his eyes through surgery."

Then I apparently spoke a bit more loudly and said the same thing over and over, something that I, of course, don't remember at all. She leaned in even closer to hear me, in fact close enough to get a whiff of the worst morning breath on record, and then realized that I was saying, "Move back." I guess she was so close that my eyes had crossed so that I could see her. She moved back, and my eyes immediately snapped back into normal position.

Chief Jim Chu said, "The most important leadership quality is the ability to inspire others so they are confident 'We can do it.' I have seen great leaders who are larger-than-life figures who inspire others with their commanding presence and charisma. I have seen other great leaders who are humble and self-effacing but are quietly confident. The leadership style that works for someone starts with his or her own characteristics, experiences, and personality."

A wonderful young OPP officer was shot and killed in Huron County in the spring of 2010. It took a bigger piece out of me than any prior death of an officer under my command, and I had never before met the member.

Vu had emigrated from Vietnam as a very young boy, as the brutal war there was just ending. His father had been killed in battle, so his mother let Vu leave for Canada, in the custody of his uncle. He eventually was adopted by a wonderful Canadian family, was raised in a devout Christian household in small-town Ontario, and married his beautiful high school sweetheart, Heather. They had three beautiful sons together as they moved around to three different communities during his OPP.

Vu wasn't a large man but was incredibly fit. He was a calm, quiet officer who could always be trusted to do his job professionally, thoroughly, confidently, and safely. His young life was taken when he was shot and killed by a troubled man who was trying to find the spouse that had left him; Vu was the first officer to approach him. It was so tragic and so senseless.

After learning of the shooting and as Vu was still fighting for his life, Julian Fantino and I immediately flew to the hospital in London and waited with Vu's family and fellow officers in the hallway while he underwent surgery. Then we learned that he had not survived.

Shortly thereafter, his two youngest boys, Jordan and Joshua, came out of the washroom with their grandfather, Heather's dad. His oldest son, Tyler, was still with his mom in another room. Their eyes were swollen, but they had stopped crying and washed their faces. Julian and I walked up to speak to them, and Jordan stood right in front of me as we spoke. He was only ten years old, and the loving father that had coached him and his brothers in hockey and taken him hunting was dead.

I put my hand on his head and asked him, "Are you OK?" It wasn't the brightest question, I suppose, given the circumstances, but it was the best I could muster. His eyes immediately swelled up, and he started to sob, burying his little face in my belly. It was a moment that I will never forget as long as I live. I could cry right now just thinking about it.

In the days following the emotional police funeral, I sent an e-mail out across the OPP expressing the emotions and pride I felt when Vu was killed and during the days to follow. I wasn't at all embarrassed when senior *Toronto Sun* columnist Mark Bonokoski obtained it from an OPP member and printed a large part of it as part of a series he was writing on posttraumatic stress syndrome.

What follows in a letter, obtained by the *Sun*, written by OPP Deputy Commissioner Chris Lewis to all field personnel under his command following the funeral of OPP Const. Vu Pham, murdered last month in the line of duty:

"I'm not afraid to admit that I cried last week. More than once in fact. I'll never be able to understand or accept the senseless death of this fine young officer and father.

"The death of Const. Vu Pham affected me more than any of the prior 39 on-duty deaths of OPP officers that have occurred since I joined the OPP almost 32 years ago, and I had never met Vu. Vu Pham had overcome incredible odds in his short life. The story of his childhood in a war-torn Saigon, the death of his father, and his loving mother's difficult decision to let her young son leave Vietnam to move to a better place, were compelling stories.

"The four loves of Vu's life were his darling wife, Heather, and their three beautiful sons, Tyler, Jordan and Joshua. The strength shown by Heather and the boys at the visitation and throughout the police funeral was amazing...those three boys will grow to be everything their dad wanted them to be.

"Vu's policing partner of two years, Const. Dell Mercey...described how Vu is a hero and how Vu had saved his life. There's no doubt in my mind that Dell is a hero, too. His actions to end this horrendous situation undoubtedly saved untold lives, as the person that took Vu's life may well have killed or injured more people.

"As Vu lay wounded and Dell was fighting for his life, officers responded from every direction, knowing fully they were going into the most dangerous of situations. I heard their radio transmissions as well as they bravely rushed into harm's way to help their colleagues and friends.

"I can't even begin to describe the feeling the commissioner and I both felt when Vu passed away. When I saw those three great little boys crying in the hospital hallway, I wondered if I had the strength to keep it under control myself.

"I spoke to Supt. Bob Bruce right away. As he was heading down to take command of the funeral preparations, he was calling those that he knew had the experience and strength to put a fitting tribute together for Vu. Bob remembered training Vu in 1995 and described Vu as a 'quiet and tough professional.' He said, 'We'll do it up right for Vu.'

"The local community supported Vu, his family and the OPP throughout this ordeal. Signs of support were posted everywhere. Offers of assistance, food, coffee, vehicles, car washes for cruisers, and accommodation never ended.

"In the last words spoken at the final meeting of the funeral command team at the arena Thursday evening, Supt. Bob Bruce...said, 'When you are driving home tomorrow after all of that is done, and you feel a hand touch your back and Vu's voice say thank you, then your work will be done.' When I drove away alone on that Friday afternoon, I thought of the strength of Vu, of his family... that's when I felt that hand on my shoulder, heard the words 'thank you,' and I had one last cry."

Some police-chief colleagues felt that it was risky for me to put myself out there in such a heartfelt communique to the men and women of the force. Of course, once I had hit the send button the day I e-mailed it out so broadly, I knew that it could end up in the media, but I truly didn't care. I am who I am, and I have no regrets about that.

Although it was not my intent but was simply my individual communication style, this e-mail went across Canada. Our members forwarded it to friends and family and law-enforcement colleagues all over North America, and it even ended up in the hands of Canadian soldiers serving in Afghanistan. Although I've always felt a strong connection with the vast majority of people I've led, this drew personnel to me and developed connections that I never dreamed of. If some folks out there thought, "The OPP commissioner is a bit of a sucky-baby," so be it. I guess I am.

Chief William McCormack said, "Leadership is about people having a passion and a desire to work for you because they want to, not because they have to. You must have the ability to empathize and have personnel see that you are always in a position of support with them and that you can stand beside them and are not afraid to do yourself what you've asked of them."

The sad reality is that many leaders don't really care to know their people. They blindly accept everything that the career-climbing employees tell them, but really don't know that some of these folks are incapable of interacting with peers and subordinates—they simply manage up well. Sadly, they never get to know the quiet, committed, and hard workers that always have their noses to the grindstone but don't try to sell themselves well to superiors. And *some* leaders don't want to see, hear, or know the bad things that may be happening out there, because if they do, they might have to actually take action.

But I'd shut my eyes in the sentry-box, So I didn't see nothin' wrong.

—RUDYARD KIPLING

Not developing a connection with those you lead does nothing to contribute to the development of trust—both them in you and you in them.

It is well worth your time and energy to develop a mutual two-way understanding between yourself and the personnel you lead. By building resilient relationships with them, you will feel connected to them and them to you, at the very least on a professional level. They need to know that their boss cares about them as more than mere employee names or numbers on a page and sees them as human beings. It's equally critical that they see you as a person as well, not some mythical creature that lives in an executive suite in an ivory tower.

People's jobs and careers are integral to their lives. The more your organization can make them a partner, the more they will deliver amazing results. This means, to the greatest extent possible, communicating your organization's strategies, goals and challenges. This builds buy-in, and again is a mark of respect. People won't be blindsided (which is a workplace culture killer) by setbacks if they're in the loop. …People's careers are a big part of their lives. That seems like a no-brainer, but leaders should have it front and center at all times. Find out what your employees' career goals are and then do everything you can to help them reach them. Even if it means they will eventually leave your organization. You will gain happy, productive employees who will work with passion and commitment, and tout your company far and wide. This is an opportunity to brand your greatness.

—MEGHAN M. BIRO

If I have a single strength as a leader and as a person, it is the ability to connect with people. Some have been critical of me for it, thinking that I overdid it, thus setting the bar too high for other leaders as a result. But I got my other work done. I didn't miss deadlines, and mail didn't accumulate in piles on my desk. I managed to keep up with my other commitments.

Regularly communicating in various ways and actually connecting with our people was my job and my number one priority. All this, in my view, contributed greatly to the development of trust.

As I wandered the halls of our headquarters or the many detachments, offices, and OPP events across Ontario, people often wanted to ask me questions about me or about my job as commissioner. I'd answer some of that, rather than look overly private and to be polite, but I always tried to steer the conversation around so it was about them and their jobs.

You can make more friends in two months by becoming
really interested in other people than you can in two years
by trying to get other people interested in you.

—DALE CARNEGIE

Speaking of leadership guru Jim Welch, Author Mary Lorenz said,

Welch developed his 8 C's of The Practical Growth Leader model after years of experiencing and observing different leadership styles. He says he found that the strongest leaders were those who established an emotional connection to their employees by embodying the following characteristics:
Caring; Candor; Confronting Conflict; Circle of Trust; Collaboration; Credit to Others; Communication; Celebration.

You can't get to know your people, know what makes them tick, and actually connect with them by sitting in your office. "Management by walking around" has become a catchphrase that denotes leaders actually getting out into the work environments and meeting with people casually. Not all leaders are comfortable with that notion. They prefer the security of their offices, their stately desks between them and any staff member with whom they are engaging, and being totally in control of the setting. That doesn't cut it in my view.

Author Deborah Mills-Scofield said, "Lesson: Remember, They're Human. Many companies treat their employees as employees—nicely and kindly, even generously—but not as humans. My manager-mentors made it clear that I mattered not just for what I could do, but also for who I was."

Surprisingly, there are still some dyed-in-the-wool paramilitary-type leaders out there (not necessarily old in age) who cannot grasp that being nice to the people you lead isn't a bad thing. They have seen too many war movies and still want to rule with an iron fist like the pre–new millennium police leaders did. What was old is now new again in their minds.

> *Nice leaders (people) don't finish last. They finish first again and again. Ignorance and arrogance are leadership killers. They're also a mark of insecurity. Treating everyone with a basic level respect is an absolute must trait of leadership. And kindness is the gift that keeps on giving back. Of course, there will be people who prove they don't deserve respect and they must be dealt with. But that job will be made much easier, and will have far less impact on your organization, if you have a reputation for kindness, honesty and respect.*

—Meghan M. Biro

As I said, we generally don't hire stupid people and we seldom, if ever, hire members that will blindly serve or be treated like dogs. There's a time and a place for a harder-line approach, obviously, but it never has to be of the master-servant conversation variety.

It may be time consuming and not within everyone's comfort zone, but getting out and walking around work sites and interacting with people is a totally different and more effective ball game. It enables you to actually see what they do and hear how they do it, learn their thoughts and suggestions and let them hear yours in a casual way, see photos of their families, plaques, and trinkets that are significant to them, all while talking in nonconfrontational and informal environments.

Police officer, military leader and author Christopher Saint Cyr's slant:

> *Each great leader develops their personal style to learn about their follow-ers and to communicate how their desires and abilities intertwine with those of the organization. Some dedicate a few moments each day to speak*

to their people and ask about important personal and professional issues. In every case, the interaction between the leader and follower is personalized in some way. The follower comes to believe the leader personally cares for them and their situation.

Part of Abraham Lincoln's success as a leader hinged on his commitment to this leadership trait. That was in the 1800s, of course—no cars, transit systems, or airplanes—but he did it quite successfully. Author Donald T. Phillips said,

> Abraham Lincoln gained the trust and respect of his subordinates by building strong alliances on both personal and professional levels. He wanted to know how his people would respond in any given situation: who would have the tendency to get the job done on his own, or be more likely to procrastinate and delay; who could be counted on in an emergency and who couldn't; who were their brighter, more able, more committed people; who shared his strong ethics and values. He also wanted his subordinates to get to know him, so that they would know how he would respond in any given situation, what he wanted, demanded and needed. If they knew what he would do, they could make their own decisions without asking him for direction, thereby avoiding delay and inactivity.

In his article "Two Things Leaders Care About," author Christopher Saint Cyr said of a Lincoln-era leader, "After the American Civil War, Robert E. Lee returned to the south to live a quiet life. He was one of the best loved military commanders in the Nation's history. Throughout the war he showed concern for his soldiers at all levels. For years after the war his followers sought him out for letters of reference, financial assistance and inspiration. It is said that he never refused a request of a veteran of his Army if he could fulfill it. Lee's obligation to his men ceased the day he surrendered and dismissed the troops. His caring continued until he died."

He went on to say, "Great leaders have two important concerns. Success of their organization and success of their people. They understand that unless the aspirations of employees are tied to the vision of the organization, neither will be truly successful. Leaders inspire their employees to succeed by learning their dreams, concerns and desires and find ways to align them with those of the vision and mission of the organization. When employees achieve success in their positions within the organization, the organization becomes more successful. Great leaders extend their influence long after formal relationships end because they genuinely care for the people they lead."

How many senior leaders in organizations retire and vanish? How many people actually care that they do? It is a personal decision on the part of the leader to stay connected or not postcareer, but at the same time it is most often the leaders' actions preretirement that dictate whether their employees will miss them when they are gone. Perhaps the leaders that fade away into the night on retirement, never to be seen or heard from again, do so because they didn't feel connected to the people that remain. Whose fault is that? I wonder.

But if the employees actually felt professionally and personally connected to the leader when they were on the job, and if the leader actually made them feel good about themselves as people and as contributors to the organization, you're darn right they'll be missed.

Effective leaders make their followers feel good
about themselves and their work.

—UNKNOWN

Emotional Common Sense

• • •

*One of the things I believe is important to being a true leader
is that you connect emotionally to your employees.*

—JIM WELCH, PRESIDENT AND FOUNDER
OF THE GROWTH LEADER INC.

MOST OF US HAVE READ articles and listened to speakers addressing the need for emotional intelligence among leaders. *Wikipedia* defines emotional intelligence as "the ability to identify, assess, and control the emotions of oneself, of others, and of groups." I personally see this as simply common sense and a trait I find to be sadly lacking in a number of so-called leaders out there. It doesn't require deep thought, an in-depth study by a team of psych majors, or several books by academics and other alleged experts who perhaps have never managed a single human being.

It should be central to all we do, in terms of our decision making, our communication style, and how we connect with our people. If we think back to the good and the bad leaders that we've worked for and with, we can remember those that didn't let their personal emotions negatively impact how they functioned and how they treated their people, and those that did. Of course, the negative impacts and experiences are much harder for us to forget.

I think this excerpt from an article I read years ago sums it up very well:

> The higher up the ladder that leaders are, the more people they impact and their EI becomes increasingly important. The person at the top sets the atmosphere that permeates the organization, including the emotional temperature.
>
> Not only does a leader with low emotional intelligence have a negative impact on employee morale, it directly impacts staff retention. We know that the biggest reason that people give for leaving an organization is the relationship with those above them.
>
> Here are five ways to spot an emotionally intelligent leader:
>
> 1. Nondefensive and open
> 2. Aware of their own emotions
> 3. Adept at picking up on the emotional state of others
> 4. Available for those reporting to them
> 5. Able to check their ego and allow others to shine

Does the list above not conjure up visions of wonderful skilled and competent leaders that you have worked with or for? Do you not also break into a cold sweat when it reminds of you of those poor leaders you toiled under that made you want to join the French Foreign Legion?

Although allowing your own emotions to improperly affect your decision making and the negative way you might speak to people is clearly a no-no, allowing people to see your softer side and your own emotions to sensitive matters can be a good thing. I never thought that way earlier in my career.

A number of years ago, I was delivering a speech regarding the Special Olympics to a group of OPP detachment commanders, community-services officers, and Torch Run representatives from several law-enforcement agencies in eastern Ontario. When I spoke about my brother Robbie, the emotion around his life, and the struggles my parents had in raising him and ensuring that he could have the most fulfilling life possible, it all got the better of me. I got choked up and couldn't finish my comments, and then I walked out of the room to get back in control and returned to the group at the break.

One of the more gruff detachment commanders, one who has always been seemingly void of any form of emotion, wandered over to me. I said, "Sorry about that. A detachment commander shouldn't have to see his chief bawling in front of a crowd." He replied with what was probably the only statement the man ever made that I agreed with: "Don't worry about it. At least we know that you are human."

I'm not sure whether he meant that as a compliment or was suggesting that it was the first time that I actually seemed "human," but it was an important point to me just the same.

For years I was embarrassed by the fact that I would often get choked up when speaking publicly about issues that had an emotional impact on me. I thought it made me appear weak to the listeners, many of which were OPP personnel. Thankfully, that is no longer the case. Although I don't want to have a breakdown and totally blubber myself to pieces in front of an audience, I am in fact human, and I should not be self-conscious about that. Thank God for that validation!

I had to remind myself of that realization a couple of years back, when I was addressing a large gathering of community-services officers from across the province, speaking of the moment when I finally fully realized the importance of the role those members play in community safety. I told them the following story:

In April 2001 I was at a large First Nations protest in Cornwall, Ontario, with hundreds of our officers and the RCMP. One cold evening, a superintendent told me that he freed up some emergency response team (ERT) members and a canine team from the event to go to Bancroft to search for a missing four-year-old girl in a desolate area. I didn't think much of it, given the volatile protest dynamics. A few hours later, the superintendent told me that the girl had been found alive and well by our local officers and the fire department. Once again, I didn't think of it as a big deal—our officers find lost people almost daily in our many jurisdictions.

Weeks later, I visited the Bancroft Detachment on the day that the officers involved in this search and their fire-service colleagues were being thanked by the little girl and her family. When I heard the full story, I was blown away.

That beautiful and precious little girl had gone into the bush to find her dog after dark. She was not dressed warmly, and the terrain was extremely rugged. Given that the ERT and canine team were so far away, a couple of detachment members and firefighters put a quick plan together and entered the woods. Within a quarter mile of the house, they found the little girl sitting on the ground and hugging a tree. She was totally fine but likely would not have survived the unusually cold night if not located quickly.

The part of the story that hit me so hard and made me emotional as I spoke was that the little girl's life had been saved by a local community-services officer, Constable Robyn MacEachern. Robyn had been in the local day care just a day or two prior and taught the young kids the "hug a tree" program. She told them, "If you get lost, don't run, don't panic. Just sit down and hug a tree until the police come and find you." That wonderful little girl did just that. It was an awakening for me: I had always undervalued the role of our officers that teach great programs to children and other vulnerable members of our communities. People like Robyn contribute immensely to public safety, and the proof was in the beautiful smile of that little girl as she handed Robyn a thank-you card she had made.

So I cried in front of the crowd, and most of them cried too. Not just because of the little girl but because they saw their boss cry and realized that they had a leader who understood what they do so well and truly appreciated their value. There was another lesson in all that for me: although it was never my intent, I developed lifelong connections with some of the people in the room that day when they saw me choke up.

Sadly, I cried again a year or so thereafter. The officer that had put the search team together that night and found that child in the bush committed suicide over unrelated issues in his personal life.

Accept feelings with an open attitude. They may be
signaling that something important is at stake, like your
values. This gives you the chance to act on them.

—SUSAN DAVID AND CHRISTINA CONGLETON

In 1994, the life of a young Toronto Police Service officer named Todd Baylis was tragically taken when he was shot and killed on duty on the streets of Toronto. During the huge police funeral that followed, I stood outside the church with thousands of law-enforcement colleagues and listened to the voice of Chief Dave Boothby as it was piped out through the sound system that allowed us all to hear the emotional service.

Dave is a very nice man and was a great officer, investigator, and chief. He's tall and striking and was a legendary homicide investigator that had seen it all in his career. Many wouldn't have expected the level of emotion Dave showed that day. As he spoke to the grieving family and friends in attendance, he openly cried. At that point, I had never seen or heard a police leader from any police force or of any rank sob.

Did I think any less of Chief Boothby? Did anyone in attendance that day feel the chief was any less of a man because he cried in public? I cannot imagine anything of the sort. He was a leader who was burying one of his people, and how much that hurt him was loud and clear to all. I couldn't have been any prouder of Dave or my chosen profession at that instant.

Sadly, I saw a similar reaction from Chief Larry Gravill of the Waterloo Regional Police in 1998 when they honored an officer who had been killed while diving to retrieve the body of a drowning victim. As the members marched down the street after the service, Larry marched behind his members, looking very much like a shepherd following his flock, with tears running down his cheeks. Larry, a tremendous and highly respected leader in his own right, was not afraid to show that he too was deeply hurting. As a friend and colleague, I was extremely proud.

In her article "The One Thing Every Great Leader Must Do?," author Mary Lorenz speaks of Jim Welch:

Welch knows firsthand what it means to connect emotionally with your employees and build a strong employment brand—and why it's essential that great leaders do both.

"Emotion" isn't often a word you see in business books; yet in Grow Now, as well as in daily conversations with clients, it is the central topic of discussion. "In the business world, emotion gets a bad rap, but the fact is an emotional connection—whether it be with your customers, your employees or your peers on the team—is critical," Welch said. Critical, because without that emotional connection, employees easily become disengaged from their jobs, their leaders and the companies they work for. Thus, today's leaders need to work to ensure that that emotional connection is there.

We don't hire robots, blind mice, lemmings, or geese. We hire human beings—hopefully the best and the brightest—and with humans comes emotion. So do problems, both personal and professional, and those life problems can bring out strong emotions in our people, some more than others. Our people are going to carry that emotion with them, whether they are at work or at play.

How many times have you seen a colleague, subordinate, or boss walking around with a morose face, seemingly mad at the world? Let's face it: some people are continually in that frame of mind, deservedly or not, but others have their moments as well.

A former colleague, long since retired, told me in so many words in 1987 that you never know what's going on in someone's life—what challenges they're facing or what they are dealing with at home. We may simply wonder, "What's his problem?" (I say "his" only because our female counterparts never have grumpy days!)

As we wander the halls and offices of our workplaces and look into thousands of eyes over time, we have to know that some of those souls are hurting. Some are facing personal or family health problems. Others are dealing with marital strife or having problems with their children. Many are hurting financially, suffering through dependency or addiction problems, or simply just having a bad day. God knows we all have them.

Recognizing this reality is key in terms of our emotional common sense. We can't make decisions about issues or people based on our emotions. Nor can we make decisions about issues or people because of the emotions of other people. That doesn't mean we shouldn't consider emotions in terms of how we approach matters. For example, how we communicate a point to a group of employees may well be influenced by how emotional the situation is for them. In addition, the way in which we communicate a work issue with an individual who is dealing with personal emotional matters is obviously a consideration.

> *The prevailing wisdom says that difficult thoughts and feelings*
> *have no place at the office: Executives, and particularly leaders,*
> *should be either stoic or cheerful; they must project confidence and*
> *damp down any negativity bubbling up inside them. But that goes*
> *against basic biology. All healthy human beings have an inner*
> *stream of thoughts and feelings that include criticism, doubt, and*
> *fear. That's just our minds doing the job they were designed to do:*
> *trying to anticipate and solve problems and avoid potential pitfalls.*
> *Everyone has felt critical, doubtful, or scared, even at work—*
> *and attempting to minimize or ignore such emotions can amplify*
> *them. Effective leaders don't buy into or try to suppress their inner*
> *experiences. Instead they approach them in a mindful, values-driven,*
> *and productive way—developing what we call emotional agility.*
> *In our complex, fast-changing knowledge economy, this ability to*
> *manage one's thoughts and feelings is essential to business success.*

—Susan David and Christina Congleton

Too many old-school leaders are as cold as ice. "The message is the message," and too bad if people don't like it. They'd never consider the emotions of the receiving group when delivering that message. But they would let their own emotions about an issue or an individual influence how or why they head in a certain direction. In other words, "I don't like him, so I'm going to hit him right between the eyes with this." Or conversely, "She's one of my favorites, so I'll let her down easy."

Similarly, issues that are close to the heart of the leader on a personal level, such as a program that he or she has never been a fan of for whatever reason, should not be influenced one way or another by those personal biases. If it's right, it's right. Always do what is right, but consider your own emotions and those of the people you lead when making decisions or when communicating the intended actions.

Author Ken Blanchard wrote a number of books in his One-Minute Manager series. One of his best theories was that of situational leadership. In a nutshell, his theory is that leaders must manage each person differently in various situations, depending on the person's individual skill level and commitment and based on the situation being faced. In other words, a very capable and experienced subordinate operating in a more routine situation can be managed much differently than a less-skilled individual in riskier circumstances. Makes total sense.

So where in that theory does the emotion of the individual weigh in? In policing, should we send a competent and committed employee who is dealing with difficult issues regarding the health of his or her child to a crib-death case? Is the right person to assign to a brutal domestic investigation an officer who has been a victim herself? Granted, there are times when we have no other deployment options, but how closely we supervise, monitor, and support that individual should be a key consideration.

The rapidly increasing complexity of operational stress injuries (OSIs), including posttraumatic stress disorder (PTSD), has to have an impact on how we lead police-service employees. If it doesn't, we're letting our people down.

Chief Rod Knecht said, "The poorest leader I worked for was void of emotional IQ. Employees were treated as a stepping-stone or a means to reaching his personal goal. The individual suffered an extraordinary ego. He validated his ego by diminishing the confidence of others."

We are all human beings, leaders and followers alike. Although we can't allow our emotions to cloud our decision making and prevent us from doing what is right, we have to recognize and understand our own emotions as individuals. At the same time, we can never forget that we lead real people who have real issues and real emotions. We must take well-meaning people who are going through a tough time as they are and accept the human frailties and emotions that come with them, within some semblance of reason.

Make Time to Connect. Remember, people do not usually leave organizations. They leave their leaders. If you lose enough good people, your organization will be unable to grow. The effective leader understands that emotional connections to the leader are the most powerful retention devices in the tool kit.

—Jim Welch

Ethical Behavior and Acting with Integrity

• • •

ETHICAL BEHAVIOR

> *If ethics is not the engine of success in the train of growth, it sure*
> *is a guard, with a flag, which may be green, or at times red.*

—PRIYAVRAT THAREJA

ETHICS. WHAT EXACTLY SHOULD WE strive to exemplify and develop in others? Is it moral conduct? Legal standards? Good character? Responsible behavior? A compass of virtuosity? Is it all that and more?

> *I had taken a course in Ethics. I read a thick textbook, heard the class*
> *discussions and came out of it saying I hadn't learned a thing I didn't*
> *know before about morals and what is right or wrong in human conduct.*

—CARL SANDBURG

We have all heard the emphasis on ethics over the past few years relating to both government and private-industry practices. This is not a new buzzword or a passing fad but an issue that is extremely important to us as leaders in police services, public service organizations, or the private sector.

> *Quite simply policing has an image problem. What the public sees on television, on the Internet, and reads in the headlines of the daily news is their reality. In the wake of the 1991 assaults on Rodney King in Los Angeles, California, the public has become adept at video-taping, photographing and audio taping the interactions between citizens and the police. Often capturing only portions of interactions, they are sold to the highest bidder and within a short period a potential scandal is in the making. These events have helped shape the perception of the police while rarely affording the opportunity for police officers and departments to exercise a "do over."*

—JOHN MIDDLETON HOPE

When one looks at the big scandals that have occurred in a few large US corporations over the past few years, the root causes all seem to relate to an ethical issue of some sort. In these instances, the public reaction to such issues could mean financial downfall for some companies in terms of the resulting loss of sales, but in the public sector, public reaction to negative ethical matters can lead to a total loss of confidence in an organization. Police forces cannot survive without the confidence of the public they provide service to, nor can companies continue to exist without the full faith of the client group.

I've always believed that ethics are nothing more than a set of moral principles or values by which we live our personal and professional lives. The word "ethics" is often used in the same sentence with "integrity," when describing people who model honesty, ideals, and virtues that are above reproach. Integrity is acting on a personal commitment to honesty and fairness and is living by one's standards. It is a navigational tool that can guide us through "fuzzy" ethical issues that we face.

Some people have different ethics at home and in their personal lives than they do at work. Is that wrong? I suppose it depends on the differences. I won't have a martini at my desk, but I certainly will at home or with friends. Most people won't spend company or public funds like a drunken sailor but might be close to broke in their personal lives owing to their own spending habits. Conversely, I wouldn't commit murder in my personal life but have often thought of it at work. Just kidding! But I'm sure you see my point.

> *Ethics is knowing the difference between what you*
> *have a right to do and what is right to do.*

> —POTTER STEWART

During a discussion group on police ethics that I participated in at a CACP seminar several years ago, we developed a list of ethical issues police officers can be confronted with:

* Abuse of rights of suspects
* "Deals"—coffee, meals, other freebies
* Lying—in court, to supervisors, on forms (overtime, expenses, etc.)
* Abuse of authority
* Disobeying laws (on duty and off)
* Abuse of government property—cars, equipment, computers, supplies
* Illegal gathering of evidence
* Participating in or observing harassment, racism, and/or sexist behavior by personnel.

Most of these are clearly legal issues whereby the decision of whether to become involved should be an easy one. Unfortunately, however, time and time again we see officers across North America violate these rules, which for good reason becomes of great public and media concern. Other issues are more gray or fuzzy and may or may not be covered by policy.

Many of these actions and others are obviously unacceptable anywhere, anytime, and I'd include lying, conniving, backstabbing, and rumor mongering in that category.

So if these activities are unacceptable to those we lead, do we not have a fiduciary responsibility to live up to and exceed an ethical code? We need to set a positive example, not a bad one. When leaders permit or turn a blind eye to such activities, we have a problem. When leaders are personally involved, we have a crisis.

Former Chief John Middleton Hope also says,

> The public recognizes there will be police officers that engage in inappropriate conduct. What they expect police executives to do is identify and punish these officers. It is the public who demands we pursue the truth. Their trust in us depends on our undying commitment to reveal the truth even if it damages the reputation of the department. The perception by various oversight bodies is that the chief of police is responsible for both the actions of the officer(s) involved in misconduct and the department's timely response to hold the officer accountable. The proverbial buck stops with the chief.

In the *CACP Professionalism in Policing Research Project*, those surveyed were asked to agree or not with the statement, "Senior management team sets an example of how to do things the right way in terms of ethics." Sadly, 49 percent disagreed, only 20 percent agreed, and 31 percent remained neutral.

The report went on to say, "Ethical leadership, which assesses the extent to which leaders incorporate ethics into their decision-making processes, was one of the most poorly rated management practices. Only 14% of respondents agreed that their senior managers demonstrated ethical leadership on the composite measure."

Obviously, our employees expect more out of us than obeying the law and following the rules. They also watch how we make decisions, how we walk the walk and talk the talk, and why. Favoritism is a glaring example of that. But clearly, employees watch and see whether we are true to our word, and so they should. We cannot say that the opinions of our people matter and then never listen to them. We can't say that we truly value our people and their thoughts, feelings, input, and suggestions and then not live up to that mantra.

> *When ethics are not followed in their true sense, he becomes a*
> *wild beast loosed upon this world. Ethics and civilization go hand*
> *in hand which teach us how to live a refined and dignified life.*
> *If you follow the ethics, you can improve your self-esteem, self-*
> *respect, your standard of living and earn a good reputation.*
>
> —POTTER STEWART

Consider these suggested ethical principles as presented by lawyer, author, and speaker Michael Josephson:

HONESTY. Ethical executives are honest and truthful in all their dealings and they do not deliberately mislead or deceive others by misrepresentations, overstatements, partial truths, selective omissions, or any other means.

INTEGRITY. Ethical executives demonstrate personal integrity and the courage of their convictions by doing what they think is right even when there is great pressure to do otherwise; they are principled, honorable and upright; they will fight for their beliefs. They will not sacrifice principle for expediency, be hypocritical, or unscrupulous.

PROMISE-KEEPING & TRUSTWORTHINESS. Ethical executives are worthy of trust. They are candid and forthcoming in supplying relevant information and correcting misapprehensions of fact, and they make every reasonable effort to fulfill the letter and spirit of their promises and commitments. They do not interpret agreements in an unreasonably technical or legalistic manner in order to rationalize non-compliance or create justifications for escaping their commitments.

LOYALTY. Ethical executives are worthy of trust, demonstrate fidelity and loyalty to persons and institutions by friendship in adversity, support and devotion to duty; they do not use or disclose information learned in confidence for personal advantage. They safeguard the ability to make independent professional judgments by scrupulously avoiding undue influences and conflicts of interest. They are loyal to their companies and colleagues and if they decide to accept other employment, they provide reasonable notice, respect the proprietary information of their former employer, and refuse to engage in any activities that take undue advantage of their previous positions.

FAIRNESS. Ethical executives and fair and just in all dealings; they do not exercise power arbitrarily, and do not use overreaching nor indecent means to gain or maintain any advantage nor take undue advantage of another's mistakes or difficulties. Fair persons manifest a commitment to justice, the equal treatment of individuals, tolerance for and acceptance of diversity, the they are open-minded; they are willing to admit they are wrong and, where appropriate, change their positions and beliefs.

CONCERN FOR OTHERS. Ethical executives are caring, compassionate, benevolent and kind; they like the Golden Rule, help those in need, and seek to accomplish their business objectives in a manner that causes the least harm and the greatest positive good.

RESPECT FOR OTHERS. Ethical executives demonstrate respect for the human dignity, autonomy, privacy, rights, and interests of all those who have a stake in their decisions; they are courteous and treat all people with equal respect and dignity regardless of sex, race or national origin.

LAW ABIDING. Ethical executives abide by laws, rules and regulations relating to their business activities.

COMMITMENT TO EXCELLENCE. Ethical executives pursue excellence in performing their duties, are well informed and prepared, and constantly endeavor to increase their proficiency in all areas of responsibility.

LEADERSHIP. Ethical executives are conscious of the responsibilities and opportunities of their position of leadership and seek to be positive ethical role models by their own conduct and by helping to create an environment in which principled reasoning and ethical decision making are highly prized.

REPUTATION AND MORALE. Ethical executives seek to protect and build the company's good reputation and the morale of its employees by engaging in no conduct that might undermine respect and by taking whatever actions are necessary to correct or prevent inappropriate conduct of others.

ACCOUNTABILITY. Ethical executives acknowledge and accept personal accountability for the ethical quality of their decisions and omissions to themselves, their colleagues, their companies, and their communities.

Society is changing rapidly. The prevalent use of the World Wide Web and the rapid response and reporting of news agencies and social media outlets allow us to know about happenings around the world within minutes. This openness has also increased the demands on public service agencies to be more accountable and more transparent in our day-to-day operations, our use of public funding and government property, our hiring and treatment of employees, potential conflicts of interest, and so on. It undoubtedly has a similar impact on other sectors.

As leaders, it doesn't go unnoticed that we can advance or damage the image or reputation of the organizations we lead and of the individuals within. We are entrusted with incredible power. Our ethical behaviors and action affect in how our client communities view the men and women of our organizations, whether positively or negatively.

If they are less than ethical, people that lead even organizations that remain ethical on all fronts will not meet the expectations of the people they lead and serve, or those of society as a whole.

John Middleton Hope said,

Ethical behavior in police organizations does not start with the introduction of an ethics program delivered to the officers on the street. It commences with a commitment by the chief of police to ensure there is an ethical climate established in the organization. In order for police departments to achieve an ethical climate in the department, the chief of police and the executive must align their philosophy and observable behaviors, their communication and their decision making processes to ethical practices, not only when it is expedient or convenient, but at all times. This behavior is observed by every member of the organization and more clearly demonstrates what the organization stands for than any rhetoric.

ACTING WITH INTEGRITY

We hear a lot about integrity, often in the negative. Statements like "He has no integrity whatsoever" and "She has tons of integrity" are bandied about regularly in workplaces. But do we really know what integrity is?

*Definitions vary. However, I like how the Concise Oxford
English Dictionary defines it: "1) The quality of having
strong moral principles. 2) The state of being whole."
For me, the "state of being whole" has particular resonance since that
is what we're talking about with leadership. We want our leaders
to be real people who understand their strengths, gifts, weaknesses
and warts. And that strong self-awareness propels them to: a) work
continuously at improving their areas of weakness, and b) surrounding
themselves with competent people to whom they readily delegate. This
is integrity with a human face. It's about being a whole leader.*

—JIM TAGGART

To me, integrity is meaning what you say and saying what you mean. It is doing what is right. It's practicing what you preach. Honesty goes hand in hand with integrity, and I don't think you can have one quality or value without the other.

Author Nikk Zorbas says, "Integrity forms the foundation of all relationships, both personal and in business. Integrity is the hallmark for a truly successful life, because having personal integrity passes on through all your endeavors. There's no shortage of business and individuals who describe themselves as having integrity, but many fall prey to dishonest business practices when they give in to greed and forfeit their beliefs. This is the main reason they fail."

Martin Luther King Jr. once said, "The time is always right to do what is right." That is entirely true. It is even more valid when nobody else but you will know what you did. I don't know who said it first, but there are words to the effect that what really counts is "doing what is right when no one else is watching." That's where the rubber truly meets the road.

I heard a story years ago where a man came out of a shopping center into the parking lot to see the side of his car all scraped and dented. He was furious, of course, that the culprit was not standing there sheepishly waiting for him so that he could confess his wrong. Then he noticed a note flapping under one of his windshield wipers. He thought, "Wow. Someone truly did the right thing here and left me his or her contact information." Then he read the note, which said, "Sorry I hit your car. There's a pile of people standing here right now as I write this note. I'm sure they're all thinking what an honest person I am and that I'm leaving you my name and contact information so that I can pay for the damage...but I'm not!" Obviously not a lot of integrity there, but a great sense of humor!

Gordon Tredgold is a reknowned leadership author and speaker whose quotes are always impactful. He says,

One of the things that defines Integrity, is how we act in private, when no one else is looking; when no one can see what we think or what we do.

We can always put on a show for others, we always can show Integrity, but it doesn't necessarily mean that we have it.

Real Integrity is a 100% of the time thing, there is no such thing as part-time Integrity.

It is easy for us to look the other way, to cheat, or to quit when no one else is looking, and then tell others what great deeds we did, but when we do that we are just lying to ourselves. We're faking it.

We have all seen—and at times have fallen victim to—leaders who don't do what they say is right or even take the types of improper actions that they are responsible for preventing. Like the human resources manager I watched rise to great heights in a police service that I know well, who then violated every HR rule that was her responsibility to enforce and was even heard to say, "I'm the queen of HR; I can do anything I want." Wonderful approach. Truly reeks of integrity. Or the manager who strictly enforced rules on the proper use of leased vehicles in a police service but hid a leased SUV away so that no one could put miles on it for valid work reasons, fully knowing he had already struck a deal with the leasing company to purchase it himself down the road. It reminds of me of the old saying "Do as I say, not as I do."

> *Honesty. Not a week goes by that we don't hear about a so-called leader losing credibility because he or she was dishonest. Often this is because of pressure to try and "measure up" and it's not coming from a place of being real—often this relates to fear of not being accepted for your true self. We live in age of extraordinary transparency, which is reason enough to always be true to your core—your mission will be revealed, your motivations will show by your behaviors. But it goes way beyond this. It's an issue that sets an example and elevates an organization. If you have a reputation for honesty, it will be a lot easier to deliver bad news and face tough challenges. Are you inspiring people from your heart?*
>
> —Meghan M. Biro

Actually demonstrating integrity is essential for the mission-critical development of trust, and we cannot survive as leaders without the trust of our people, those we serve, the media, public officials, governing bodies, and partner agencies.

When asked what the most important quality that the great leaders possess was, Chief Robert Lunney said, "Integrity—the chief's position requires uncompromising character and honesty in dealings with members and employees, the police authority, the media, and the community. The chief is also responsible and accountable for establishing high standards of integrity within the service."

Senior managers and leaders in organizations, whether public, private, or not for profit, carry enormous clout. People around and below them know that they can make or break careers. They have tremendous influence in terms of who goes where and who gets what perks, what courses, what travel, which promotions, and what office spaces. They have the positional power to abuse or take advantage of physical and financial resources or processes. In many cases they also have the political influence to make many things happen or not in communities, including building organizational or individual reputations or destroying them.

That can be a tremendously positive or terrifyingly negative power. Some people end up being corrupted by that authority.

Regarding integrity, Gordon Tredgold goes on to say,

If we are prepared to be underhand to achieve positions of Leadership, then people will have little faith or trust in us as leaders.

This is all related to Integrity, the more Integrity we have the less political we will be perceived. With Integrity comes the desire to do the right thing.

When we do the right thing it's easier for people to understand and accept our motivation. It's true that we can't please all the people all the time, but if we do the right thing, then at least they will understand and might be able to accept our decisions, even if they don't like it.

We all know that in policing, even the perception of wrongdoing by one officer can hurt all of the personnel within the organization and sometimes further. Some people remember reading in the paper that a cop was guilty of some offense and quickly forget what organization he or she was from. All police agencies end up getting tarred with that all-encompassing brush. If the guilty party happens to be a senior officer or manager or, God forbid, the chief, the impact can be nuclear in nature.

I love this quote by one of the leading writers of the Victorian era, George Eliot:

Keep true, never be ashamed of doing right; decide on what you think is right and stick to it.

We haven't seen any cases of blatant corruption at the chief level in Ontario that I recall, but I have seen chiefs forced to step down over illegal activity or inappropriate behavior a few times over my career. Those few instances hurt the community trust in that agency, likely significantly affecting the morale of all therein and once again harming the reputation of policing in general. Such dark moments can haunt an organization for a generation.

If the corrupt activities are broader in scope, like the involvement of an entire unit or more serious illegal activity (e.g., the LAPD Rampart Division), we have an international incident that will be studied and reported on for decades.

An author on leadership integrity and organisational change, Margaret Thorsborne says:

The greatest fallout from a lack of integrity is the loss of trust in institutions, industries, management and individuals. In the vacuum created when trust is lost, suspicion and paranoia thrive. Is it any wonder that we have lost faith in our institutions, management, the business world and those who lead us, and have become distrusting and cynical about the ability of those in authority to give priority to our welfare and wellbeing?...Integrity is an old-fashioned virtue that has become a low priority somewhere in the quest for increasing profit, market share, votes and tenure.

We can never forget that the integrity by which we live our lives and demonstrate to those we lead and serve will make or break us in terms of our credibility internally and externally. Trust in us is totally lost at the drop of an unethical hat. We must continually and consistently set a positive example for those around us.

Margaret Thorsborne also says,

> Understand that your integrity in dealings with others (and yourself) is an essential component of the glue in your relationships. It delivers respect, loyalty, commitment and trust. It's a virtue worthy of your interest.
>
> Find role models who are known for their integrity and watch their values playing out. Watch their behaviour. Learn from their example how they "do" honesty and openness, how they walk their talk.
>
> Have courage. Integrity is hard work. Be prepared to be disadvantaged sometimes when you make a stand over an issue, or to be inconvenienced when you made a promise.
>
> Do what you say you will do. Don't let people down.

Author and CEO Amy Rees Anderson also makes an incredibly valid point: "If I could teach only one value to live by, it would be this: Success will come and go, but integrity is forever. Integrity means doing the right thing at all times and in all circumstances, whether or not anyone is watching. It takes having the courage to do the right thing, no matter what the consequences will be. Building a reputation of integrity takes years, but it takes only a second to lose, so never allow yourself to ever do anything that would damage your integrity."

I've personally heard senior executives preach of the importance of integrity in the workplace, only to regularly violate every rule known to man. These same individuals hold the smallest of infractions over the heads of colleagues and subordinates forever, only to do the same and worse with great frequency.

Forbes' Magazine and leadership athor Jack Zenger said, "There is too much evidence in the news regarding top executives' ethical breaches to not question the validity of these inflated scores. Perhaps ethical lapses tend to occur most often in senior executives because of new and different combinations of forces that are impinging on them. The tendencies to give in to unethical behavior may be latent in many leaders, but there are few opportunities to express this behavior while serving at middle levels in the organization."

It is challenging enough for leaders to avoid unfair rumors of inappropriate actions in this social media–rich, competitive environment in which we toil. False and real tales of infidelity, illegal and immoral activity, and the bending of company rules will plague some executives for all eternity, rightly or wrongly.

Zenger continues: "Whatever the cause, it is clear that the egregious acts of dishonesty that destroy careers (and in many cases have destroyed entire organizations in their aftermath) have been generally executed by people who hold the most senior roles in their firm."

The importance of integrity in leadership transcends all vocations and callings.

> *The supreme quality for leadership is unquestionably integrity.*
> *Without it, no real success is possible, no matter whether it is on*
> *a section gang, a football field, in an army, or in an office.*

—DWIGHT D. EISENHOWER

And as Chief Jim Chu said very well, "My favorite quote originated with Warren Buffet. When you look to hire/promote someone, look for intelligence, initiative, and integrity. But of all these three, look for integrity first. Because if that person doesn't have integrity, you'd better hope he or she doesn't have intelligence and initiative."

Fair Is Fair!

• • •

Why are some leaders bullies, when everyone agrees that treating
people fairly always works much better? "We already know that
fairness is the goal," says Professor Steven Blader, a management
professor at New York University's Stern School of Business,
who studies, among other things, what sort of management style
motivates employees. "Why isn't every manager out there acting
fairly?" he asks. "People care more about fairness than they do
about self-interest." The study makes clear that leaders who have a
strong sense of their status within an organization tend to act more
fairly than do those who are most concerned with their power.

—SUSAN ADAMS

WE CAN ALL FALL INTO the trap of favoring some employees over others.
I've been there and done that. It's human nature. Some people are easy
to like and others aren't, but does the likeable employee outperform the
unlikeable employee? Sometimes yes and sometimes no. Many leaders
assume the people they like are better employees, when in reality the
leaders are simply being snowed. Conversely, when you don't particularly like individuals, it is much easier to find fault in all they do, when
the reality of the matter is that they may be hard workers that do things
perfectly right.

*Every person should be treated fairly in an organization, but
every person should be treated differently in an organization.*

—JIM WELCH

Some leaders are guilty of being blindly loyal to all the people they lead
and never seeing a single fault, or at least being willing back them until
their dying breaths. That can result in not taking on employees that need
to be challenged. That in itself is totally unfair to the good employees who
follow the rules and always give their best.

Commissioner Bob Paulson said,

> My greatest challenge was found within myself, and it was discov-
> ering that I had to get past the personal loyalty trap that besets
> many leaders. Recognizing that leadership, to be effective, must
> be exercised in the much broader context respecting public, or-
> ganizational, and mission interests. It was a profound shift in my
> thinking and my actions. I remember clearly my first assessment
> as a commissioned officer in the Canadian Armed Forces. It was
> very critical of my performance and featured a line that, while
> I've always remembered, took me some time to actually figure out:
> "Lt. Paulson displays an excessive amount of downward-flowing
> loyalty."

Forgiveness is not easy for some, including many leaders. But it is key to
remember that our people are human, and they will err. We all do. But we
cannot forgive only those whom we like. If there was no malice involved
in an error or a lapse in judgment, we should apply our forgiveness in a
fair manner.

*Leaders must be firm and foster accountability, but they also
must know when to forgive past wrongs in the service of building
a brighter future. One of the most courageous acts of leadership*

*is to forgo the temptation to take revenge on those on the other
side of an issue or those who opposed the leader's rise to power.
Those whose main motivation is to settle scores and get payback—to
obstruct rather than construct—are on the wrong side of history.
Their legacy is not rebuilding, but rubble. From (ahem) members
of Congress to leaders in any turnaround situation, it's a lesson
worth remembering: Taking revenge can destroy countries,
companies, and relationships. Forgiveness can rebuild them.*

—ROSABETH MOSS KANTER

Shortly after Julian Fantino was appointed OPP commissioner in 2006, he and I were being driven to an event when his cellular phone rang. When he answered, even I could hear the loud voice on the other end. Something had apparently gone terribly wrong.

The day prior, our drug-enforcement officers had arrested a group of narcotics dealers following a lengthy undercover operation. In the twenty-four hours that followed, a harried media-relations officer in the local detachment had prepared a media release and had quite accidentally included the name of a young offender and issued the release to the press. This, of course, resulted in an outcry from the young person's family and a number of advocacy groups. The government was very concerned about the apparent violation of the legislation, and someone had called Fantino to say that the attorney general was very upset. I'll never forget his reply.

He said, "Tell the AG to take a pill. The officer didn't do it on purpose, and it will be fixed. It won't happen again." I harkened back to other days in our history when the officer involved would have been drawn and quartered over this. He or she would have been known forever as "the one who..." But to this day I don't even know the offending officer's name. There was no malice involved. A tired officer simply screwed up, as we all do.

The legendary tough-guy police chief from Toronto did the right thing and, after setting the caller straight, returned to the conversation with me as if nothing had happened. Many would not have thought that

Julian would have responded in that fashion, but I saw true and fair leadership from him in that moment and in many more to follow.

Author Robert Andrews said, "If we're honest, there are no ideal leaders. Even what we perceive as great leaders have their faults. But despite their faults, we agree that most good leaders are fair. Whether we like their decision or not."

Fairness is extremely important, but admittedly, I haven't always thought that way. I overreacted when people that I wasn't particularly fond of did something that I didn't like. Conversely, I was quick to reassure those I did like when they made similar errors.

Sometimes people simply perceive unfairness in how we treated an employee through some process, disciplinary or otherwise. At the same time, cries of favoritism permeate the air when someone isn't disciplined over some perceived lapse in judgment, or when a certain person is selected for a promotion or some opportunity that others sought. Those are tough things to deal with. We can't always explain the "what" in terms of disciplinary matters. The punishment meted out can't be published or communicated in most cases, leaving some with the perception that nothing was done. We get that. In addition, we cannot always communicate why a certain employee was promoted over another, or why we chose a specific individual for an opportunity of some sort and not another person.

American CEO and leadership author Rob May:

If you want to be a better leader, focusing on fairness is a good place to start. Here are some things to try:

* Be open and honest about the reasons behind your decisions.
* Create processes that are transparent, so that people understand how decisions are made.
* Listen to both sides of the story, and make sure everyone's voice is heard.
* Communicate clearly.

As chief superintendent in the OPP, a common perception is that my wife is favored and has excelled only because she is my wife. Given that I became commissioner, every transfer, promotion, or course she's enjoyed since has been because of me. Some of the doubting minority out there will never know her education, her commitment, the many difficult jobs she's held over her career and how well she carried them out, her personality, or how well she treats people and builds morale wherever she goes.

Nor will they know how being married to me has hurt her on a number of fronts *because* she is my wife. In one case she was the only rank-qualified applicant for a job that she had tons of experience for. In any similar case, we would have simply laterally moved the applicant into the vacant position and run a promotional process to back-fill the person that was moved. But we still made her study and go through an interview panel (without me on it!) just because of perception. I get that. In addition, there were other cases where she wasn't sent on sought-after courses, because it would have raised a bunch of eyebrows. She's actually OK with all of that—she gets it too.

So fairness can actually cause some people grief through its application, but we have to do what is right.

As leaders, if we don't dot our i's and cross our t's, if we aren't as open and transparent as the rules allow, and if we emit any perception of favoritism or bias, our credibility will be in question, and potentially all the good and fair decisions we make will be forever tainted. Let's judge ourselves accordingly and act in the best interests of the organization—*fairly*.

These men ask for just the same thing, fairness, and fairness only.
This, so far as in my power, they, and all others, shall have.

—Abraham Lincoln

Only the Resilient
Will Survive

• • •

Resilience is not what happens to you. It's how you react to,
respond to, and recover from what happens to you.

—Jeffrey Gitomer

In her presentation to the FBI National Executive Institute Session 35, Cycle 2, in 2012, a friend of mine, then Deputy Chief Constable Judith Gillespie of the Police Service of Northern Ireland (PSNI), walked the participants through the thirty-year organizational and sometimes personal struggles that the former Royal Ulster Constabulary (RUC) faced in Northern Ireland; this is now commonly referred to as "the Troubles." Her resounding and overarching message from start to finish was that she and the PSNI had to "remain relentlessly optimistic," something she completely ascribes to, to this very day.

This wonderful lady and intelligent police leader enlisted in the then RUC in 1982 in the midst of a violent and turbulent multidecade period that saw the murders of more than three hundred police officers, both on and off duty. Some were killed at home, in front of their families, while others were attacked on the streets. Police stations had to be heavily fortified to prevent attacks. Those years saw multiple RUC officers responding in armored vehicles and accompanied by squads of heavily armed soldiers to what would be routine calls for service for most Western police forces. Schoolchildren had to be escorted by the military as they walked to and from school for fear of terrorist acts. The Troubles all but totally destroyed the people of Northern Ireland.

A young Judith not only joined the RUC during a highly charged and dangerous period, but she was one of very few female officers within the RUC in those early days. She never expressed any sentiments regarding how she was or wasn't accepted by her male counterparts, nor did she cite any tales of harassment or abuse; however, I can only imagine how challenging those days were for her as a female member of the RUC. The many years to follow would be only more difficult for her, I'm sure. That would include the many dark days associated with the morphing of the RUC into the current day PSNI: hiring practices that forced them to have not a single more Protestant member than they had Catholic members, an oversight Policing Board that some suspect at times included members with previous ties to the very groups that brought terror to the streets during the Troubles, and a very long and arduous peace process.

However, to this day, Judith Gillespie truly does remain relentlessly optimistic. Now retired, she stays positive about her beloved country and the future of the PSNI. Although a state of fragile peace remains and the acts of terrorism and other forms of violence have dissipated tremendously, volatile public protests do continue fairly regularly. Depending on the effectiveness of the response of the police to those incidents, that relative peaceful state is forever in jeopardy. I'm sure that without the strong personal resilience that Judith marches forward with, she and her family would have long fled to another continent. However, she remains in Belfast, strong and optimistic, healthy, happy, and forever loving her homeland.

*Success is not final, failure is not fatal: it is
the courage to continue that counts.*

—WINSTON CHURCHILL

As we march through life at work and play, as we grow up, and as we decline, we face a never-ending series of hills and valleys. They might be as simple as not making the cut when trying out for a sports team, getting divorced, not getting promoted, or being turned down when asking someone for a date, or they may be life-altering situations we encounter. We cannot give up hope on every occasion. If Judith Gillespie had, she wouldn't have become a police officer, or she would have quit ten minutes into it. But she persevered.

In her October 22, 2013, speech to the British Irish Parliamentary Assembly, Judith stated the following:

> Policing in a politically polarised context is hugely challenging and there's a constant need for consistent engagement at community and strategic level to clearly communicate positioning on the big issues. Public trust and confidence remains a challenge. Notwithstanding high confidence figures there remains a significant minority who have no confidence in PSNI.
>
> Despite all of this, I remain relentlessly optimistic—and with a focus on the possible.

A good friend of mine in the OPP, S. Sgt. Joe Girard (now retired), applied twenty-six times for promotion from sergeant as vacancies at the staff sergeant level came up. A former Canadian Forces Airborne soldier, Joe has never been one to fold his tent quickly. He remained positive and optimistic and eventually did get that promotion. He then said, "Twenty-six times is a charm, Chris."

The *Psychology Today* website states (author unknown),

> Resilience is that ineffable quality that allows some people to be knocked down by life and come back stronger than ever. Rather than letting failure overcome them and drain their resolve, they find a way to rise from the ashes. Psychologists have identified some of the factors that make someone resilient, among them a

positive attitude, optimism, the ability to regulate emotions, and the ability to see failure as a form of helpful feedback. Even after a misfortune, blessed with such an outlook, resilient people are able to change course and soldier on.

Some people go through life seemingly with little effort, without trying hard and having things always go their way. That ease of life they enjoy may be only our perception and not the reality. But if it is reality, then good for them. They won't develop any scar tissue and won't necessarily develop the resolve that will enable them to take on the direst of challenges, if any come their way.

All of us pass through a series of ebbs and flows in terms of our optimism about life, both personally and professionally. But the great leaders strive to remain resilient on a personal level and continuously make every effort to maintain resilience in those they lead. You can't have one without the other, and the success of the organization as they labor to deliver to a needy customer base completely depends on it.

In her article "Cultivate a Culture of Confidence," Rosabeth Moss Kanter says,

> Nothing succeeds for long without considerable effort and constant vigilance...a key factor in high achievement is bouncing back from the low points. Long-term winners often face the same problems as long-term losers, but they respond differently...
> Consider first the pathologies of losing. Losing produces temptations to behave in ways that make it hard to recover fast enough—and could even make the situation worse.

Leaders with defeatist or "the sky is falling" attitudes do nothing to help those they lead develop resiliency. Eventually their followers succumb to that negative outlook, and they too begin to feel that the situation is hopeless. Those are the people that focus their every thought on how bad things are and are continuously heard saying, "This place is going to hell in a handbasket. I can't wait to retire." Even sadder is the fact that quite a few of them have many years of service remaining before they are pensionable.

A competent leader can get efficient service from poor troops, while on the contrary an incapable leader can demoralize the best of troops.

—Gen. John J. Pershing

Kanter goes on to say, "Resilience is not simply an individual characteristic or a psychological phenomenon. It is helped or hindered by the surrounding system. Teams that are immersed in a culture of accountability, collaboration, and initiative are more likely to believe that they can weather any storm. Self-confidence, combined with confidence in one another and in the organization, motivates winners to make the extra push that can provide the margin of victory."

The mind-set and spirit of the leader of the pack undoubtedly either positively or negatively influences the speed of the pack. If the leader is continuously whining about every decision made by those above, can never accept change or the reality of the environment he or she works in, and is always crying, "Woe is me," that attitude will undoubtedly impact those he or she leads. The lack of resiliency in the leader and, downstream from him or her, in the workforce almost always translates to poor morale across the board.

A little known leadership blog I stumbled across contained the following quote, the validity of which really struck me:

To thrive in turbulent times, companies must become as efficient at renewal as they are at producing today's products and services; renewal must be the natural consequence of an organization's innate resilience. To be resilient an organization must dramatically reduce the time it takes to go from "that can't be true" to "we must face the world as it is."

—Shawn

The rapidly growing state of flux that police services and public and private organizations have been in for the past decade or more has had a significant impact on the resilience of their leaders and on the organizations as a whole. We all know the phases of any change-management process and the resulting impacts on people. The end state of the change cycle is never fully attained, except in isolated situations that relate perhaps to specific projects. Ongoing change is here to stay, resulting in an even-greater demand for personal and organizational resiliency.

When asked about the importance of leadership in policing, Senator Vern White said, "We live in an ever-changing environment where we have to have leadership qualities to survive and, more importantly, for our respective organizations to survive."

The need for resiliency transcends our role as leaders. If we are to remain healthy, engaged, and effectively functioning leaders for our people, we need to remain resilient in our personal lives too. We cannot be train wrecks in our off-duty worlds and then go to work, flip a switch, and suddenly have immense strength. Of course, I recognize that all of this might well be easier to say than to do.

I love this quote from author Dick Ruhl:

I define resilience as the capacity to carry on—to withstand, persevere, or recover from challenging circumstances.
Resilience involves acting as though it is impossible for you to fail. This may sound counter-intuitive, but dealing with challenge may be the best opportunity to tilt the game in your favor. Don't look at crisis as something to survive. It's actually an opportunity to thrive.

Things can and do go bad. Some situations feel hopeless at times, but wandering around looking as if the world were soon coming to an end helps no one, including yourself. Keep your chin up, get over it, resolve to fix things, focus on the positive, and never quit on the hill you're facing.

Some might say that I'm more stubborn than I am resilient. I believe that the two qualities work hand in hand.

When I had brain-tumor surgery in May 2000 and a large portion of my skull and a piece of my limited gray matter were removed, I was determined to do two things. Firstly, live. I have never been afraid of the act of dying; I just don't want to go too soon and miss anything! Secondly, after surviving, I wanted to return to work in some capacity. I'm sure some colleagues hoped I'd become a compost heap, many others prayed I'd live, and some in the middle didn't want me dead but certainly hoped I wouldn't return to what was a great superintendent role and a career opportunity for someone else. Every cloud has a silver lining, and my early retirement because of health issues would have led to the promotion of an inspector into a vacant superintendent position, and the downstream career opportunities would have been numerous. However, I did survive, and following months of rehabilitation, I did return to the OPP, into a part-time and then eventually a full-time role. But it was at least a couple of years before I felt I was fully recovered, if ever.

My doctor credits, at least in part, my presurgery fitness level. I also know that he and my neurosurgeon would have both supported me if I had been inclined to never work again. However, I believe that the human mind is a power influencing factor in how one survives such an ordeal. My resilience and stubbornness prevailed.

In the mid-1990s, I had two friends whose wives were diagnosed with breast cancer, in two different cities on the same day. They were both mothers of two children and were roughly the same age. They had mastectomies the same day, went through the same regimes of chemotherapy, and convalesced over the same months. One of them was determined that this would not beat her and continued to live her life, attending events, shopping, and meeting with friends, smiling and wearing a kerchief. She is alive and well until this day.

Sadly, the other passed away within the year. From day one, she never left the confines of her house except for medical appointments. She remained inside, alone and crying. No one ever saw her outside. Even if someone went to her door, she opened it only a crack to whisper minimal words and then returned to the darkness of her house. It was so sad to watch. She was a wonderful person.

I'm not being critical of that delightful lady at all, but was it simply genetics that allowed the other woman to survive at least twenty more years? Was it the health care differences between two great hospitals in two major cities in Ontario? Was it shit luck? Or did the sheer will of one to live result in a positive outcome, while the other poor soul cried herself to death?

Many of us have known people who were at death's door but willed themselves to stay alive until all of their families were at their bedsides. Good luck or resiliency?

Translate that, if you will, to day-to-day life. Some people feel that they are always unlucky. My father is one of those people, and at times he has influenced my outlook when things didn't go well for me. He calls it the "Lewis luck," or lack thereof, when anything goes bad. So was getting a brain tumor simply the Lewis luck for me, or was it actually good luck that I survived? It's a "glass half-empty or half-full?" scenario. I much prefer the glass to be half-full.

There are other personal factors that can contribute greatly to our resiliency. Fitness is key, both emotional and physical, and in my view they are directly related. The ability to deal with the hours, volatility, and stressors of police work and of many other careers, the demands of supervisory and management positions, health challenges, and recovery from such curveballs all require a strong mind and body.

As a young officer, I thought physical fitness was all about being able to leap tall buildings in a single bound, about being physically able to save my life and to save the lives of others, including fellow officers. Many years passed before I fully understood the links between physical and mental health. During my years on the tactical team, which had enormous fitness standards, I never leapt over a single building. I seldom had to run more than several yards on a single gun call. But I was ready for that and more should the need arise. What my fitness level did prepare me for, however, was what we faced in every call: stress. Whether we were guarding dangerous prisoners, raiding biker clubhouses, or lying outside a gunman's

house all night in the cold while he was being skillfully negotiated to sur-
render, there was always lots of stress.

Stress can have tremendous impacts on our bodies, even when we are
only intermittently exposed. Some people get very stressed just by waiting
for the phone to ring and anticipating the need to make life-and-death
decisions. Others suffer from years of cumulative stressful events. Yet others are seemingly unaffected. That doesn't make them any stronger than
those that are impacted; it's not something that you can control. But there
is no doubt that maintaining a high level of fitness and overall physical
health go a long way in helping you deal with stress. The bonus is that
you'll look better, feel better, and be a great example to those you lead.

In *A Leadership Primer,* Gen. Colin Powell states,

Perpetual optimism is a force multiplier.
The ripple effect of a leader's enthusiasm and optimism is awesome. So is the impact of cynicism and pessimism. Leaders who
whine and blame engender those same behaviors among their colleagues. I am not talking about stoically accepting organizational
stupidity and performance incompetence with a "what, me worry?" smile. I am talking about a gung ho attitude that says "we can
change things here, we can achieve awesome goals, we can be the
best." Spare me the grim litany of the "realist"; give me the unrealistic aspirations of the optimist any day.

Because police forces are generally considered a part of the public service sector, at least in the Western world, there may be inherent challenges within the policing context that further inhibit the building of
organizational resiliency versus life in the private sector. Risk taking is
often frowned upon by political masters. It's difficult if not impossible
to terminate the employment of individuals in the policing environment
in Canada (not so much in the United States), so those that never do buy
into the organizational goals and subsequently act like a rapidly spreading

malignant mass on the otherwise healthy employees are tough to get rid of. Flexibility is not always a prevalent feature of governmental or para-military organizations. Fiscal pressures are most often out of the hands of public service leaders. So adapting to changing environments, building resilient cultures, and confidently moving workforces forward can be try-ing situations within law-enforcement organizations.

Chief Rick Deering faced a number of cultural and personal obstacles when he took over the Royal Newfoundland Constabulary in 2001 and in the years to follow:

> My greatest challenge as police leader involved dramatically al-tering a culture that had existed, unchanged, for more than one hundred years. Everyone supports value-added change until it af-fects him or her personally. When this happened, things got very interesting and clearly put my leadership skills to the ultimate test. Against my better judgment and usually reliable intuition, I fell into the trap of trusting those whose agendas were not in sync with mine or the organization's. Eventually, this small group of ill-intended senior officers threw many obstacles in the way of much-needed progress.

As police leaders, we don't have to like those challenges, but we have to accept them as part of the playground that we volunteered to play in. We must acknowledge that a continual barrage of change processes will be a part of our way of life until we retire. That is reality. There is no mileage to be gained by fighting it to the point that it negatively impacts all those around us.

Communication remains key. Our people need to know that change is inevitable, that we accept it, and that we *will* continue to succeed and be viewed as a team that expends energy trying to make the change positive for clients and employees, as opposed to digging in as if we were preparing for an armed conflict.

As we're developing and selecting leaders within our organizations, their ability to successfully manage change is key to their future success and that of the organization as a whole. Those that have continually demonstrated a reluctance to change will not model the leadership behaviors that we need to keep our organizational resiliency at a high level.

Dr. Roger Gibbins is a Canadian author, professor and former CEO, who has written many books relevant to leadership. He says:

> Rigid organizations tend to break rather than bend in the face of organizational change, and "bounce" is not a characteristic commonly associated with the hierarchical characteristics of the public service.
>
> …Greater resiliency within the public service is far from an unattainable goal. At the same time, we must keep in mind that the traditional value proposition of the public service—to its political masters, to the community, and to employees—is the promise of continuity in the face of change. This is not an easy balance to strike, but not impossible.

Just Make a Decision!

• • •

A true leader has the confidence to stand alone, the courage to
make tough decisions, and the compassion to listen to the needs
of others. He does not set out to be a leader, but becomes one by
the quality of his actions and the integrity of his intent.

—GEN. DOUGLAS MACARTHUR

DECISION MAKING HAS NEVER BEEN an easy thing. When making decisions, every police chief, commissioner, president, or CEO since time began likely faced his or her unique challenges and considerations while dealing with the issues of the day, thinking that it simply couldn't get any worse. Although the current decision-making issues are daunting and at times seem so much more complex to executives than those faced by their predecessors, I'm certain this is merely their perspective. The issues our bosses were challenged by decades ago were surely as troubling to them as our issues are to us now.

However, it is a fact that the environment around is us changing with an unprecedented speed.

Getting to the right answer is tougher these days. It's not just the
greater number of variables to consider; executives also need to
make subjective judgments about highly ambiguous factors that are

moving targets. The usual competitive analysis doesn't work well when technology keeps erasing industry boundaries and the pace of change is so fast that you can't wait for things to stabilize. And any decision you make will be judged in the court of public opinion. You have to take into account potential consequences for a range of constituencies who may have no direct long-term economic interest in the business—regulators, shareholder activists, societal watchdogs, the media. These conditions were beginning to emerge 10 years ago, but now they're dominant.

—Ram Charan, in "An Interview with
Ram Charan," by Melinda Merino

Too many managers who think that they are actually leaders continue to make decisions based on their own agendas and what will make them look good. They are often not the right decisions for the right reasons and are not in the best interests of the communities they serve (clients) or the people they lead. Why? Because their every move is about them.

Author Les McKeown speaks of what he calls "the enterprise commitment": "When working in a team or group environment, I will place the interests of the enterprise above my personal interests." That's what counts to the true leaders, as opposed to "What's in it for me?" Those who don't follow that mantra are failing their clients and their people.

The need to make ethical decisions under the growing media and public microscope has grown as well. It's always been an important issue for leaders to consider, but errors in judgment seldom go unnoticed or unforgiven in our current environment. Having said that, I believe that the ethical tests of today remain unchanged from days gone by.

Some years ago, one of our OPP provincial commanders assigned the commander of our Professional Standards Bureau to develop an "ethical decision-making tool." When I asked what exactly this tool would look like, I was told that it would be a laminated card that we could carry and turn to when making decisions in different situations. It would help guide us ethically. My laughter wasn't well received. Nor was my reply. At that time, I considered myself the president of the Persona Non Grata Club in the eyes of that provincial commander, so I had resigned myself to never being regarded as relevant anyway.

I said, "It is not complicated. *All* of our decisions should be ethical. All we have to do is ask ourselves: Is it the right thing to do? Is it the best thing for the communities we serve and our people? Would I be embarrassed if my mom found out or if my decision ended up on the front page of the paper? If the answer to all of those questions is no, sounds good to me. I don't need to carry around a card to guide me." I don't recall the end result of this ridiculous assignment to my beleaguered colleague, but I never did see a laminated card produced or issued—thank God.

> *The four-way test of the things we think, say or do: is it the truth? Is it fair to all concerned? Will it bring good will and better relationships? Will it be beneficial to all concerned?*

—Rotary International, "Four-Way Test"

There are as many decision-making models, frameworks, and templates in existence as there are academics. They show a variety of quadrants, considerations, dynamics, influencing factors, and quotients.

I am not an MBA or an academic. I haven't studied and written theses on such issues. No disrespect to those who have, but I'm a small-town boy who worked hard, was lucky enough to be in the right place at the perfect time on occasion, treated people well, learned through my many mistakes, and took some risks along my journey.

But I am also someone who has made decisions for many years: some potentially life-altering decisions, many career-limiting decisions, some good, many not. But I accept all of that and take the bad with the good. I'm sure I've learned more from my mistakes than from any successes I might have had along the way.

*There is only one way to avoid criticism: do
nothing, say nothing, and be nothing.*

—ARISTOTLE

My scar tissue has been earned—in tactical operations, major crime investigations, major protest events, large joint-forces operations, First Nations conflicts, and many more, often in highly charged political environments and always fueled by a concentrated media focus. That's not me bragging; that's simply me saying that I survived all of this as a former tugboat sailor from northern Ontario. If I could do it, millions of much smarter, more qualified, and more educated people can accomplish anything that they set their minds to.

Successful leaders have the courage to take action where others hesitate.

—UNKNOWN

I think that many leaders, far too many, are afraid to make decisions, because they don't want to take any risks out of fear that an error will jeopardize their careers. Instead, they risk their careers by not making decisions! Or as I like to say (hopefully this is one of those quotes that will be engraved in granite somewhere, someday), "Their fear of career risk risks their careers."

Only those who dare to fail greatly can ever achieve greatly.

—ROBERT F. KENNEDY

Many of the decisions we make as leaders are relatively simple, based on our experience, organizational knowledge, and good old common sense. However, when those decisions may have a significant impact on those we lead, it can become even more challenging.

Chief Barry King said,

My greatest failure as a leader was sometimes not making the hard decision to move from his or her position someone who was interfering with the progress we were trying to achieve. This occurred after I took over as chief. I wanted to leave one particular senior member with pride as opposed to demonstrating that failure to commit to work with me will leave you out of the loop, regardless of whether you are a senior officer. Over time, this occurred twice, and then I soon learned that after giving someone an opportunity to get on the train before it leaves the station, it is that person's problem when he or she misses the ride and destination.

The most seasoned of employees are not all-knowing or brilliant when they reach supervisory, management, or executive levels. We are all learning every day as leaders. Many of our best lessons are cultured as we toil away in these positions. So when time permits, why would we not seek the input of our people? Supervisors should be seeking the input of workers. Managers should be listening to supervisors, and on it goes. If chiefs, presidents, and CEOs are making decisions without all the facts and input to consider, they'll fail.

In his article *5 Habits of Effective Executives*, Author George Ambler quotes prominent leadership author Peter Drucker:

Effective executives, finally, make effective decisions. They know that this is, above all, a matter of system—of the right steps in the right sequence. They know that an effective decision is always a judgement based on "dissenting opinions" rather than on "consensus on the facts." And they know to make many decisions fast means to make the wrong decisions. What is needed are few, but fundamental decisions. What is needed is the right strategy rather than the razzle-dazzle tactics.

How many times as entry-level employees did we wonder, wouldn't it make more sense to do that some other way? Or, why do we do things like this? Or better yet, why do we even do this at all? We have all been there. The difference is that thirty-five years ago, you didn't dare ask those questions. You'd be branded as a know-it-all, a troublemaker, or worse. In fact some of the old corporals and sergeants in the 1970s just might have pulled you into the garage and pounded you. That was then.

Just as we should be doing in terms of encouraging innovation in our people, we should, when practical, seek the input, thoughts, and ideas of those we lead when making decisions. At times we'll get wonderful ideas from them based on their boots-on-the-ground knowledge of the community. At other times our people will see their suggestions put into action and feel some sense of satisfaction. In addition, it will help them grow as employees and as leaders themselves.

CEOs face countless decisions. The best executives understand which ones they need to focus on and which ones they can delegate. They also know when to make a decision. And they've debated the risk of not doing it. Any change in the landscape creates opportunities for somebody. The decision to grab a big opportunity can be destiny-changing.

—Ram Charan, in "An Interview with
Ram Charan," by Melinda Merino

There are other situations where decision making does not allow for in-depth discussion and a group think. Sensitive personnel issues arise. Decisions are required that may result in disciplinary action against staff, or in extreme cases, people lose their jobs as a result. However, there are still outlets and resources available to assist. There are actually people out there who know more than we do! HR experts, lawyers, accountants, peers, former mentors and bosses, and more. Sometimes sucking up your pride and admitting that either you don't have a clue where to go next or you need the opinion of a trusted colleague or friend to run ideas by or to simply validate a train of thought is actually a good thing.

In their best-selling book *The Decision Book—Fifty Models for Strategic Thinking*, authors Mikael Krogerus and Roman Tschappeler, state,

> We are often forced to make decisions based on limited or ambiguous information. At the beginning of a project, for example, when the finer details are yet to be clarified, we need to be bold in our decision-making—particularly because these early decisions have the most far-reaching consequences. Towards the end of a project we know more and have fewer doubts, but by then there is no longer anything fundamental to decide.
>
> But not making a decision is a decision in itself. If you delay a resolution it is often an unconscious decision, one that you do not communicate. This leads to uncertainty in a team. So if you want to make a decision later, be sure to communicate this clearly.

Knowing my interest in leadership and having previously sat through one of my presentations on the subject, OPP sergeant Mike Harrington once sent me an article written by Elbert Hubbard in 1899, entitled "A Message to Garcia." It chronicles events that occurred during the Spanish-American War, when US president William McKinley decided that he needed to quickly communicate with the leader of the Cuban insurgents, Gen. Calixto Garcia, prior to invading the Spanish colony there. Garcia was believed to be fighting Spanish troops somewhere in a remote mountainous region of Cuba, in an unknown location where he could never be reached by the conventional means of communication at that time. Finding him would not be an easy or a safe task. In fact, it might well be impossible.

When President McKinley expressed his wish that his critical message be delivered to Garcia without delay, US Army lieutenant Andrew S. Rowan readily accepted the challenge without question or comment. He took the letter, "sealed it up in an oil-skin pouch," and set off on his mission to "carry a message to Garcia!"

Hubbard's article was reportedly written in an hour on a winter evening in February 1899. Its focus is to query the reader as to the measure of a man that would accept such a daunting, seemingly impossible, and extremely dangerous assignment without question.

We all know people who have a thousand reasons not to do the simplest of problematic tasks. We are also familiar with subordinates, leaders, and colleagues who ask hundreds of questions as to how they should approach an assignment far less difficult. How to get to Cuba, how to determine Garcia's whereabouts, how to get to his location, how to avoid the enemy, how to locate supplies—these might all be questions they or even *we* would ask before accepting the mission. In addition, how many times in our careers have we heard people say, "It's not my job" or "Why can't someone else do it?" or even worse yet, "Do it yourself"? We also know those that might say, "I tried, but I couldn't find Garcia," without honestly trying. But Rowan apparently just took the package from the commander in chief and set about his way.

Hubbard states,

My heart goes out to the man who does his work when the "boss" is away, as well as when he is at home. And the man who, when given a letter for Garcia, quietly takes the missive, without asking any idiotic questions, and with no lurking intention of chucking it into the nearest sewer, or of doing aught else but deliver it, never gets "laid off," nor has to go on a strike for higher wages. Civilization is one long anxious search for just such individuals. Anything such a man asks shall be granted; his kind is so rare that no employer can afford to let him go. He is wanted in every city, town and village—in every office, shop, store and factory. The world cries out for such: he is needed, & needed badly—the man who can carry a message to Garcia.

In addition to the obvious portrayal of the positive traits we want in all of our subordinates, the article also encourages self-analysis in terms of how the reader can develop these traits in his or her own life. It is touted as being one of the most widely read literary pieces in history. In fact, many military academies have made it mandatory reading for officer cadets, and it is presented to noncommissioned officers on promotion within various US military divisions.

As I reflected on the essay and the writings of various authors that have examined its meaning, I came to the conclusion that the reality of the applicability of this article has greatly diminished over time. In our para-military organizations, police leaders have long pushed the notion of having their subordinates not ask any questions but simply get the job done. I fully believed in that approach myself over the years, both as a frontline officer and as a leader. In fact, as a young constable in the 1970s, I had corporals whom I lived in fear of ever questioning or challenging in anyway.

At the same time, for many years we taught theories of participative management to new supervisors, and in fact in the OPP it was required reading in preparation for promotional interview panels at one time. The whole theory was simple—those folks out doing the job day after day know it best and can offer the best advice on how to do it better. But God forbid we'd ever actually ask them what they think.

We don't hire lemmings. We recruit intelligent and educated person-nel. We encourage them to be innovative and to be in a state of continuous learning throughout their careers. We want them to make decisions that may jeopardize their lives or those of a colleague, and we authorize them to use deadly force. Although some might think that in a perfect world they would all be like Lieutenant Rowan and accept the most difficult of assignments without hesitation or question, we cannot expect that to be reality in this millennium. Our people ask questions, want to understand "why" we do certain things in a specific way, and constantly look for easier or safer approaches and technological solutions to challenges. They also expect to be consulted on issues that impact their lives and careers when appropriate. They are often not afraid of supervisors and senior officers.

Is that a bad thing? Do they have a problem, or do we, as rapidly aging old cops from the paramilitary environment, have the problem?

If you're wise and not a know-it-all, you have a spirited, candid dialogue with your team, and you listen. Listening isn't just hearing; it requires the willingness to entertain other viewpoints—especially opposing ones. You extract the inner feelings of your people, get them to explore the depth and breadth of their thinking. Of course you need to bring people along with you to carry out the decision. You can begin by explaining your reasoning. Strong leaders ask people to get on board or depart honorably. The other side of the equation is where the CEO makes little effort to socialize the decision and loses the support of his or her direct reports.

—RAM CHARAN, IN "AN INTERVIEW WITH
RAM CHARAN," BY MELINDA MERINO

If we as leaders are not picking the brains of these young and capable folks, we are missing the boat. When difficult decisions need to be made that will impact the employees of the organization, we owe it to them to seek their input. If we are making decisions without that input, then we are making them without necessarily having all the facts. That's not fair to our people, it's not fair to the communities we're sworn to protect, and it is not true leadership.

Chief Bill Blair said, "I've had to teach myself to speak last. Even if I have a strong opinion about something, I wait until it goes around the room, and sometimes my opinion changes. But if I speak first, it's over. Everyone just agrees with me. I need the opinion of others. It should be *our* decision, not *my* decision."

In the most dire and extreme situations, there isn't time to seek the counsel of anyone, let alone to call for a group hug, lock arms, and sing "Kumbaya." When the bad guy is running out of the back of the house with a gun, there is not sufficient time for the leader to say, "Excuse me,

Mr. Deranged Killer, but we need a minute here to look at our whiteboard and develop an airtight strategy on how to ensure that you either never see the light of day again for the rest of your natural life or perhaps never breathe another molecule of our precious oxygen. Hang tight and we'll get back to you in a wee bit."

The true leader has developed the confidence and trust of his or her people and responds posthaste when snap decisions are made and direction is given. "Run here, shoot there" is followed to the letter because the leader has built trust through the more routine and mundane work days and events by seeking the input and suggestions of his or her people. But when forming operational goals and strategies, and time permits, why wouldn't we get the thoughts and suggestions of our people? If we do, we'll make better decisions, and we'll have more buy-in from the troops on those decisions. That is true participative management.

We will still always have Lieutenant Rowans in our services and companies, and God love them. Most of us can name some we've worked with or for or have supervised. We'll also always have some people who couldn't make the decision to come in out of the rain. Unfortunately, some of these people we have promoted. But the vast majority of people that make up our services want to do the right things for the right reasons. They will, however, question the how and why of that along the way, and we should question them when feasible as we lead them and our organizations into the future. There is nothing wrong with that, because we are in this together.

Anything less is a failure of leadership.

Author George Ambler said,

Effective executives consider the following guidelines when making effective decisions:

- Seeking dissenting opinion. Effective executives approach decisions by seeking dissenting opinions rather than seeking consensus.

* Make decisions actionable. The toughest part of making a decision is getting it implemented.
* Set decision boundary conditions. Do not make decision based on what is acceptable. You will need to compromise in the end. Don't start with the compromise, start with what's right.
* Effective decisions are based on facts. When making a decision you're making a judgment call not a choice between right and wrong.

The first step on the road to effective leadership is the decision to take responsibility for managing oneself.

Many leadership and, more specifically, decision-making lessons can be gleaned through the various studies on the US Civil War, in particular the three days of July 1–3, 1863, in Gettysburg, Pennsylvania.

As I've said publicly on probably more occasions than most would like, leadership is not rocket science. The loss of fifty thousand US soldiers in the fields of Pennsylvania 150 years ago is clear proof of that statement. The same leadership failings that we sometimes see around the world now—in both the private and public sectors and in policing—clearly contributed to the loss of the Confederate army (Southern states) in the Civil War. Although the war continued for almost two years after the Gettysburg conflict, the Union army (North) clearly gained the upper hand during these historic three days of fighting.

Gen. Robert E. Lee was the supreme commander of the Confederate army. A brilliant strategist and legendary leader, he was at one time the commandant of the US Military Academy. While at West Point, he was classmate to, or personally trained, many of the military officers leading both armies. He had under his command in the Confederate army trusted generals and colonels that he had total faith in, but some of them let him down and in doing so contributed to the failure of the South. In addition, there were times when he should have listened to those that reported to him but chose not to, thereby unnecessarily putting his soldiers in harm's way.

In a nutshell, some of the leaders under Lee's command did not agree with his strategy at Gettysburg. Although the South had recently completely overwhelmed the North at nearby battles in Virginia under Lee's leadership and were on the verge of overall victory, his subordinate generals were not united in agreeing with his decision to attack the North directly on two hills they had fortified just outside of Gettysburg. Some generals proceeded as they saw fit; in other cases, their delays in enacting different aspects of the attack resulted in several tactical errors. The result was a complete slaughter of the Confederate army.

A number of generals had perished in earlier skirmishes or were sick or injured, and unfortunately there were not enough leaders trained, developed, and ready to fill their shoes.

Some decisions were made in a "self over mission" fashion, whereby leaders were out for themselves. Some leaders took responsibility for their errors, where others blamed subordinates for their own blunders. At least one key general was out doing his own thing with a key group of soldiers and couldn't be easily contacted by Lee, leading to a tremendous gap in the intelligence information with which Lee might have made alternative attack plans. Lee didn't have all the facts regarding where the enemy was, where they were going, how many of them there were, and what their overall strengths and weaknesses were.

Personality, politics, communication, motivation, and relationships ended up playing a larger part than they should have in terms of planning and executing the attack.

Of course, digital radios, cell phones, satellite phones, and Blackberries weren't part of the issued kit of the armies of 1863, so communication between elements was a huge planning and execution challenge. Weak leaders added to the problem by not properly supporting their commander by doing all they could to provide timely and accurate information. Additionally, some of Lee's orders weren't always crystal clear, which furthered the communication-gap problem. At the same time, it appears that he didn't heed the advice of his key team members when planning the attack. Whatever the root cause, not getting the proper information and not listening to the suggestions of his team became critical factors in his failure. Then when he made his decisions, the leaders he led did not leave the room united to enact his plan. It became a recipe for disaster, and a disaster it was.

Does any of this sound familiar to modern leadership? Do new-millennium leaders always sing from the same song sheet? Do leaders consistently have adequate background information before they make plans and decisions? Do all leaders seek the advice of experienced subordinates when planning their approaches to emerging problems? Do leaders always properly train, develop, and select leaders effectively and in a timely way? Do some leaders make decisions based on their own agendas versus what's good for the entire team? Unfortunately, no one is perfect, and no organization is without its scars and warts. We are humans, not androids.

However, it is the responsibility of leaders to do all they can to make those they lead be the best they can be. I am certainly no better than Robert E. Lee—far from it. But I did have the benefit of his hindsight as well as the learnings of many who followed him, including the twelve OPP commissioners before me, the many police chiefs past and present across Ontario, Canada, and the world, and I proudly led an organization that is as well trained and equipped as any in the world today. Unfortunately for General Lee, that wasn't the case for him.

Gen. Robert E. Lee had tremendous credibility among his troops. I suppose that's why he is so highly regarded to this very day. Credibility like that doesn't come cheap; it is hard earned. But a leader's credibility is undoubtedly a key factor in terms of getting employee buy-in to a decision, as is the need for soliciting input where feasible.

When commenting on misconceptions held by leaders who have failed as decision makers, author Ram Charan, in "An Interview with Ram Charan," by Melinda Merino, says,

One is that they know it all. That they can figure it out on their own. A second is that if your decision doesn't work out, your career is done. That's not true if you have established credibility. Credibility of the CEO is the number one thing. If you lose it—with your direct reports, the board, key investors, the rest of the company—then you are done.

(Without credibility) none of your decisions will be executed. Credibility also helps you gain access to the right people, the right information, investments, and support. In some cases, it's what allows you to make the right decision in the first place.

Right or wrong, my decision-making model in my role as OPP commissioner in terms of corporate issues at the "Commissioner's Committee" (executive) table, comprising myself and the four deputy commissioners, was simple. I tried to make it as democratic as possible, but that didn't always work. Sometimes a decision just had to be made, and sometimes that wasn't easy or popular when we were trying so hard to be democratic.

> *But it's not a democracy. I've seen some executives become prisoners of their direct reports. They succumb to endless debate, or they may just want to be liked. They lose time and respect. If you're the CEO, you decide.*
>
> —Ram Charan, in "An Interview with Ram Charan," by Melinda Merino

The OPP Commissioner's Committee generally operated like this:

Firstly, I encouraged the deputies to constantly seek the input of those they led on all organizational matters. That was not a tough sell at all, as that's how they led as well.

Corporate decisions required the presentation of a written business case (usually by subject matter experts, committee chairs, or project leads) that explained the background of the issue, the decision point being sought, the rationale, options, a suggested option, and lastly a documented consultation record.

The four deputies expressed their opinions, thoughts, and concerns, as well as their preferred directions. If it wasn't a slam-dunk decision, I would ask questions to provoke more discussion and influencing considerations.

Then, the majority ruled. If it was a two-two tie, I'd break the tie, and I always reserved the right to invoke my five votes. I seldom used that positional power, but when I did, I'd explain my rationale and take the blame if it didn't work out.

And sometimes, "You've just gotta do what you've gotta do."

In his article "How to Make Good Decisions as a Team," Les McKeown said,

Data; debate; decide or defer.
That's it. That's the rhythm of successful team-based decision-making. Data; debate; decide or defer...that's just what it is, the underlying drumbeat to the decision-making discussions of a high-performing team.

So gather the information, data, stats, or opinions; debate the issues, pros and cons, and positions; and either make a decision or defer it while you gather more data to enable it.

My friend Chief Jim Chu says, "Never make a decision when you are mad." That's great advice. I am guilty of making career-altering decisions regarding people I led when I was mad. Sometimes raging mad. Nothing good can come out of that. I also made decisions based on whether I liked the individual involved. No good can come from that either. I fought that tendency hard because it was so wrong, but I am human.

Author Francesca Gino said,

High-stakes decisions...have something in common: they involve high levels of uncertainty. When so much is unknown or unknowable, trying to decide what the right course of action might be, triggers anxiety. In response, many of us seek the counsel of others to help us make these weighty decisions.

The anxiety prompted by high-stakes decisions can be so great that it can overwhelm our careful plans and analysis.

Eliminating the emotional turmoil of high-stakes decisions may not be always possible, but there are ways to minimize your likelihood of falling prey to bad advice.

1. Refrain from making major decisions until you are in a relaxed state and can clearly reflect on the matter at hand.
2. Avoid making a quick decision or obsessing over details.

Decisions need to be consistent and fair, with all personal biases pushed aside. That's not always easy to do, but leadership isn't always easy. Is it the right thing to do or not? That should always be the question, as opposed to "Do I really like this guy?"

I once offered advice to a good friend who was an extremely capable leader. His total dislike for a manager under his command was obvious to all. His perception was that she had wronged him at some point, but his facial expressions and the tone he used when speaking to her did nothing but give her ammunition for a poisoned-workplace case the moment she walked into the office each day. My suggestion was that he smile and say "Good morning" to her, then pour her coffee as if she were one of his A team, while not giving off any outward signs of his disdain. It seemed like pretty rudimentary advice, but we all forget the basics at times, and some, including me, have allowed their likes and dislikes of certain individuals to cloud the decision-making process.

Conversely, I'll be the first to admit that at times I've avoided making decisions that were truly the right thing to do, solely because they would negatively impact a personal friend. In fact, in one case, it involved moving functional units from under the command of one deputy to another to better align roles and reporting structures. It was clearly the right thing to do in the minds of the majority of our senior leaders but was delayed on my part out of my loyalty to a deputy who was a longtime friend and very committed to me. That was so wrong on my part. When I finally made the decision and discussed it with him, I told him, "I've wanted to do this for three years. The only reason I didn't was because you're my friend. I can't lead this organization that way."

> *There are risks and costs to action. But they are far less*
> *than the long-range risks of comfortable inaction.*

—JOHN F. KENNEDY

Decisions most often go well and are huge successes. Some decisions don't go particularly well, but life goes on. Other decisions are total train wrecks, unfortunately. The test of the true leader is his or her reaction to all of those scenarios.

I firmly believe that the real leaders give credit to those they lead when things go well. When things go bad, the leader assumes responsibility and does not pass the blame on to his or her people. We have all experienced the opposite: weak-kneed leaders accepting credit for someone else's efforts or, similar, folks passing blame for their own blunders. Do either of those things even once, and your goose is cooked. Word of your actions will spread like wildfire, and you will lose whatever credibility you may have had, perhaps forever.

We must learn from the decisions we make, whether they appear to be good or are proven to be bad. If we don't debrief our decisions to some degree, how will we know whether they were truly right or wrong? On many occasions we won't know whether they were wrong unless things go to hell in a handbasket.

American author Rita Mae Brown said, "Good judgment comes from experience, and often experience comes from bad judgment."

We review major police operations routinely, whether the result was extreme (e.g., we took or lost a life) or not. I'm a firm believer that as time permits, we need to consult the right people, weigh the risks, make and communicate the decisions made, and then debrief and tweak as necessary. I'm sure OPP folks throughout our senior management team heard me say many times, "If it doesn't work, we'll fix it." However, we can't forget that it may appear to have worked, but some elements of the plan could have been better and we can learn from them. That approach applies to corporate decision making as much as it does operational policing calls.

> *Systematically review your work. Here's another tip decision-makers can borrow from the managers of "real" work: decisions will get better if you establish the habit of reviewing them after the fact. This requires "a culture of honesty and self-examination," as a manager at Chevron told us when we visited there. If your organization can't shine a light on past decisions to learn what went well and what didn't, you are very likely to make bad ones.*

—Tom Davenport

The admission of a mistake by a leader resonates greatly, probably because the men and women of the organization so seldom hear such a declaration from above. Why are many leaders so reluctant to admit they were wrong, but then expect their people to fess up when they are? They likely view admitting that they are, in fact, human as a frailty when in reality it is a strength.

A LinkedIn article, "What Amazing Leaders Do Differently," states:

One of the most courageous things a leader can do is admit when he or she is wrong, and admit it often.
On the flip side, crappy leaders dig in their heels when they're wrong. They'd rather assert authority than admit a mistake. But owning up to one's faults is a greater sign of strength than the ability to stand one's ground.

As always, we need open and honest feedback if we as leaders are going to really know what decisions went well and which ones failed to meet the mark.

Although I cannot determine the source, I was told long ago that Abraham Lincoln once said words to the effect that "you need people that will tell you the honest truth and will point out the foibles. A compass will tell you where north is but won't tell you of all the traps, dangers, and pitfalls you'll encounter along the way."

A long-serving OPP member and friend, Chief Superintendent Rick "Cliffy" Turnbull (now retired) consistently said to the people he led, "You'll always have your say; you just might not always have your way." That's very true. There will be times that all the honest input and feedback in the world, all very legitimately sought, will not influence the decision of a leader to go a certain way. There may be other political factors at play, or the leader may just go with his or her gut feeling and take a certain fork in the road. That's reality. But as much as possible, we should try to explain the rationale for our decisions, particularly to those reporting directly to us, for their edification. To not do so does nothing for their personal development and may impact their confidence that we truly consider and value their input. At other times, it may well prove to them that you haven't completely lost your mind—yet.

> *When we are debating an issue, loyalty means giving me your honest opinion, whether you think I'll like it or not. Disagreement, at this stage, stimulates me. But once a decision has been made, the debate ends. From that point on, loyalty means executing the decision as if it were your own.*

—Gen. Colin Powell

The people we lead also need to understand that as leaders themselves, they won't always get their way, and when they don't, they still need to leave the boardroom standing shoulder to shoulder with us. Too many leaders want to blame a decision that they don't agree with on the boss.

They may well believe that the decision is the right way to go, but because it is controversial with the troops, they roll their eyes and say, "The boss said we have to do this." I can't even begin to imagine how many decisions that I knew nothing of have been blamed on me. We have all seen leaders blame the boss for a decision that he or she wasn't a part of and may not have supported. That's simply the easy way out for weak-kneed leaders who are afraid to tell those they lead, "I made the decision, and here's why," when they know that the decision may be not be well received.

It drove me insane that some senior officers and managers—albeit, hopefully, a very small minority—would sit back and offer no suggestions or input, then hold court with their direct reports at another place and time and be critical of the decision. Abraham Lincoln once said, "If you have no will to change it, you have no right to criticize it." I wish that more leaders, as well as their followers, lived by that axiom. None of us can force them to, but we can sure encourage the heck out of them, and in turn we will be better leaders as a result of considering their advice.

I'd rather regret the things that I have done
than the things that I haven't.

—Lucille Ball

Other Vital Leadership Qualities

• • •

Encouraging Innovation

Leaders instill in their people a hope for success and a belief in themselves. Positive leaders empower people to accomplish their goals.

—Unknown

Within the public service, innovation is a matter of "assessing risk and then testing and applying a creative idea to solve a problem or improve a policy, program, product, or process" according to governance and management consultant and author Lee McCormack. At first blush, this sounds much more applicable to the private sector than to the policing context.

Traditionally, police agencies haven't been into innovation in a big way. New programs thrown at us over the decades, such as community policing, did not go over incredibly well, especially if they were simply old programs with new monikers.

Although policing always has been and remains a risky business, changing the model by which we deliver the service was not necessarily a risk many leaders were willing to take. Any paradigm shift was fraught with the risk of offending old-school police leaders, and implementers would likely be painted with the "dreams and schemes" brush. No "real cops" wanted that label. After all, "we have always done it that way."

> *While kindness was the very foundation of his personality, Lincoln*
> *also understood that if people were going to come to him with ideas,*
> *suggestions and better ways of making things work, he had to*
> *provide the climate to allow it. He actively encouraged innovative*
> *thinking and the participation of subordinates. Lincoln wanted*
> *"adopt new views so fast as they shall appear to be true views."*

—DONALD T. PHILLIPS

Besides old-school perception risks and a general malaise in response to stepping outside the box, barriers to innovative thinking have historically been resource or time shortages. After all, "we have work to do and no time to deal with that crap," and "we barely have enough people to answer calls, so I'm not wasting the boss's time with that crap." Crap always seemed to be the common denominator.

> *The best executive is the one who has sense enough to pick*
> *good men to do what he wants done, and self-restraint to*
> *keep from meddling with them while they do it.*

—THEODORE ROOSEVELT

However, our people often have wonderful ideas; they just haven't always been supported to bring them forward. There hasn't been an incentive for original thought. In fact, many of our people have never felt empowered to try on their own anything that is not etched permanently within our policy-bible granite.

> *I think leaders most effective influence on their people's creativity*
> *is in how they shape the social environment. We need a lot of things*

inside ourselves to work out to tap into our creativity, but most
of all we need a social environment that supports us expressing
ourselves. Do leaders encourage risk taking or punish failure?
Do they promote knowledge sharing or prevent their people from
interacting outside their domain? Do they give their people enough
autonomy to pursue projects that might not work out in the end,
but that everyone can learn from? All of these are questions leaders
have to ask in order to diagnose the social environment and make
the cultural changes needed to enhance creative potential. Most
people already have the skills they need to be creative, they just need
to be in an environment that helps them express their creativity.

—PAUL SOHN, IN AN INTERVIEW WITH DAVID BURKUS

When I arrived on the doorstep of the old Number 15 District Headquarters in South Porcupine in 1978, en route to my first posting in Kapuskasing, the old district superintendent gave me my joining instructions. He quite eloquently said, as only a 1970s superintendent could, "My advice to you is keep your eyes and ears open and your mouth shut." The word "innovation" didn't come up in the conversation. He went on to give me even wiser counsel when he added, "Women, booze, and guns will get you in trouble, son. Stay away from all three." I was proud to tell him, "I've never been much into guns, sir." I then got the questioning glare that I would eventually be on the receiving end of many times, the stare that asked the question, "Are you screwing with me, kid?"

All joking aside, I certainly did not feel empowered whatsoever. It was obvious I wasn't being paid to think. Not being a very big man, I also assumed I wasn't being paid for my brawn, so I left confused.

Lesson: Light the Fire and Clear the Path. Guide your people's
passion and get out of the way: the autonomy and freedom I was
given to create and do my job exponentially increased my passion,
excitement and success. My manager-mentors made sure my passions

aligned with organizational direction, gave me some high-level boundaries, resources, and introductions to make it happen. They removed obstacles, showed me how to handle challenges, provided opportunities, and took the blame while giving me the credit.

—Deborah Mills-Scofield

Most often, we do not need to spoon-feed our people. They are bright folks. Sometimes we need only to ask them thought-provoking questions to help them get their thoughts flowing in the right direction. That isn't easy for some bosses, because they want to tell others exactly how to do things. Author Geoffrey James said,

> Average bosses think their job is to know all the answers and to provide those answers to their employees as frequently as possible. However, each time a boss answers an employee's question, that boss robs the employee of an opportunity to think and grow. Extraordinary bosses know that people don't learn when wisdom is handed to them on a platter, much less forced down their throats. They know that a manager's job is to ask the questions that will spark, in the employee's own mind, the thought processes and ideas that will make that employee successful.

Here is Chief Frank Elsner's take: "My greatest failure as a leader was that I didn't listen closely enough to the people around me and that it took me too long to become an active listener. In my early years, I was so preoccupied with pushing my agenda that important things were missed and had to be corrected later. My predecessor used to say, 'Two ears, one mouth—there's a reason for that.' Now I know he was right. A good leader should spend about twice as much time listening as talking."

Some private companies provide financial incentives to employees if they come up with ideas that save the company time, effort, resources, and ultimately money. They also have contests to drive innovative thinking, like the "identifying the stupid things we do" concept. However, cash or vacation awards, company trophies, and "Employee of the Month" honors are not commonplace within police services or government ministries.

I suspect that if surveyed, not many police employees would feel that they are encouraged and supported to come up with innovative ideas in terms of service delivery or efficiencies within their agencies or departments.

How do we overcome that disquieting mind-set? Firstly, leaders have to truly develop employees' trust that their opinions are valued, encourage them to bring ideas forward, and provide feedback through implementation or a response as to why the idea cannot be further developed. The old "we tried that and it didn't work" response won't hold water. What was tried and failed once in a specific time and place in an organization's history might work now in different circumstances. Surely if someone had suggested in-car computers in the 1960s, it would have been a nonstarter, since the computers of that era were the size of a small house. But since then, it has become an effective and efficient model.

> *You encourage innovation—When employees feel trusted they are more willing to take risks, explore new ideas, and look for creative solutions to problems. Conversely, employees that don't feel trusted will do the minimum amount of work to get by and engage in CYA (cover your "assets") behavior to avoid catching heat from the boss.*

> —RANDY CONLEY

Being innovative doesn't mean that the world is going to completely change as a result, which unfortunately is the fear of some when they hear that word. It certainly can mean a totally new approach to business or to dealing with a specific task or challenge, right up to and including the total elimination of a program. But it can also simply mean a more subtle change: adapting, modifying, consolidating resources, replacing pieces of a procedure, creating new entities to augment existing structures, and more. We can't be expected to have all the answers and ideas, however.

Do we really know it all? Do we have such a firm handle on what is happening throughout the organizations we lead that we can make, in isolation, every decision regarding where we should be going, what we should be doing, and how? I know that wasn't the case in my world. Far from it. I continued my learning every day. I did not and do not profess to know it all.

The real leader has no need to lead—he is content to point the way.

—Henry Miller

I recently found this quote from a leadership speech that I delivered in 2009. It was untitled, so I'm not even sure whom I was speaking to, but hopefully they had a sense of humor: "I've never been afraid of those that don't know, if I at least know that they are aware that they don't know. Nor am I afraid of those that really do know what they are doing. But leaders that 'think' they know but don't really have a clue are what puts all of us in danger and scares the crap out of me."

Chief Clive Weighill said, "Leadership does not mean taking complete control of decision making and sending down directives. It means challenging staff to find solutions and then encouraging them to implement those strategies. This ensures that people grow from experience and reap the benefits of success or learn from strategies that did not produce results."

In his article "The Hands-Off Approach to Leadership: *Do Nothing!*," Harvey Schachter says,

> J. Keith Murnighan, a professor at the Kellogg School of Management at Northwestern University, says leaders often feel responsible for every team member and under enormous pressure to keep doing more—to do everything they possibly can. "Conscientious, dedicated leaders do too much—way too much," he writes in his provocative new book, *Do Nothing!*

Nature may abhor a vacuum. But he argues that employees benefit from a vacuum. If managers move aside and do nothing, their team members will not become lethargic but instead will fill the vacuum created.

"People on your team will reveal skills you never knew they had, and will accomplish things that go far beyond your estimate of their capabilities. They might not do things the way you would do them, but they will get results you never expected—positive results—because everyone has hidden talents, and most leaders never discover them," he argues.

In *A Leadership Primer*, former secretary of state Gen. Colin Powell said, "In a brain-based economy, your best assets are people. We've heard this expression so often that it's become trite. But how many leaders really 'walk the talk' with this stuff? Too often, people are assumed to be empty chess pieces to be moved around by grand viziers, which may explain why so many top managers immerse their calendar time in deal making, restructuring and the latest management fad. How many immerse themselves in the goal of creating an environment where the best, the brightest, the most creative are attracted, retained and most importantly, unleashed?"

In the pressure-filled change-management worlds in which we now function, we not only need to hear the thoughts, suggestions, and ideas that our people have as we make decisions and set agendas, but we owe it to them to let them be heard. In addition, the organizational buy-in that will emanate is priceless.

BEING ACCOUNTABLE IN ALL WE DO

The buck stops here.

—HARRY S. TRUMAN, FORMER US PRESIDENT

There are thousands of quotes attributed to Harry S. Truman, but none are as widely remembered as this one. It was clear that he meant that he had ultimate accountability.

Truman was known to be very blunt and extremely outspoken. He reportedly once said, "Richard Nixon is a no-good, lying bastard. He can lie out of both sides of his mouth at the same time, and if he ever caught himself telling the truth, he'd lie just to keep his hand in."

As a leader and public figure, I try not to make Truman-like quotes, but I'm only human. On occasion I will say something bordering on stupid. However, when I do, I will be accountable for my error in judgment or slip of the tongue!

As the overall leader of the organization, the commissioner or chief is accountable to his or her government (municipal, regional, provincial, federal), the communities served, police-services boards and other governing authorities, oversight bodies, and the men and women of the police service. He or she also has to ensure that accountability exists from top to bottom within the organization. All leaders should accept the positional requirement of accountability and carry it out as part of their duty in all they do, whether public or private sector employees

Accountability is a value that should be innate to us all as public servants, regardless of rank. We are bestowed with extraordinary authorities that far exceed those of the citizens we serve, including the power to violate specific legislation in the lawful execution of our duty, up to and including the authority to take away people's freedom and to use deadly force in specific circumstances.

At the same time, we are funded through the tax dollars of the public we serve and are sworn to perform specific duties under provincial and federal legislation and government and police-service policies and in accordance with our contractual obligations to the municipalities we provide service to. That responsibility carries specific demands of accountability, and while exercising our responsibility, we must treat all people that we deal with internally and externally with dignity and respect. We will be held responsible for that, and so we should.

Be accountable.
Excuse making is contagious. Answerability starts with you. If you
make excuses—which is first cousin to "alibiing"—so will those
around you. Your organization will be soon be filled with finger-
pointing individuals whose battle cry is, "It's his fault, not mine!"

—BILL WALSH

Our need for accountability also extends to our conduct, both on duty and off, as we are expected to set a positive example of professionalism at all times. We should do that for our own reputations and out of respect for our organizations, the people we lead, and the people we serve, but we should never forget our colleague leaders. That includes those in other police services, not just our internal colleagues.

Commissioner Giuliano Zaccardelli said,

> Ultimately we have to be accountable as role models and living to a higher bar than any other profession. There is harassment, sexism, corruption, and so on in every profession; however, in policing, every such incident becomes front-page news.
>
> Decisions we make as police leaders will inevitably impact police leaders across municipal and provincial boundaries. Whether [they] be professional decisions regarding labor issues or policy matters, or personal life decisions that could end up shedding a dark light over the police profession, we all must be considerate of the broader impacts of what we say and do.

We also must be accountable in terms of our producing an honest day's work for the pay we receive. We should and do expect that out of those we lead, so the onus is on us to lead by example in terms of personal accountability. Supervisors, managers, and the senior executives of any organization must work hard for their salaries and, as leaders, must ensure that the men and women under them do the same. We should all do what we can to make sure our fellow employees are pulling their weight and not letting the clients and the rest of the organization down.

That doesn't mean that all of us can give 100 percent every minute of every hour of every day we work. As human beings, we have days when we feel more physically and emotionally healthy than others. We may have personal life or family issues that impact our performance. Our best efforts one day may not equal our best efforts on another. That's human nature. However, over time we all have to try our best and be answerable in terms of our overall performance.

We have all worked with or for those who have not been accountable as individuals throughout their careers. The "I can do whatever I want" mentality is alive and well within them.

There is always a social element to a leader's role: attending functions like retirement luncheons and dinners, fund-raising events like golf tournaments, police association/union happenings, and more. To not be seen at some of these things and interact with people, internally and externally, is simply not right. That type of activity may come easier to some than others, but it is part of the role of the leader.

Unfortunately, if it weren't for social events, some leaders would never be seen. There are those who have never missed a social event and spend more time golfing and curling than leading. That is a sad reality for some leaders, but we all know it's true. That's not leadership and is not the example that true leaders should be modeling as acceptable behavior for those they lead—particularly in a police service, where "honesty" is either engraved in granite somewhere prominent in the police headquarters wall or remains an assumed core value of the organization.

We have to set a positive example for others, and anything less is a failure of leadership.

Acclaimed author James O'Toole was quoted in an article by John Huey and Ricardo Sookdeo as saying, "Ninety-five percent of American managers today say the right thing. Five percent do it." As true leaders, we should always do our very best to be in the 5 percent.

I don't believe in performance quotas in a police organization, but at the same time, we have an obligation to perform as we protect communities and prevent crime. We all contribute differently to those goals depending on our individual roles within the organization, but we all must contribute in a commensurate way. Those who aren't contributing must be held accountable. That includes the leaders within the service.

> *True accountability is a multi-dimensional activity that takes into account both the systems and culture of the organization, as well as the interpersonal aspects of the leader's own actions. An organization needs to have a culture of accountability. In other words, where it is the norm for individuals to understand and meet their obligations, and to speak up about obstacles to meeting those obligations. Leaders need to build and nourish this kind of culture, which means they need to understand what accountability is, to demand it of themselves, their reports, and the organization.*

> —Thomas R. Krause and John Hidley

At the same time, leaders should ensure the accountability and performance of those they lead with an element of common sense.

I've been told of alleged instances (I assume some to be true examples, and others may well be urban myth) whereby leaders have held people accountable to demonstrate their own high level of responsibility and perhaps to build a repertoire of "holding people accountable" examples for future promotional interviews. If this does occur and people are being overly documented, that's simply not appropriate and not an example of doing the right thing for the right reasons. Simple discussions and verbal warnings should be a critical part of our performance-management process; not every little issue has to result in disciplinary documentation. If leaders aren't talking to their people and understanding why certain things are or are not occurring regarding their performance, but are simply handing out documentation at the blink of an eye, then they're not doing themselves any favors in terms of any performance reparation.

> *If your team is not functioning well, not performing and you*
> *want to know where the problem lies, then get a mirror and*
> *the person responsible will usually be looking back at you.*
> *Teams reflect their leadership, so if they are not functioning*
> *well then it's usually due to the leadership, i.e. you.*
> *If you want to know whom to blame, then get a mirror.*

—Gordon Tredgold

We all need to be accountable and perform to the best of our ability, from the bottom to the top of the organization. We owe that to the public or clients we serve, our personnel, and each other.

Thomas R. Krause and John Hidley are the authors of many publications on health care safety. They say:

Leaders need to be accountable themselves and responsive to the accountability, or lack of it, in others. This element is what makes accountability a personal practice of the leader; by demonstrating that he is himself accountable and expects it of others, the leader sets the example for others in the organization. Leadership accountability is an expression of the leader's personal values, supported by his or her personal use of best practices and use of the appropriate leadership style for the job at hand.

Their comments certainly apply to leadership accountability in any sector.

Supporting and Caring

When leaders actually know their people, they'll see changes in their demeanors and actions when they occur. They'll be able to distinguish behavior that differs from the norm and can then delve deeper to see whether there is anything they can do to help. Sometimes, simply asking and opening the door to further discussions or support is all that is needed by an employee who is going through a tough time in his or her life. In other situations, leaders may well end up hearing things they wish they didn't have to know, but that comes with the turf as well.

In any police department or company, there are members living in their own personal hell: spousal abuse, substance abuse, personal, family, or mental health issues, financial hardships, marital discord, and more. We hire humans, and no human is immune from the curveballs that life can throw.

For police officers or civilian employees of a police service, there is a higher level of reluctance to admit such issues. Our people often feel they need to rise above such challenges out of a fear of being labeled as weak, or not trusted to be armed, and more. Police officers believe that they fix the problems of society; they don't add to them with their own personal hardships. It's a sad reality of our profession.

Leaders need to model caring and supporting behavior and encourage others to do the same through all of the management and supervisory ranks. It needs to be the normal, expected action and simply "what leaders do," not some one-off fad that is merely a flavor-of-the-month leadership style.

Unless it's a very small police service or company, the chief or president cannot know all members in the department, what makes them tick, what their strengths and weaknesses are, and what challenges they are facing in their personal lives. But the true leaders will know all of that and more about their direct reports and many more. They'll know their names, their family members, and they'll know by looking at them whether they are having a good day or something is bothering them. They will consistently model the positive leadership behavior that they expect of all the leaders within the organization. In addition, they will do all they can to ensure that all the leaders under their command are supporting their people and doing all *they* can to keep morale high from top to bottom.

That's not an easy task in a large organization. It's tiring, actually, but it is more than worth the effort.

SETTING THE RIGHT EXAMPLE

I have ever deemed it more honorable and more profitable,
too, to set a good example than to follow a bad one.

—THOMAS JEFFERSON

Author Stephen Gower poses the question, "What do they see when they see you coming?" In other words, are you modeling the behavior and image that you expect those you lead to copy? What perception of who and what you are do people have when they see you? Do you stay in half-decent physical condition? Do you take pride in ensuring the uniform or suit that you're wearing makes you look like a professional? Do you walk and talk and carry yourself with a bearing that makes others proud to call you a boss or a colleague?

If not, why not? You should have all of those expectations of your subordinates and they of you.

On a lighter note, I read this unknown quote on Twitter: "My boss said 'Dress for the job you want, not the job you have.' Now I'm sitting in a disciplinary meeting dressed as Batman."

Albert Einstein said, "Setting an example is not the main means of influencing others; it is the only means."

When you watch CNN and see the US president land in Marine One on the White House lawn and walk past the reporters, whether it be George Bush Sr., Bill Clinton, or Barack Obama (George W. was intentionally omitted!), you see professionalism, bearing, and power. Even if you didn't know exactly who the person walking by was, you'd think, "That person is someone important." He would be well attired and groomed, not slumped over and totally out of shape.

There was a case in Ontario many years ago—and I'm not even sure what police service was involved—but the story goes that a wanted killer was stopped by a professional, fit officer who looked every bit a strong and confident officer. The killer was arrested without a fight. Legend has it that when subsequently interviewed, he was asked why he didn't shoot the lone officer who stopped him. His answer was something to the effect that the officer appeared so professional and capable that he decided not to mess with him. I'm sure that there are a hundred similar stories out there, fact or fiction.

In his article entitled *14 Tips for Developing Leadership Presence*, author John Keyser says, "Appearance is important, dress neatly and for the occasion. Being well groomed and smiling helps, as do comfortable eye contact, a firm handshake, standing tall, shoulders back, and walking purposefully like an athlete. We can all do that."

Close your eyes and imagine the most professional-looking person that you ever worked with or for, in uniform or business attire. Now do the same for the most slovenly-appearing person that you worked alongside or reported to. Do you see the difference? Would you not actually *feel* the difference if you saw them both in the same room?

I attended a community event in dress uniform some years back, alongside OPP and municipal-police colleagues. I was in my dress uniform, pressed, neat, and with shined shoes. I'm no Charles Atlas, but at least I did my best to be fit, stand tall, and look proud. No big deal. The deputy chief from another service walked into the same event in uniform pants, a police shirt, no hat or tie to be seen, and a hockey jacket. He wore black high-topped running shoes with the laces undone and dragging behind one foot. His pants had permanent knee shapes in them because they hadn't been ironed since God knows when, or ever. His hair was long and unkempt, and he sauntered in with his hands in his pockets as if he were meandering into a strip joint. I couldn't help but look good next to him. I actually felt sorry for him. He looked like an unmade bed. His appearance was the talk of the members from his service, OPP officers, and the political officials present.

My point here is simple. It took very little effort on my part to look professional and to set a good example for OPP members in the room. It might have cost me five extra minutes in total. The resounding and differing impression left by the two senior police leaders in the room was everlasting for all present.

A University of Maryland article "Setting the Example" said, "The most persuasive Leadership skill is the personal example of the leader. Employees often will copy the actions and behaviors of leaders they like and admire. They will literally walk, talk, and act as the example set by the leaders of their unit."

We all join the job as physically fit people. We have to. Many stay that way for at least the first several years of their careers, some forever. Our uniforms must be kept clean and well pressed, and our boots and belts black and shiny—at least initially. Good supervisors ensure they and the people they lead maintain that appearance forever. My coach officer in 1978, the late Matt Spaans, used to tell me to wipe my boots and brush my hat off every day. I never stopped doing that for thirty-six years. That didn't make me a hero; it just helped me set the right example.

Your attitude matters more than everyone else's. As a leader, they are looking to you, watching for clues and modeling your attitude. Remember that someone must inject the positive attitude, must smile first, and must make it ok to think about problems proactively. If you don't do it, who else will? Every leader wants those they lead to be learning, developing and growing. It is hard to convince them to do so if they don't see you doing it. The expectations you have for others will impact their performance, positively or negatively.

*If you want to affect and implement change you must be a champion
of it. If you want the change to be successful, you must lead people
towards it. If you want others to be, remember who they are watching.*

—KEVIN EIKENBERRY

As leaders, we can't do things one way and then expect those we lead to
do it another. The old "Do as I say, not as I do" expression died its death
twenty years ago. We must obey the rules if we are going to enforce them.
We must model the behavior we expect of others. That is not a complicated way to look at things. We must in fact *do what we say.*

*The first thing you will want to do is promote the exact behavior that
you want to see in your followers. When they see you following the rules
that you want them to follow, this will send a powerful message to them
saying that you practice what you preach. If you want your followers
to make a change, you should become the embodiment of that change
yourself. Always follow any rules or changes you make. When you do,
this will show that you are serious about your employees following it
as well. Even if you are a leader, you will not want to act in a way
which makes it appear that you are better than those that follow you.*

—EXFORSYS INC., "HOW TO SET AN
EXAMPLE FOR YOUR FOLLOWERS"

I was always harder on supervisors and managers for their indiscretions
than I was on constables and civilians. My expectations for the former
were higher; they should set the example for those they were entrusted to
lead, such as wearing their uniforms properly, not looking or acting like
miscreants, not saying or doing things not in keeping with the values of
the organization or flagrantly breaking the code of conduct. They should
know better and should do better.

That same standard should apply even more stringently to those above them on the organizational food chain.

Example is leadership.

—ALBERT SCHWEITZER

Change Leadership

• • •

Leadership is vital to the success of a police service or any other organization. The environment in which we live is constantly changing, and for organizations to be successful, they too must change. The roles and responsibilities of the police are intrinsically linked to all aspects of the environment that surround us. Therefore, CHANGE invariably will occur. The only question that remains is whether a person influences and leads this change or becomes victim to its impact. Leadership is the difference maker.

—CHIEF EDGAR MACLEOD

I DON'T KNOW WHO COINED this phrase, so I cannot give him or her credit, but I love it: "The new norm is that there no longer is a norm." How true!

In policing, we once carried on for years and decades with very little change. Then, on rare occasion, we would draw entire operations to a halt and make significant change. That scared the heck out of everyone.

The challenge of change in policing is that from the beginning, including in the 1970s, the 1980s, and even much of the 1990s, we were more firmly fixed as paramilitary organizations. So we didn't allow much room for debate and functioned for the most part under the Nike Corporation slogan, "Just do it." We were terrified to question leaders as to why we were doing things a certain way or, God forbid, why we were making changes, or even worse, when and how we would make much needed changes.

However, that was then. The twenty-first-century workforce, comprised of generation X or Y folks, or the millennials, think much differently than old farts like me did in the early days. I like to call them the "why gens." They continually question "Why?" (rightly or wrongly) or "What's in it for me?" They are not likely to blindly accept at face value every policy, protocol, guideline, direction, or even order that we might throw at them.

The one unchangeable certainty is that
nothing is unchangeable or certain.

—JOHN F. KENNEDY

Leadership is key to enabling people to go from change avoidance to change acceptance. If we are going to get organizational buy-in, our people need to understand the why and preferably have a say in the what, when, and how.

Chief Paul Shrive says, "Police officers know their jobs, and most complete their day-to-day tasks in an efficient and effective manner. They don't often need to be spoon-fed. What they do need is a clear understanding of why the organization is suddenly changing/moving in a new direction. They need to feel that the decision to move in a particular direction was made with their input and that their experience is respected by the decision makers within the organization."

A good example of how change is coming at us now at an unbelievable rate is on the technology front.

In the OPP we acquired a new radio system in the late 1940s. The next one came to us in the 1980s. That was a full forty years of communicating through the old transistor radios.

The newest generation of radio network was implemented in the OPP in the early 2000s. That was twenty years in the making—half the time of the evolution of the early system. It wasn't that many years ago that we had computers, telephones (both landlines and cellular), and radios. Now we have digital technology that blends all of these tools in one environment. Thus, we are only ten years into that new digital network, and we're almost out of parts and equipment to sustain it and are rapidly developing a new system. How long will the next one last us? We'll need to begin planning for the future-generation network as we're building our next one.

People fear change because the status quo is too easy. We are in a state of constant environmental change. Changes in crime trends, cybercrime, efficiency reviews, "do more with less," "do everything with nothing," mass retirements, job rotation, morale, impactful court decisions, the threat of terrorism, economic slowdown, traffic trends, budget pressures, demands for more accountability, increasing oversight, a changing recruit pool, social media, immigration, morphing jurisdictions, newer and newer technology, increasing social issues, climatic-change impacts, focus on prevention, "cops on the dots," COMPSTAT, real-time twenty-four-hour news coverage, civilianization, private policing—and more.

We must continually analyze the changing environment and stay ahead of the curve. The only way to survive is to reshape to the needs of a rapidly changing world. Resistance to change is a dead-end street for us and the organization. Organizations are continually reshaping themselves to change quickly to meet the needs of their client bases. Customers are not only demanding excellent, cost-effective, and accountable service; they are also demanding more for less. If we do not supply it, our competitors will. That may be through customers contracting with other police services or employing private security firms, but they will get what they want.

As leaders, we need to take action to change as quickly and smoothly as possible, and that effort needs to be both ongoing and fluid. We can't stop the presses every few years and make significant organizational changes. We must be doing it 24/7, 365 days a year, or we'll fall behind.

Chief Robert Lunney describes his biggest challenge as a police chief as "influencing cultural change to ensure true commitment to the mission and values of the service." He then describes his greatest success in a leadership role as "influencing and guiding the organizational culture toward one that accepted and welcomed continuous change."

Below I've reprinted parts of an article that comes from the transcript of an extensive interview I did for the OPS newsletter *TopSpot* in September 2012 regarding change management. Although somewhat lengthy, it captures many of my personal thoughts on managing change. Right or wrong, grammatical errors included, these are my off-the-cuff responses to the author, Pankaj Tripathi:

> To individuals within any organization mostly change means "something bad" is about to happen, someone is about to lose their job or some program is going to be eliminated therefore causing change in people's lives and that is never necessarily viewed as a positive thing. But if we are not making change to the organization constantly in the terms of the way we deliver services and its structure then we are going to fall behind the curve. Change is inevitable. The environment is changing constantly and we have to stay ahead of the curve and try and anticipate that through analysis. We should try and make positive changes before we are forced to make them, because then it is too late.
>
> People are afraid to change, because they are comfortable doing the things the way they do it. Change is often viewed as unneeded stress. For example, "I might have to come in five minutes earlier or might have to stay five minutes later." It is the stress that accompanies the end result of the change process that people don't necessarily like.
>
> Change has to be done for the right reasons and not simply to "shake things up."
>
> Like all aspects of leadership, one has to do the right things for the right reasons. It should never be about the leader, his or her personal agenda, but about the people they lead, organizational

priorities and objectives, all of which should be in the best interests of the people they proudly serve.

Effective communication is probably the key to successful leadership. I have to stress the most critical word in that statement (effective). During the change process, from commencement until full implementation, communication is crucial. People need to understand the rationale for the changes they are going to buy into. If you don't have good communication as to the "why"; "how" it is going to impact people (they will always fear the worst unless it is communicated to them up front); and what the rationale for change is, then you are never going to get the necessary buy-in.

How do we effectively communicate change? Number one, be upfront. Determine your audience groups; their fears; and the appropriate key messaging.

We have brought in a new set of tools. Our blogs, forums, groups, face-to-face employee engagement and other platforms provide various channels for our people to share feedback and give inputs. All these help us ask our people—what do you really think? We should always be listening to them. They are doing their job day in and day out and know it best. They know how to do it more efficiently, more effectively and produce the best results. They know how to do it better.

People want to put up their hand and speak, "I have an idea." So when you look at making a big change, you can't make it in isolation of the thoughts of the people that are going to be impacted by it. You have to communicate the rationale of the change. Our new tools give people the opportunity to do so, and people are using them and we have to listen to their feedback.

Address the "why" first. Develop the rationale for the change. You can't do it in isolation as a leader. You develop your ideas and then develop your key people who will be managing this process and get their buy-in as to why we need to make the change. Your key team managers who are going to lead the change initiative need to be on the same page. Then you have to think what will be the reaction of the people who are going to be impacted by this change. What are their fears going to be, job loss, change of role or a move to a new organizational unit. How are you going to address that? Then you have to develop your communication strategy, look at all their fears and apprehensions and come up with ways to mitigate them. Get your team together, get their buy-in and develop your key messaging.

When the process starts you need to communicate all that stuff upfront and try to get everybody on the same page as to why this is occurring. Get it through the organization far and wide. You need to pick key people that are influential, whether it be union leaders, senior people or simply natural and respected leaders at any level, and get them on your side to help you deliver the messaging.

…You have to consult. Get the input from key people that truly understand the organization and its people. Ensure that there is continuous dialogue. If any bargaining groups are involved, you have to have them at the table as opposed to merely seeking their input. If you can have association (union) members sitting as a part of the change management team, that greatly helps build trust with the broader membership, in addition to the great input you will likely receive.

Communications must be consistent and then once strategies have been developed you have to go back to the table and run them by others, fine tune them and get further feedback. This way you are building a culture of cooperation and buy-in throughout the entire process.

Once you start with the change initiative you have to have regular report backs. People need to know where it all stands and how it is all coming together, and then be prepared to change the strategies as something unexpected turns up. The guiding principle is "if it doesn't work we will fix it."

What do the famous say about change? There is so much to be gleaned from the following quotes on change:

It may seem easier for our life to remain constant. But change, really, is the only constant. For an organization such as ours, change is the engine of growth and the muse of creativity.

—MICHAEL D. EISNER, DISNEY

Change is the law of life. And those who look only to the past or present are certain to miss the future.

—JOHN F. KENNEDY

Change will not come if we wait for some other person or some other time. We are the ones we've been waiting for. We are the change that we seek.

—BARACK OBAMA

Be the change that you wish to see in the world.

—MAHATMA GANDHI

Never doubt that a small group of thoughtful, committed citizens can change the world. Indeed, it is the only thing that ever has.

—MARGARET MEAD

The world as we have created it is a process of our thinking. It cannot be changed without changing our thinking.

—ALBERT EINSTEIN

I have accepted fear as part of life—specifically the fear of change…I
have gone ahead despite the pounding in the heart that says: turn back.

—ERICA JONG

How do we do it?

We should never be offended when our people ask the question "Why?" Anticipate that and proactively develop your communication strategy accordingly. It's not always a statement of resistance. The old Fram Oil Filter Company advertising slogan regarding preventative maintenance on your automobile holds very true: "You can pay me now or pay me later." Make the investment up front. Communication at the front end and throughout is paramount.

Anticipate the "What's in it for me?" questions. Address those issues proactively at the front end and consistently throughout the exercise.

Be a positive influence by focusing on the benefits that the change will provide them and the organization. True leaders should not blame those higher up the food chain. Although at times the rationale for change is totally beyond our scope as leaders—there are, for example, fiscal realities—and there's nothing to be gained from hiding that, leaders should focus more on the positives than the negatives and avoid passing blame. Our people can be dragged down emotionally by the negative attitudes of their leaders and, thankfully, can be excited by our confidence when we properly display it.

Leaders should not feel uncomfortable if feeling any hesitation about the change on a personal level. Leaders are also human (mostly). By spelling out the benefits, they will not only comfort their people but help to convince themselves at the same time.

In her article "Ten Reasons People Resist Change," author by Rosabeth Moss Kanter states,

> Change interferes with autonomy and can make people feel that they've lost control over their territory. Smart leaders leave room

for those affected by change to make choices. They invite others into the planning, giving them ownership.

If change feels like walking off a cliff blindfolded, then people will reject it. People will often prefer to remain mired in misery than to head toward an unknown. Leaders should create certainty of process, with clear, simple steps and timetables.

Decisions imposed on people suddenly, with no time to get used to the idea or prepare for the consequences, are generally resisted. Leaders should avoid the temptation to craft changes in secret and then announce them all at once...and seek input.

Within the OPP, any major change initiative that we undertook that struggled getting traction or was never fully accepted almost always floundered because of ineffective communication at the front end.

In the early 1990s, the OPP undertook an immense multiyear reorganization project to meet difficult funding targets. Some good things came from what most refer to as "reorg," with sarcasm and a grimace much like when Jerry Seinfeld used to say "Newman" upon realizing that his neighbor had just pulled another fast one.

Some would subsequently say, "Reorg was a mistake; all they did was screw things up and promote a bunch of people," and much more—most of which is not fit to print. Although I agree with bits and pieces of the discourse, I think that many good things came from our reorg and that some of the lingering negativity is due to the failings of the communications strategy around the initiative, as opposed to the change exercise itself.

Many senior officers eventually gathered at a hotel in Orillia to partake in the presentation of the results, which many didn't have a clue about until they heard what they believed to be already set in stone. The meeting was not well received and led to an almost all-inclusive lack of support by OPP commissioned officers. Rightly or wrongly, the majority felt they hadn't been properly consulted; although there was a trifling number of strong operational senior officers involved in some of the working groups, there was a feeling that many of the key players were largely void of operational police experience and that life in the OPP would be no longer worth living.

Again, some good things emerged from reorg, and it was not the ruination of the OPP. However, it did get off to a terrible start, resulting in excruciating slow progress and constant pushback. Then, during the years to follow, some had a fear (real or imagined) that we could never change anything back, because it would be an insult to those involved, some of whom remained very senior officers in the force. However, if we truly gave it an honest chance and if elements of it needed to be changed back to the way they were or a new course of action implemented, why should there be fear in that? Change doesn't have to be absolute and forever binding—but requires real leadership.

Rosabeth Moss Kanter went on to say,

> By definition, change is a departure from the past. Those people associated with the last version—the one that didn't work, or the one that's being superseded—are likely to be defensive about it. When change involves a big shift of strategic direction, the people responsible for the previous direction dread the perception that they must have been wrong. Leaders can help people maintain dignity by celebrating those elements of the past that are worth honoring, and making it clear that the world has changed. That makes it easier to let go and move on.
>
> The ghosts of the past are always lying in wait to haunt us. Old wounds reopen, historic resentments are remembered—sometimes going back many generations. Leaders should consider gestures to heal the past before sailing into the future.

In the early 2000s, we launched what we called "the promise of the OPP." In essence, we were doing only what other major organizations had done decades prior: etching our core values in stone. One of them, the one that caused and still causes the most consternation, was professionalism.

Now how could anyone in policing argue that professionalism is something that should not be front and center in all we do? How could anyone be offended with the notion that as police personnel, we should be professional at all times? Well, that one foundational core value offended many, merely because of the way we delivered the messaging.

In addressing groups of personnel under my command as the promise of the OPP rolled out, once I convinced them to open up with their reactions—which was a challenge in itself—the overwhelming majority said, "If you don't think we're professional, get rid of us." With the odd individual, I thought, "I wish." But many were missing the point, and it really wasn't their fault, because we—and I—had dropped the ball at the front end. Our folks thought we were saying that we suddenly needed them to be professional because they apparently were not already, as opposed to "We always have been professional; we're known internationally for our professionalism; it's important that we maintain that professionalism for reasons of public trust in a changing society" and more. We then played catch-up for months and years because we started off on the wrong foot.

The key lesson here is that we hadn't really thought out what the fears, apprehensions, and reactions from the masses would be. We didn't consult with any representative group of our people for feedback going in. We (including me) sat back on our haunches and figured we were all-knowing. How wrong we were. We never totally recovered from that debacle, and to this day our people have never really accepted the promise of the OPP, although the vast majority practice its contents every day. There were huge lessons in that for me.

Senator Vern White said, "When I look at great leaders, I see them as being creative visionaries and change-management gurus. Looking at creativity (generation of new ideas or concepts), but more importantly, or as important, it is about change. The leadership requirement I see is the one that defines a leader, someone who is willing to create and implement change."

In his 2000 book *Leading at the Edge: Leadership Lessons from the Extraordinary Saga of Shackleton's Antarctic Expedition*, author Dennis N. T.

Perkins outlines the challenges faced by polar explorer Ernest Shackleton and develops leadership learnings from his adventures for the reader. Amazon previews his book in part, as follows:

> Stranded in the frozen Antarctic sea for nearly two years, Sir Ernest Shackleton and his team of 27 polar explorers endured extreme temperatures, hazardous ice, dwindling food, and complete isolation. Despite these seemingly insurmountable obstacles, the group remained cohesive, congenial, and mercifully alive—a fact that speaks not just to luck but to an unparalleled feat of leadership. Drawing on this amazing story, *Leading at the Edge* demonstrates the importance of a strong leader in times of adversity, uncertainty, and change. The book reveals...timeless leadership lessons that show readers how to:
> Instill optimism while staying grounded in reality
> Have the courage to step up to risks worth taking
> Consistently reinforce the team message
> Set a personal example
> Find something to celebrate and something to laugh about
> Never give up

I always preach that "a leader is someone who always puts the good of the people he or she serves and the good of the people within the organization before any personal needs or agenda." That, of course, applies to our every decision as leaders and, accordingly, when to make change, why, and how. It should always be in the best interests of delivering service to the community, closely followed by what is best for our people. Change should never be about making ourselves look good. In fact, sometimes the required change will hurt some dedicated employees through job change or the loss of employment. At the same time, the change considered or implemented may hurt us as leaders in the eyes of some (political figures and others). But that's why they pay us the not-so-big bucks: to do what is right.

Leadership is about understanding your current context, and anticipating the future context and creating a vision for a better future. It's being inspiring and being inspired. In short, leadership is about change and understanding the complexities to affect change.

—CHIEF EDGAR MACLEOD,

The Good, the Bad, and the Ugly

• • •

WHENEVER I LECTURE ON LEADERSHIP, I preface each talk with the following comment:

"While I'm speaking here today, I want you all to think about two things. Firstly, think of the best leader you ever worked for and what made them that way. Why would you walk through broken glass for them? Conversely, think of the worst boss you ever had. What was it about them that made you want to quit the job, go home, and suck your thumb and cry yourself to sleep? I know that all of you are now picturing those great and poor leaders in your mind."

I immediately see the gears turning among the audience as they picture the worst and the best leaders that have impacted their lives. Some smile, some grimace, and others do both.

We have all worked for and with the best of leaders and at times with the worst of leaders, and let's face it: some have been downright evil and nasty. However, we've learned from them all, and if we don't think of the lessons we learned from them, both good and bad, then we're not leading in the best interests of our followers. Those leaders significantly impacted us in wonderful, disappointing, and disturbing ways, so we owe it to those we lead to use the positive attributes and not the negative qualities that we experienced.

On a personal level, I worked for grumpy old men who were still good leaders because although they weren't all smiles and chuckles, they did care about their people and did their best to support them and help them be good employees.

On the other hand, I worked for funny and friendly supervisors that couldn't make a decision to save their lives and would hightail it if things looked even remotely as if they might go bad.

I'll bet toonies to Timbits that you're already picturing a number of leaders you've been exposed to as you ponder those last few paragraphs!

I have also worked for combinations thereof. Some were wonderful, humorous, and caring bosses that were decisive, were not afraid to make tough calls, and would live with the fallout if things went south. They did everything they could to make those around them feel that they were vital members of the team. Others were hateful human beings, and they did everything in their power to make everyone around them just as bitter and evil as they were. I learned from them too and decided very early on that I would never treat anyone so horribly.

I fully believe that the negative impact bad leaders can have on the people they lead is far greater than the constructive impact that good leaders can have. I suppose it's because negative experiences can have a far-reaching impact on a person, much more so than positive impacts can. There is hurtful memory contained in scar tissue.

I think bad boss experiences stay with us much longer
and have a much bigger impact on us…
With my bad boss, I can honestly say that his negative impact on me
lasted at least 6 months after I had left and joined another company.
Both in terms of my own self-confidence and self-esteem, for a while
I thought the problem was with me, even though I knew he was a
really bad boss and saw how he treated some of the other staff.
The amounts of stress generated by bad bosses is not good for our physical
health, let alone our mental health or emotional wellbeing. Their impact

can even spill over into our private lives too, where we bring the bad boss
into our homes, through conversations with our partners about them.

—Gordon Tredgold, "The Impact of Bad Bosses"

As I passed through the organizational hierarchy, I saw glaring examples of the good, the bad, the ugly, and the evil at every rank. We all see examples like this. I couldn't help but wonder how the hell some of them got past their probationary years, let alone successfully got through a promotional interview.

I asked the chiefs that I surveyed to describe the best and the worst leaders that they ever worked with or for and what it was about them that made them either good or bad. There is something to be learned from every response, so I have documented them all below. I've included my own examples as well.

Chief Bill Blair:

Deputy Chief Bob Molyneaux. He was courageous and decisive and in tune with the people more than anyone that I ever met. He'd stop and talk to people and make them feel special. He put me out front and center and supported me at a time in my career when I had been sidelined and wasn't on the A team. I would have walked through hell for him.

Chief Jim Chu:

Chief Jamie Graham was the best chief I worked for in Vancouver. Jamie has a great sense about people. He promoted the right mix of deputy chiefs who all wanted to work with each other as a team and wanted to work hard for him and the organization. He also has a great sense of humor, which helped in the many difficult times.

Ian Davidson, deputy minister:

One of the best police leaders I have ever worked with was my staff sergeant in the patrol division in Ottawa, who later was my superintendent of investigations. At a certain time in my uniformed career, I allowed myself to be influenced by some negative members of the uniform branch. They often expounded critically about organizational decisions, leaders in the organization, and even our colleagues. Although I was not comfortable with the negativity and found myself in disagreement with many of their observations, I found it very difficult to challenge them. Being junior and with a dissenting opinion to the vocal minority, it was difficult to challenge. Many other officers and civilian staff found themselves silenced or adopting the views of the loudest voices. It was easier and avoided being labeled.

One time while I was talking to my staff sergeant on the road, he asked me how things were going. I launched into the small-minded groupthink criticisms on a couple of matters that I had foolishly adopted for a short period in my career. He listened intently, as if he understood and maybe even supported me. When I finished my comment, he asked me if it was really that bad. I rather mindlessly complained because it seemed like it was the practice.

It was then he said, "Ian, if you really feel that way, drive back to the station, take off the uniform, and find something more suitable for you to do. Maybe this profession isn't right for you." He appeared mildly offended and probably surprised that I would allow myself to be like those who had little to offer but criticism.

I was truly shocked that he said that to me. I knew immediately he was right, and this bothered me immensely, as he was a role model and mentor to me. Simply put, I allowed the negative critical voice of others to speak for me. And worse, I was actually was part of the problem, if even for a short period of time!

His few words were some of the most meaningful in my thirty-five-year career. Thanks, Bob, I needed that!

Chief Rick Deering:

The best leader I had the pleasure of working for was Roy Gordon, a commonsense, soft-spoken gentleman with a quick wit and a sense of humor that was appreciated by all. He taught me many valuable lessons regarding the art of leadership through the humility, empathy, and honesty that accentuated every decision he made, particularly the difficult ones. In particular, he had the innate ability to accurately assess every situation on its own merits and apply the best resolution for all involved. Succinctly put, he was a master at both talking the talk and walking the walk.

Chief Frank Elsner:

S/Sgt Jim Bulduc, my watch commander in Thunder Bay. He cared about his folks, and we knew it. I mentored under him as a newly minted sergeant. He taught me to be courageous and stand up for what is right. Lead from the front and apologize when I make a mistake. He had a wicked sense of humor, but you always knew where you stood. He demanded perfection from himself and from us and helped us achieve it.

Chief Jennifer Evans:

I would say the best leader I worked for always took the time to listen to what everyone in the room had to say. He recognized and valued the importance of hearing from different perspectives before he made a decision. He took the time to listen, evaluate, and analyze a situation before making a decision. He also took the time to get to know his team, and his personal approach and strong work ethic were contagious.

The Honorable Julian Fantino:

I have worked for many such individuals, each with uniquely different approaches to getting things done. However, each demonstrated a number of common and consistent traits and value systems, such as being knowledgeable and experienced, trustworthy and loyal, as well as having the innate ability to apply common sense and a tempered approach to situations, and maintaining a calm and reassuring presence in the face of adversity or heightened challenges.

Chief Leanne Fitch:

Sergeant Gary Arbour would certainly rank up at the top. He was fair but strict; he wasn't afraid to hold officers as accountable as the public he policed. He was a Christian man who loved his community and was a true professional in every sense. Always well turned out, taking pride and care of his kit and his health. He was deeply involved as a volunteer in our city. He demonstrated compassion in leadership and always respected others. He was slow to anger but very effective in jumping into police action as needed. He always had a calm demeanor and was consistent in his disposition. He was quick to smile but quick to pull someone up short if need be. He didn't mince words or talk behind anyone's back. Gary was well respected by the respectful...and was criticized only by those officers who discarded the rules of the organization or disrespected their own profession. That says a lot about the integrity and the heart of the man right there! A fine leader whom I have always held up as a role model.

Chief Kimberley Greenwood:

I have had the good fortune to work with great leaders, I felt that they were/are willing to put themselves at risk to make a difference, and all of them stood out in a crowd, they were not/are not satisfied with status quo, and they were/are responsible, courageous, and caring.

Chief William Blair is a great leader; no matter how tough it has become for him, he keeps on leading and never gives up. He has distinguished himself by making the tough calls for the sake of his members and the betterment of the service and the community.

Chief Glenn DeCaire is a great leader and mentor; he accesses how people are in handling relationships and coaches individuals in connecting above, beside, and below people in the service chain of command. He assists those who need to grow in an area by giving them assignments/projects that help them show initiative and become more responsible.

Chief Laurie Hayman:

I have been fortunate to have worked with several chiefs who each in their own way inspired me to work hard and to continuously improve my leadership skills. It would be very challenging to name one individual as the best, as they each provided a different style of leadership that I was able to benefit from. Brian Collins, although quiet, was an excellent, brilliant thoughtful chief. I would enthusiastically work for Brad Duncan again and believe him to be one of the hardest-working police officers I have ever had the privilege to work alongside. Carl Johnson, who hired me as the first woman police officer in Saint Thomas, was a chief who worked diligently and modeled what he expected, was willing to make difficult decisions, listened to the viewpoint of those around him before implementing change, and encouraged people to do their best in serving the community.

As chief, I would hope to model some of the characteristics of each of these three great police leaders.

Chief Barry King:

The absolute best leader I ever worked for was Chief Douglas K. Burrows, Peel's first chief. He was the only chief in Canada, at that time, to possess a university degree and was a strong proponent of training and education and staying ahead of the curve.

Chief Burrows was selected as the first chief of police and immediately met with the Planning Team and confirmed operational decisions, discussed concerns we had, and then informed us he had great confidence and appreciated the effort put into the plans and gave the green light. His direct, yet arms-length involvement gave us the reassurance that he was appreciative, his vision had been respected and acted on, and he had faith in our continuation. He earned our respect, trust, loyalty, and appreciation. The Planning Team members, and by extension most other senior members, supervisors, police, and civilian members, identified with his vision to be the best we could be, progressive, proactive, and proponents of Sir Robert Peel's philosophy. It took this full explanation to clarify that it wasn't any singular action or act but rather a collection and progression of inner strength, intelligence, motivation, and professional and astute leadership skills that clearly earned him my respect as the best leader I have ever worked for and what he did that made him great.

Chief Rod Knecht:

Constable Ernie Harapiak—my trainer at my very first detachment in Kyle, Saskatchewan. He retired as a constable a few years back. He emulated what a great human being is and what a great human being does. He had an unfettered belief in what is right and what is wrong. He was a commonsense, salt-of-the-earth guy that loved the profession of policing, despite many challenges. It was all about helping the underdog and looking out for and protecting those people that were unable to take care of themselves. He had an extraordinary ability to detect criminal behavior and solve crime almost effortlessly. He showed me the importance of being part of your community and personally and professionally investing in your community through your own time and sacrifice. He demonstrated the importance of establishing strong relationships and always treating everyone with respect, despite position, status, ability, or background. He also had one of the most extraordinary senses of humor of anyone I have ever met. He always found humor in everything and taught me the importance of not taking anything life has to offer too seriously. As I typed this, I caught myself laughing out loud about some of his antics. I still consider him one of my best friends thirty-six years later, although we rarely speak.

Commissioner Chris Lewis:

I already spoke of Wayne Frechette and the positive impact that Wayne's leadership ability had on me. Wayne and I both worked with a man named Bob Adams at one time or another. Bob "Pookie" Adams (don't ask—it's a long story) retired from the OPP as a detective superintendent. He spent much of his career in criminal investigations, from fraud to homicide and much in between. Although I never actually reported to him, he remains someone that I will always look up to as a leader.
Bob has both incredible people skills and a wonderful sense of humor. He could laugh with the troops or at himself. Although a tremendous investigator, he never got wrapped up in what rank

he was or the fact that he was the boss. He could make decisions, take it on the chin if necessary, and deal with the good and the bad of investigators and support personnel. He really cared about the people he led, always ensuring they felt that they had a say and were important team members, regardless of rank or status.

When I was living in Cornwall in a hotel for two years on assignment, separated from my wife and daughters at the same time as I was dealing with a considerable health issue, Bob was there for me. He's never let me down on either a professional or a personal level. He was and remains the best of the best, in my view.

Chief Robert F. Lunney:

My principle mentor in policing continually challenged me to perform at a higher level and held me accountable for results. He had a propensity to focus on the elements of the task necessary for success and to pursue them relentlessly.

Chief Dan Maluta:

The best police leader that I have had the pleasure to know is not one that I worked for but one of my peers, Paul Shrive. Paul is a retired chief superintendent of the OPP and also served as the chief of the Port Moody Police Department here in my home province of British Columbia. I believe Paul's career as a police leader spanned over forty years, and he left both organizations with distinction. The fact his members were honored to have followed him was obvious on the occasion of his retirement from the Port Moody Police. Paul was a great mentor to me when I became a chief, and I could depend on his counsel no matter what challenge was presented. What made him great was his consistent display of integrity. He possessed the ability to make the right call on a myriad of problems facing a police leader in the modern era. It seemed intuitive, but his decision making was always logical and methodical, was ethically based, and sent a clear message. Through it, he earned the respect of everyone he dealt with.

Chief William McCormack:

Jack Ackroyd, chief of Police Toronto (1980–85). I believe that this questionnaire in regard to leadership fits Jack Ackroyd. He had great respect for the public, the media, senior command officers—right down to the constable on the street. Jack Ackroyd was creative. He had a great understanding of police and the public and was a catalyst for opening up lines of communication between both.

Chief Dale McFee:

Two mentors come to mind. Both very different, one very much focused on details and tactics. The second was very much focused on changing the direction. Both knew each other but never ever valued each other's work. The interesting part of this for me was to take parts of each person's qualities and use them to enhance my skills.

Chief Edgar MacLeod:

Difficult question! I have worked for and beside many fine police officers, including chiefs of police. The best leaders within my cohort group came from frontline supervision or simple on-the-street police officers. The tactical leadership was unbelievable. It was leadership in the moment by taking a crisis and resolving the sense urgency in record time. Unfortunately, that tactical leadership often does not transcend into strategic leadership. Tactical leadership is essential, even critical to the success of a police service. However, tactical leadership occurs in a command and control environment where systems are better understood. Tactical leaders can also quickly adapt and modify systems as the circumstances. The competencies of great tactical leaders often conflict with the competencies required in strategic leadership. The strategic leader needs to occur more in a collaborative environment where creativity and relationship have a much higher value. Strategic leadership needs to consider and take into account complexities of many factors. It's about channeling those complexities into one strategic direction (that may or may not be clearly understood).

So to answer the question, I have been more influenced by community leaders who have brought together many people and many agencies to focus on one common purpose. There were many individuals who have influenced me. All were ordinary citizens who did extraordinary deeds in helping others.

Commissioner Thomas B. O'Grady:

Thomas Chambers was the deputy chief of the Ajax Police Service, which was eventually absorbed into the Durham Regional Police Service. His approach to dealing with all situations (crisis or otherwise) was always calm, clear, and consistent. His approach to discipline was low key and usually left the offender feeling badly that he had disappointed the deputy and resolving to do better in future. I was not surprised when he was selected as the deputy chief to coordinate the amalgamation of all the police services into one cohesive unit as Durham Regional Police, which he did with ease and great vision.

Chief Paul Shrive:

Many years ago I worked for a corporal named Bev Britnell. He led by example yet did not expect his subordinates to necessarily match his level of perfection. He did all he could to see that I performed at my personal best, and was not shy about complimenting me when appropriate. His personal style and level of professionalism caused me to try to do my best at any assigned task. He was a great role model both on and off duty. I never told him that. I should.

Chief Clive Weighill:

I wouldn't name any person in particular. The best leaders I've witnessed had a combination of

* Empathy for others
* Making decisions for the right reasons, not to better their statuses or positions
* Not letting their egos get in the way
* Confidence in what they were doing, but not being overconfident
* Giving credit to those who did the work
* Allowing individuals to be actively involved in decision making
* Willingness to acknowledge if they made a mistake

Senator Vernon White:

There are many great leaders I have worked with/for. The best for me was Inspector [name removed] of the RCMP in Inuvik. He carried the torch for every member and was there through the good times and tough times. When his wife was arrested for stealing narcotics at the local hospital, by me, he made a number of gestures to distance himself from me and the investigation (I was a constable) and, following her conviction, made a special outreach to me to ensure I was OK.

Commissioner Giuliano Zaccardelli:

The best leader I ever worked for was Deputy Commissioner Henry (Hank) Jenson. He was an intelligent, energetic, and hardworking person. He had a vision and a strategy of how to make sure the RCMP's Economic Crime Program was a world-class program. He was able to energize and get full commitment from everyone who worked in the program throughout the country. They became disciples and strong supporters of the program because of Jenson's vision and leadership. Because of his leadership, he was able to attract the very best candidates to his program. They were proud to be part of something special that Jenson was responsible for creating. Jenson's leadership was the major reason for the highly successful program.

Now let's see what they had to say about the bad leaders (or perhaps at times "ugly"):

Chief Bill Blair:

The worst leader—unethical. Would not tell the truth or stand up for people. Would be AWOL when things got tough and would run away and try to blend into the crowd. Suddenly you'd be standing alone.

Chief Jim Chu:

I worked for a chief who didn't work very hard and was openly pessimistic. I worked for another bad chief who did not consult and ended up listening only to yes-men in the months before he was fired.

Ian Davidson, deputy minister:

I won't go into detail, but one leader was the classic carrot-and-stick boss. The problem was that in time the stick was slowly and often silently used against him by many who lost fear of his style; the carrots he offered became unworthy of eating! He had lost his influence and relied entirely on his rank and the stick that came with it! I knew I had to move on in my career to continue to grow as a leader.

Chief Rick Deering:

The worst leader that I ever experienced is one that I never worked for but worked very closely with for a number of years. In fact, I am disappointed to say that I had a large hand in this individual's development. An intelligent officer, with a gift for marketing himself and using in-vogue buzzwords in the proper context, he was eventually appointed to a senior position.

Unfortunately for both the police service and him personally, it became clear in a relatively short period of time that he was overmounted. A litany of poor decisions based on personal biases and personality conflicts quickly undid years of hard-won progress. Fortunately, he moved on to bigger and better things outside the police culture.

Chief Frank Elsner:

I worked with a leader that often talked about leading from the front, putting our people and community first, being fair, ethical, and forward thinking. Over the years I found that he was more concerned with his own reputation and what was in it for him. The rank and file, especially the female staff, saw through the façade, and he lost his legitimacy with the troops. He held family and close friends to a far-different standard than others, so when it came to discipline within the organization, it was seen as punitive and personally targeted. He was seen by all to be feathering his own bed at the expense of everyone around him. He was incredibly self-serving, thinking only of himself.

Chief Jennifer Evans:

A poor leader is one that makes decisions based on what is best for himself. He listens to only those who are like him or who agree with him and surrounds himself with yes-men. Another poor quality is a leader who punishes everyone for the mistake made by one or one who forgets that sometimes mistakes are mistakes and people should not be punished for an eternity for simple mistakes. A poor leader is lacking in character and ethics.

The Honorable Julian Fantino:

Here again, I have worked for many truly lousy leaders whose only authority was their ranks, absent any other credibility whatsoever. Showed a lack of judgment and common sense, always quoting policy and telling untruthful stories about their escapades.
Very insecure and prone to panic in stressful situations— untrustworthy and abused people verbally.

Chief Leanne Fitch:

The poor leaders, it seems, are easier to point out than the precious few who rose above. Bad leadership I have witnessed includes everything from field trainers who are in leadership roles over cadets, up to and including senior managers. The things I have seen include drinking on the job, breaking the law, disrespecting the public and/or officers, embarrassing people intentionally, being abusive in language and deeds. Applying double standards, outward display of favoritism, racism, sexism, and homophobia, adultery, and excessive uses of force. And yes, in some cases, all of that has been rolled all into one person who was deemed to be a leader; in others it has been seen in bits and pieces.

Chief Kimberley Greenwood:

I worked with an individual who would assign a task or project with limited instructions/guidance and within a short period of time take over the assignment, making all those involved feel deflated and unappreciated.

I also worked with an individual who was a great visionary but was unable to communicate it effectively; the person's passion was not transferred in a productive manner.

Chief Laurie Hayman:

Two challenges with leaders that I have worked for have been at opposite ends of the spectrum. One was an inspector who micromanaged his people to the point of both resentment and lack of self-confidence in their decision-making capacity. The other leader demonstrated a very poor work ethic and delegated away all of his responsibility and refused to make a decision.

Chief Barry King:

The worst leader I ever encountered was a patrol sergeant in Mississauga PD who had fewer qualities, attributes, and redeeming features than any of the eighteen members on the platoon he was responsible for. A true holdover from the strict seniority-only-based school of promotion, he was vulgar, full of entitlement, dictatorial, and disliked. He would attend calls, interrupt in the midst, and instruct on what action was to be taken, oftentimes worsening the situation. His ideal call was where there were a number of officers and many members of the public and spectators present and, being a very tall, lanky individual, he could yell orders, wave his arms, instruct everyone where to stand, what to do, and display for all to see that he was the boss. Enough said.

Chief Rod Knecht:

The poorest leader I worked for was void of emotional IQ. Employees were treated as a stepping-stone or a means to reaching his professional goal. The individual suffered an extraordinary ego that was founded on intimidation, threats, demeaning commentary, and derogatory behavior. I found this person to be tremendously insecure, and he validated his own ego by diminishing the confidence of others. He often surrounded himself with people that were willing to leave his behavior unchallenged and attempt to ingratiate themselves with him through praise, atonement, and self-deprecation. Working for this individual was, however, beneficial. I was able to witness the impact that this style of leadership has not only on the individual employee but that individual's family. The lesson is that negative leadership has an impact far beyond the work environment, and so positive leadership can have an impact far beyond the work environment.

Commissioner Chris Lewis:

I have worked with and for some leaders that were the worst of the worst, both uniform and civilian. They worked hard, managed up very well, and always looked after their chosen few subordinates but made no bones about ruining the lives of those they didn't like. How did these people get promoted? Everyone in the organization below them (unless they were part of the leaders' handpicked in-crowds) knew full well how incompetent and mean spirited these people were. How sad.

One corporal I reported to years ago in the north had six of the hardest-working constables in the OPP working for him. We cleared up virtually every crime that was reported, worked hard to prevent occurrences, laid tons of proactive liquor, drug, and weapons charges, and had some laughs along the way. However, he spent every waking minute trying to drag morale down. Nothing was ever good enough for him. He truly made me want to quit the job. In later years, I worked for some senior people that knew nothing, had virtually no experience regarding anything that remotely resembled law enforcement, and surrounded themselves with similar people. Insecurity at its finest. If you disagreed with them, you were ostracized. They would jump to conclusions based on the word of one of their minions or believe rumors about people they didn't like, as if it were a blood sport.

One executive-level member took pride in forcing out senior people that she didn't like. When one senior officer couldn't take it anymore and retired, she said, "I killed another one." Nice. Although she was very bright and driven and had tremendous capacity, she'd lie to government officials and to the commissioner to ruin the reputations of good, honest people that didn't drink her Kool-Aid. I'm convinced that she kept a hoard of voodoo dolls that looked like me and others she despised, just to shove pins in them at night. What a way to go through life. I eventually became very bitter, started to doubt myself, became afraid to make decisions, and even suffered some health issues as a result, until I made the conscious decision not to let her kill me too. God only knows how many other lives she negatively impacted, but I do know that there were many. My blood pressure still goes up when I think of those years.

Chief Robert F. Lunney:

The worst leader was a top executive, full of himself and reveling in the perks of the position, who proved oblivious to the challenges facing the organization.

Chief Edgar MacLeod:

This too for me is a difficult question for me to answer. My dad, who was a coal miner, had reminded me on many occasions that "good people do bad or dumb things." So for me I have a lifetime of finding the good in everybody and doing my best to focus on that goodness.

So with that in mind, there was no shortage of police leaders doing bad or more often dumb things. There was one common denominator among these individuals: that is the lust and enjoyment of power through their authoritative positions. These people loved being looked up to because of their positions. They also loved instilling fear and exercising power just because they could.

Chief Dan Maluta:

The worst police leader I ever worked for used coercion to get results, displayed no integrity, and did not lead by example. Leaders who don't set an example by walking the walk, even occasionally, eventually lose credibility and fail to create empathy with their officers. This is an inevitable progression, when leaders become detached from the workforce environment—from "the street"—and disappear to issue edicts by e-mail and memoranda from an ivory tower. This is particularly true when their followers know or suspect that the leader never did share their experiences and challenges; there is a disconnect that becomes irreparable. I can't help but think of British general Alexander Haig not witnessing the reality of hundreds of thousands of his soldiers being pulverized by machine gun fire on the western front, still insisting that future wars would be won by the horse and sabre.

Chief William McCormack:

Leadership that was counterproductive to good policing was from someone who

- Had a lack of understanding of certain factions within policing
- Had tunnel vision

* Disregarded the human aspect of the job
* Had a bad temper
* Would not listen to others' points of view
* Ruled with an iron fist—"me and no one else"

Chief Dale McFee:

I could name a few. Some think they are bigger than the game! When this happens, the game eventually removes you from the job. Following the sports theme, when you tend to play for the name on the back (of the jersey) and not the crest (on the front), leadership is short lived and often not in the right direction.

Commissioner Thomas B. O'Grady:

An OPP inspector who consistently avoided difficult decision making and usually addressed the issue to his subordinates with the advice "play it by ear." In spite of his lack of leadership abilities, he was a very likeable person, which probably explained his rank.

Chief Paul Shrive:

I once worked for a person who was famous for not making decisions. You might work months on a particular project and, when it was presented, find that it never again saw the light of day. His fear of disapproval from above prevented him from advancing any controversial report or project. This caused a significant morale problem for his subordinates.

Chief Clive Weighill:

I've found on many occasions I learned more from individuals who were not good supervisors or leaders. I watched and learned how they negatively impacted people and the service in general. Some of the most striking examples of this were people who

* Had an ego so big they could never allow anyone to receive credit except themselves.
* Were micromanagers that had to have control over all details. This rarely allowed anyone under them to feel confident making decisions or to grow with experience.
* Thought they were smarter or better qualified than those that worked around them.
* Became angry with staff when things didn't go right, rather than listening to the problem and trying to find a solution. I've always found people are more apt to assist you when you acknowledge the issue in a calm manner and ask for their support to help solve it, rather than yelling at them and demanding explanations.

Senator Vernon White:

I worked with a senior leader who specifically made reference to have people follow his or her lead rather than to lead themselves. This person made specific reference to people getting in line rather than leading, a real damper on young leaders.

Commissioner Giuliano Zaccardelli:

The worst leader was a deputy commissioner who said all the right things, but no one believed what he said or believed that he meant what he said. His actions never supported what he said. People were in a constant state of uncertainty and at times feared him. It was well known and assumed that his principal objective was his own self-promotion and advancement. People did not feel comfortable around him.

In my opinion, there is a striking theme in all that the chiefs have said: the positive aspects that made leaders great and the negative issues that made other leaders fail are all people skills. Only one or two brief remarks above focused on job-knowledge qualities, and only in general terms like "knowledgeable" and "experienced." None of chiefs said, "The best leader I ever worked for really knew the criminal code front to back." Conversely, none of them identified that the worst leader "couldn't write a good search warrant to save his soul" or "didn't know how to balance a budget."

Within hundreds of years of experience among some of the top police leaders of today and yesterday, within police services of varying sizes from coast to coast in this great country, none of those surveyed cared one iota about the good or lousy leaders' ability to know the law, know policy, or do police work or administration. Do we consider that when we are selecting and promoting leaders? Do we *all* think in that context as we ourselves try to be effective leaders and as we model leadership for those who will someday replace us?

Sadly, I think not, but we certainly should.

Leadership is action, not position.

—Donald H. McGannon

It's a "Me, My, I" World

• • •

I believe that the first test of a truly great man is humility.

—JOHN RUSKIN

THERE'S A DISTURBING TREND AMONG some police leaders out there that I don't recall seeing and hearing about years ago. Maybe it was there and I was oblivious to it, or maybe years ago many police leaders were anti-media and weren't in the spotlight as much as they are now. Or perhaps it's the 24/7 news coverage we live with in the digital age. I call this trend "me, my, I" leadership, and it applies to those leaders who seldom speak of the men and women in the organization they lead without making them sound like personal property: "My men." "My detectives." "I this" and "I that." "My city." "I believe…" "My strategy…my approach." "My stations, cars, guns, dogs, cats, gerbils, bullets, squads, investigators, spaceships, fighter jets, zombies…yadda, yadda." Enough already. What do the hard-working people of the police force think when they hear their leaders refer to them as if they were chattel?

Did any of those subordinate folks contribute to the strategy? Did any of them have an idea or an original thought? Was it all the chief or commissioner or ranking officer? Did he or she do it all—think it through, consider the options, develop a strategy, implement it, and risk life and limb while doing so? I think not. Lots of bright and committed people make it happen as a team. No one person ever does it all in any organization.

Chief Rod Knecht says, "It has been my experience as a witness of police leadership that a big ego is a sign of selfishness, while being humble is a sign of selflessness, and selflessness is the lifeblood of great leadership."

A close friend and colleague, OPP Chief Superintendent Dave Crane (Ret.), some years ago participated in an executive assessment exercise conducted by an outside consultant. During that session, he was asked to give an example of something he did in his executive role of that time that met certain parameters established by the interviewer. Dave went on to give a fitting example, citing wonderful things done by a team he led. When the interviewer probed and asked, "Yes, great, but what was it *you* did?" Dave clarified that at his rank, he really didn't do anything other than encourage, support, remove roadblocks, inspire innovation, and so on. The interviewer wasn't satisfied and aggressively pushed him to explain what he *himself* did in this example. She expected him to say that he did everything—thought up all the good ideas, made them all happen—and without him, nothing would have ever worked successfully. Things went downhill from there.

Dave expounded on his view of leadership, as only Dave could, explaining, "I didn't do anything. *They* did it," at which point he walked out of the room. Knowing Dave as well as I do, I'm sure the lady was seeking therapy and doubling up on her meds before the day was out!

The scary part of that story for me is that most of those interviewed would have told wonderful stories of how they single-handedly accomplished amazing feats, and it would all be crap. Dave was honest, and it did not help him in that exercise at all, but he really didn't care. He was not going to compromise his values.

Average bosses put most of their attention on customers,
investors, other managers, and their own career. In this priority
scheme, employees rank dead last—if they're even on the list.

*Unfortunately, employees can sense when a boss doesn't care
about them, and they respond by not caring about their jobs.
Extraordinary bosses know that the best way to please investors, peers,
and customers is to put the employees first. They realize that it's
employees who create, build, sell, and support the products that customers
buy, thereby creating investor value and advancing a manager's career.*

—GEOFFREY JAMES

I heard a joke somewhere about a man going for a job interview and the interviewer asking him to name a negative quality that he had. He said, "I'm too honest sometimes." The interviewer said, "I don't think that honesty is a negative quality," and the man replied, "I don't really give a shit what you think."

US Army major Henry A. Courtney said, "The bigger the man's head gets, the easier it is to fill his shoes." I've always enjoyed replacing weak leaders. They are easy acts to follow. It's also always easier to succeed an egotistical person than it is to succeed a down-to-earth one. Our people aren't stupid; they pick up on the egos. Then they quickly see that the more grounded leader actually knows he or she isn't God's gift to the world and that they (the boots on the ground) actually count.

Humility is not thinking less of yourself, it's thinking of yourself less.

—C. S. LEWIS (NO RELATION!)

I once lectured on my experiences in the fight against smuggling in the Cornwall, Ontario, area to a group of private sector company presidents and CEOs. The speaker before me was a decorated military hero from the first Gulf War. When I saw the agenda, I thought that the crowd wouldn't be too interested in hearing my tales after hearing about the war in Iraq. I wasn't in battle and never served in a foreign land. But his stories were all about *him*. His inflated ego was apparent to all these bright and success-ful people in the room. The speaker's use of the words "I" and "me" were not missed by the audience, and despite the galaxy of egos present in that group, he was not a hit.

I simply got up and talked about the dangers and operational chal-lenges *the team* faced, how *we* addressed those problems, the successes of *our people*, the leadership lessons learned, and more. The story was not about me. That approach was considerably more positively received by the audience.

Consider the first public quote by Captain Chesley "Sully" Sullenberger, who landed US Airways flight 1549 on the Hudson River in New York in 2009, saving the lives of 155 passengers: "Circumstance determined that it was this experienced crew that was scheduled to fly that particular flight on that particular day, but I know I can speak for the entire crew when I tell you we were simply doing the job we were trained to do."

It wasn't about him. It was about the crew. It was about "we." Captain Sully Sullenberger is a leader. I'd bet dollars to donuts that his crew would walk on broken glass for him.

> *"Who knows himself a braggart, let him fear this, for it will*
> *come to pass that every braggart shall be found an ass."*
>
> —WILLIAM SHAKESPEARE

Where did this "me, my, I" attitude come from? Why do so many lead-ers have the ability to manage up much better than manage down? In my opinion, it's either a learned behavior, or it's all ego.

> *Successful people are always looking for opportunities to help others.*
> *Unsuccessful people are always asking, "What's in it for me?"*
>
> —BRIAN TRACY

I'm convinced that if some of those leaders who tell every story as if they did it all themselves took a polygraph test, they'd pass. In their minds, they are truly the only people in the organization capable of pulling off whatever great accomplishment that has occurred. They believe their own headlines and their contrived inaccuracies.

Likely, through much or all of their earlier careers, they took credit for the work of others and exaggerated their involvement in any operation or project that went well. At the same time, I'm sure that when things went bad, they were the first to point the finger at others rather than take the potential career hit. They wouldn't do it in front of the people they led but behind closed doors so that they wouldn't lose the support of the staff that continued to carry them and make them look so good. What they'd tell their bosses would be a far cry from reality.

Then, as they progressed through the hierarchy, they saw others' methods of operation and quickly learned what would get them promoted and what wouldn't and then modeled themselves accordingly.

Author and speaker Robin Sharma said, "The best leaders are (more) interested in the benefit of the company than their own egos. The best leaders are more interested in impact and not just income. They are more interested in growing more leaders as opposed to stroking their ego. That's the difference between a great leader and a bad leader."

Think about this: If a young up-and-coming executive, who presumably isn't stupid, sees that those colleagues who continually agree with everything their managers and the CEO say tend to get the better jobs and advanced courses and other career opportunities, and those that don't get pigeonholed, it takes incredible strength of character to not fall into the career-lapdog trap.

Conversely, if your colleagues at the senior-executive table that actually have the parts to disagree with the executives next to them, even in the most respectful of ways, are sidelined or put into the organizational penalty box, what's your reaction going to be? Once again, it's a learned behavior. The dilemma for that young executive is then, "If I agree to everything, including the dumbest of ideas, I'm in good stead. If I disagree, even when asked my opinion, and do so in a professional and respectful way, I'm done." Most will, unfortunately, take the path of least resistance. Sad but true. I've been there; I've seen otherwise-good people either clam up tight or agree with an inane suggestion out of fear, and I've seen others speak honestly and go down in flames. In addition, I suffered on a personal level when I respectfully disagreed with a superior. I'd rather be permanently sidelined and still be able to look myself in the mirror the next morning than to sell my soul.

In reviewing the book *The Wisdom of Failure* by Laurence Weinzimmer and Jim McConoughey, author and book reviewer Harvey Schachter points out:

> Self-absorption: The biggest mistake, the authors say, is leaders who allow their ego to run wild. Those folk believe they are invincible. But they aren't, and crash and burn, taking others with them.

I speak fairly regularly on leadership to frontline supervisors, midmanagers, right up to and including executive leadership teams within policing and, at times, to government ministries and agencies. It's a passion of mine, and I personally grow from every session.

What is always abundantly clear to me as I speak and read the reactions of those looking back at me is this: *People get it.* They know and feel the differences in leadership styles. They smirk when I speak of the "me, my, and I" leaders, because they are picturing a leader who talks just like that. They look at each other and smile when I mention bosses who are in it only for themselves, don't care about those they lead, and often can't even name their direct reports. They laugh out loud when hearing of leaders that take credit and pass blame, or never emerge from the sanctity of their offices if things are going bad—because they have lived it.

Do you want them thinking of your smiling face when discussing the perfect example of all those things that leaders should never be? I certainly don't.

*It is amazing what you can accomplish if you
do not care who gets the credit.*

—Harry S. Truman

Commissioner Giuliano Zaccardelli said, "A challenge in policing is often the lack of humility in many of its leaders. Too many type A leaders have difficulty admitting that they do not know everything, and are too proud to admit it. Humility enables a leader to recognize his or her limitations and surround himself or herself with people who possess talents that he or she does not possess. A great leader is willing to show his or her vulnerabilities. Many leaders possess humility."

Be humble. Show humility. Ensure it's never about you but about them. They will recognize and appreciate the difference.

Forging and Maintaining Relationships

• • •

There is only one thing worse than fighting with
allies, and that is fighting without them.

—WINSTON CHURCHILL

I WAS BORN A PEOPLE person. I will die a people person. Sometimes it is a blessing for me, and other times a curse. My wife leans toward the "curse" side of the equation. But it's who I am, right or wrong—and it's what I do.

In the fall of 2001, my wife and I were in Myrtle Beach at a resort. It was a month after 9/11, and the resort was almost empty. When we got to the pool, there was only one other couple there. Angie saw me looking across the water at the pair and said, "I know what you are doing; you are trying to see if you know them. You don't, Chris. You are going to go places where you don't actually know anyone."

As she continued her diatribe, a third couple entered the area, and as they passed us, the man said, "Hi, Chris." He was a retired police officer from Ontario that I knew. That shut Angie up quick!

But I wasn't done. I meandered to the other side of the pool and asked the man in the first couple, "Are you from Sault Sainte Marie?" He said,

"Yes." I asked, "Is your name Richard?" He replied that it was. As it turned out, we had worked together one summer during high school and hadn't talked in over twenty-five years. It's a small world.

My point here isn't "Look at me: I know lots of people!" My message is that people count. Life is about people and the relationships between them. You can't control whether others will remember you or will even care to look around the pool when on vacation to see whether they know anyone. But I guarantee you Richard will never forget that chance meeting, that I remembered him, and that I made the effort to go over and say hello.

The key to building successful relationships at any level is making the effort.

Leadership often entails conflict. In the business world, I assume that customers are always king, but competitors and suppliers and contractors might be the Antichrist in some situations. In the military, the enemy is often clear—at least it was until domestic and international terrorism increased. But generally, in the heat of battle, the enemy is relatively apparent.

In policing, conflict with criminals and other offenders is frequent, but it is not an absolute. I survived many years of dealing with the good and bad of society, and I guess that very few of even the most hardened criminals walked away from me thinking that I was a complete goof. A wise man once said to treat everyone, including offenders, as you would want your mother treated.

No, I don't hug and kiss criminals and tell them I love them as I did my dear mother, but as a human being, I have always tried to treat people respectfully.

Business is an ecosystem, not a battlefield.
Average bosses see business as a conflict between companies,
departments and groups. They build huge armies of "troops"
to order about, demonize competitors as "enemies," and
treat customers as "territory" to be conquered.

*Extraordinary bosses see business as a symbiosis where the most
diverse firm is most likely to survive and thrive. They naturally
create teams that adapt easily to new markets and can quickly form
partnerships with other companies, customers…and even competitors.*

—GEOFFREY JAMES

From the police-leadership perspective, the potential for conflict with
some governing officials, political figures, special interest groups, or police associations/unions can be expected, but the leader needs to carefully
manage those relationships to mitigate conflict and to support healthy and
fruitful interactions. We can control only our own tempers and emotions
and can bite only our own tongues if situations get heated, but we must
do all we can. It is the right thing to do, and it's also part of the concept of
leading by example.

One of my personal challenges has always been to keep my temper in
check. I've become angry with subordinates, peers, and even bosses in a
way that I was not proud of at times. Most often when that occurred, one
of them had become pushy or aggressive with me—although this is not
an excuse. Some of these incidents in fact hurt me in the eyes of decision
makers, and I can't blame them for it. Thankfully, my flaw has improved
with age, but I still have to constantly tell myself that there's more to be
lost than gained by flying off the handle.

In his book *Policing Ireland's Twisted History*, my friend Alan M. Wilson
said, "It's easy to make war but very difficult to make peace."

I've always done my best—with some success and some disappoint-
ment—to proactively build positive relationships with everyone around
me, especially key players that I have had to interact regularly with. Most
bosses have liked me, and most have respected me as a person, a hard
worker, and a committed member of the OPP. The odd one hasn't, but
hey, they were entitled to their mistakes! I never kissed up to them; I just
worked hard, was honest, and told them my opinion as what I believed
to be right. Some liked that approach; some didn't. The odd relationship

with those above me was subsequently challenged as a result, but rightly or wrongly, I was always true to myself, and I made the effort.

Our lives begin to end the day we become silent about things that matter.

—Martin Luther King Jr.

In the past twenty years, policing has become a competitive business, at least in Ontario and some other parts of Canada. As policing costs go up and municipal revenues go down, the math isn't always good. Municipal leaders are struggling with policing-service delivery options, such as maintaining a stand-alone service, amalgamating with neighboring police services (regionalization), or contracting out service delivery to the provincial police—which in eight of ten provinces is the RCMP. It is sad to see the decline of many smaller police services, but from a strictly business sense, the larger services offer substantial savings through their economies of scale. These are difficult and emotional decisions all around. This pattern is starting to grow in the United States and in some European countries, and I predict it will expand to a much greater degree.

Ontario has just over fifty police services, including the OPP. There were closer to two hundred police services fifty years ago. So back then, there were two hundred police chiefs, who had two hundred personal secretaries, two hundred police-chief cars, two hundred stand-alone police stations, often two hundred independent radio networks with two hundred independent dispatch centers, and on and on. Not necessarily a cost-effective way of doing business. Times have greatly changed since those days, in terms of us now having less but mostly larger police services.

On the other hand, Pennsylvania, which has approximately the same population as Ontario (thirteen million), currently has about thirteen hundred police departments despite being about one-eighth of the land mass of Ontario. That will inevitably change, as Ontario and Quebec have, as Netherlands and Scotland have, and more. The conflict among law-enforcement leaders will be incredible when it does.

Ontario has been dealing with this trend in a big way since changes were made to the Police Services Act in 1998. It happened in dribs and drabs prior to that. Relationships between some police chiefs have suffered as a result, particularly toward the leadership of the OPP, as small and midsized police-service chiefs have feared the OPP "takeover." That has not been an easy situation to manage for the OPP's various leadership teams over those years.

However, we brought some of that negativity on ourselves. Some past OPP leaders in various capacities made it known that the OPP was going to aggressively take over smaller police services. Some joked about it, not really meaning it, and underestimated the impact their statements had. Unfortunately, the OPP's vision at one point was to be "the police service of choice." That went over like a fart at a wedding. Nothing good came from it, and it sent a clear message to many police chiefs and senior officers that we were taking over the world. That became a huge ship to try and turn around. Frankly, we have not yet totally recovered.

As a regional commander at the time, I found it very challenging. Many small police services refused to call us for help as they did not want to admit they couldn't handle operations on their own. They'd rather not have had access to an aircraft, a scuba diver, or a canine unit than to call us. Separate meetings of police chiefs were held outside of the normal Ontario Association of Chiefs of Police (OACP) meetings, to which OPP senior officers were not invited. Closed-door bad-mouthing, as well as public criticism of the OPP and its leaders in the media, became commonplace among a number of chiefs. Some chiefs and senior officers that I considered friends totally avoided me or stopped talking when I walked up to them. Even chiefs of some large police services that had nothing to fear turned against us.

The members of the region that I led were very frustrated with the public criticism. Our senior officers were refusing to go to OACP meetings and events, and at least one deputy commissioner made the pitch that the OPP entirely pull out of the OACP entirely.

I had to lead by example and take the high road. Through a region-wide communique and at a number of personal meetings, I directed our people to do the same and to not become engaged in the bad-mouthing. I struggled to stay out of the media mudslinging but met personally with chiefs that cast stones, and explained my concerns. I brought every OPP senior officer that was available to OACP meetings with me as a team, and we walked up to every chief we met, shook his or her hand, and tried to engage him or her in friendly conversation. I still regularly visited police chiefs in my travels and invited them to OPP events. I bit my tongue until it bled on many occasions but also stood up for our people when a chief said something totally inappropriate about us at a meeting or event.

As challenging as it was, it was the right thing to do. We developed good relationships with some chiefs and improved relationships with others in the process. Our senior people did the same and made me very proud as they went to those meetings, held their noses, and took the high road.

In her article "How to Transform Difficult Relationships," speaking about colleague Bob Burg, author Dorie Clark said,

> Mastering these skills is necessary for career success, he (Burg) says. "You can have so many of the other qualities that help toward success—great talent, very high character, being ambitious, kind, charitable, or hard working…they're all great, but let's face it. Unless you can influence others—that is, moving people to the desired and appropriate action—you can only accomplish so much."
>
> Meanwhile, he says, "When you utilize these principles, your life will be a lot more fun and a lot less stressful and more profitable, both personally and in business. You know you've got the ability to have people work with you and not against you…Expecting another person to be helpful, friendly, and benevolent changes you—and that changes them."

When I was seconded to work with the RCMP in Cornwall in 1993, we formed a task force of over seventy officers. RCMP, OPP, Cornwall Community Police Service, and what was then Canada Revenue Agency (now Canada Border Services Agency). Typical of any joint-forces operation (JFO), within the Cornwall Regional Task Force (known as the RTF), several players from all of the agencies did not want to work with some of the partner organizations. Bad feelings and jealousies permeated the air whenever certain participants were in the room, over real or perceived injustices from days or years gone by.

At the inaugural group meeting, it was clear to me that the room resembled a high school dance, where boys stand on one side of the room and girls on the other and eventually start to mingle. The RCMP guarded one corner as a group, the OPP glared from another, and so on. It was typical of some other JFOs I had been involved in, just on a larger scale.

I remember my initial speech to them very well, in fact almost to the word. I said, "I know there are people here that don't trust some members in the room for whatever reason. Some of the RCMP members feel that sometime, somewhere, they got screwed over by an OPP officer. Some of the OPP and Cornwall members similarly feel they got screwed by a Mountie or a customs officer. We have to leave our shoulder flashes at the door and remember that we're all part of the RTF. No one is going to screw anyone on the RTF. We're one big team here."

From then on, ensuring members from different organizations were paired up and placed on different teams so that they would be forced to work together, trying not to favor any individual or group over another, became the game. Social team-building functions, joint training sessions, making sure that all four organizations were appropriately profiled and recognized in all our operations, getting everyone jackets and ball caps that said RTF on them, spreading the good and the bad assignments equitably, and so on were the only ways to build relationships among the services and the members.

The high school kids indeed started to dance. To the untrained eye, one would never know who was from what police service when the members were together. They were simply the RTF and proud of it. It was a huge success from both operational- and relationship-success perspectives. Lifelong friendships and professional partnerships emerged from that task force.

Then, two years later, when I left the RTF, they had a party for me. In my farewell speech, I reminded them of my comments at the original briefing regarding the fact that no member of the RTF was "going to screw another member." I pointed out how wrong I was! Some of the relationships that had formed among RTF members had become very personal and everlasting. A few relationships had blossomed far beyond my expectations. So I guess our attempts at Relationship Building 101 were effective after all! The most important aspect in my view was the resounding operational and history-making successes.

Another interesting exercise and learning experience for me in terms of proactive relationship building was between the RTF senior leadership team and the thirteen chiefs of the Mohawk Territory of Akwesasne, as well as the leaders of the Mohawk Warrior Society (MWS).

When we first established the RTF in the fall of 1993, there was a lot of tension in the air between non-Aboriginal people and Ontario and First Nations leadership and community members on Akwesasne. There was often automatic gunfire on the Saint Lawrence River at night, there were many dangerous high-speed chases of suspected smugglers through the city of Cornwall and surrounding areas, and the mayor of Cornwall was wearing a bulletproof vest while living with a police security team. The public announcement of a task force did nothing but heighten that ongoing tension.

I understand the benefits with much more clarity twenty years later than I did then, but I and my RCMP partner, Inspector Harper Boucher, decided to meet with the Akwesasne chiefs and subsequently the Mohawk Warrior Society leadership on Cornwall Island. When we arrived at the meeting, we found them in a heated argument, and to our surprise, the MWS reps were in attendance as well—also arguing with some of the elected chiefs.

Despite our initial response of wanting to run to the car and escape to mainland Ontario unscathed, we stayed and began the arduous journey of developing credibility and a working relationship with both elected chiefs and MWS representatives, which lasted many years and undoubtedly mitigated many potential pitfalls along the way. They knew we would do what we felt was right as police agencies, and we knew where they stood on specific issues. Neither side wanted to see anyone hurt, either police or those running contraband across the international border. At one point, one of the MHS spokesmen said, "If one of our people gets hurt by your officers, we'll make Oka look like a pillow fight."

The Oka standoff in Quebec in 1990 saw a violent confrontation initially between First Nations protestors and the police, in which a Sûreté du Québec officer was fatally shot. The resulting protracted military deployment there cost millions of dollars and created bad feelings that will last for many generations. However, through our many regular meetings and a number of ad hoc discussions, we successfully dealt with concerns from both sides, which may well have saved lives in the long run.

We met regularly, sometimes simply over coffee or lunch, to discuss key issues and even just to build the relationship further when there was no specific agenda. When I left the RTF in 1995, I called my MWS contact for a meeting and introduced him to my replacement. The MWS rep was smuggler, ran a multimillion-dollar criminal enterprise, and was a convicted criminal and one tough individual, but he got somewhat emotional that I took the time to say good-bye and to introduce the incoming OPP lead. He knew we would bust him in a heartbeat if we could, but he respected us. I didn't develop a professional relationship with this man because I liked him as a person, but it was the right thing to do on many fronts.

The view of educator and best-selling author Ed Fuller:

Solid relationships are not formed overnight, however; and they are defined by culture and community. Different values and customs can sometimes make genuine connections difficult to build and maintain.

A strong connection may begin with untold hours of dining to-gether and mingling at social events. But to reinforce a productive relationship you need to demonstrate fairness and evenhanded-ness. It's hard work but the rewards of getting out from behind your desk and making the effort to build strong relationships face-to-face are many.

The need for effective relationships far transcends internal and personal dynamics. It's more than building a positive working relationship with the police union or political masters or even the media. Leaders must strive to maintain and build upon effective relationships with people and organizations that surpass their own personal needs. They have to consider the benefits to the organization and the people they lead, not simply their quests to fulfill their own aspirations or to feather their own nests.

Unfortunately, that is not always the case for many modern leaders in policing. We've all seen police leaders who stonewalled people and agen-cies over issues where their own egos had been bruised.

There are some organizational heads, private sector executives, politi-cal staff, and even the odd police leader that I didn't particularly like as individuals, but it was not about whom I liked or who could help me. Some of them criticized me or the OPP behind my back or publicly. I always dealt with that as appropriate, but I didn't make a spectacle of it or sever all ties either. I still went out of my way to acknowledge and speak to those individuals in future. Sometimes I had to bite my tongue so hard that my sinuses filled with blood, but I smiled and moved forward as I took the high road.

Author Victor Lipman said,

Recognize this is business, not pleasure, and drain the emotion out of it. Remember these are business relationships, not friendships. Even turbulent business relationships can yield business benefits. Compartmentalize.

Try as best you can to see things through the eyes of others. No one's perfect; all of us of course have faults. It's entirely possible some of the fault in a fractured relationship is yours.

In the best interests of the organization, I had to be professional and ensure I did all I could to keep the relationships strong. On the political front, as commissioner, I knew most of these folks couldn't hurt me, but I wouldn't walk away having the OPP clearly in the cross hairs of those that could forever harm our people and the good work they did by letting my personal pride or ego get in the way of our organizational goals.

Author Michael Simmons' opinion really resonates with me:

Relationships are more than just strategic chess pieces that help us achieve our goals efficiently.

Approached properly, they can help us both create and achieve goals beyond our wildest dreams. They can last for decades; well beyond the length of individual deals, transactions, and companies. As relationships deepen, their mutual value often compounds as each is willing to do anything to help the other person during the ups and downs of their career and life.

What's amazing about relationships is their ability to transcend professional boundaries and have a huge impact on our behaviors, well-being, income, happiness, and even longevity.

Our network of relationships constantly and independently evolves as the people in it grow.

Effective leaders should never hesitate to laud or give credit publicly to other organizations, no matter how insignificant their roles in something may have been. Acting as if your own organization is the only one that knows anything or does anything right will do more harm than good, in terms of relationship building. Leaders should never be critical of other agencies or people in front of those they lead. They shouldn't get caught in the vortex of negativity that surrounds those leaders who never have anything good to say about anyone else around them, internally or externally.

Admittedly, there were times when I could have lived up to that statement more professionally than I did.

Les McKeown said in his article "4 Signs You Will Fail as a Leader,"

When truly effective leaders talk, one thing becomes noticeable. When discussing others, whether their employees, vendors or customers, the conversation typically trends toward the positive. Strong leaders look for success in others. They focus on what has been done well, and seek to build on that success.

You have to work at relationships. It requires contacting people when nothing is happening and there are no favors to ask. Just saying hello to people, keeping communication channels open, congratulating someone on the good days, or offering support during tough times should be a part of your every day as a leader.

> *I'd certainly rather have them inside my tent*
> *pissing out than outside my tent pissing in.*
>
> —Chief Wayne Frechette

Personal Attacks:
Survival of the Fittest

• • •

Don't Worry about Criticism
1. Remember that unjust criticism is often a disguised compliment.
2. Do the very best you can.
3. Analyze your own mistakes and criticize yourself.

—DALE CARNEGIE, *DALE CARNEGIE'S GOLDEN BOOK*

I WON'T LIE AND SAY that criticism has never bothered me. I've certainly had days where it got to me, both professionally and in my personal life. However, I have learned that fair or not, it comes with the turf.

I always knew that the insanity of vicious personal attacks occurred across all major organizations, including policing, but it was never more real to me than when I was a young chief superintendent who had a shot at being a deputy commissioner someday. The fact that at that time I didn't care to ever be a deputy was of no consequence. What mattered to some was that I might be a contender. The claws then came out. In addition, being in charge of a large region of twelve hundred personnel—not all handpicked folks like I had been fortunate enough to have led in my several positions prior—meant I now had to deal with the best and sometimes the worst of supervisors and managers. That in itself led to rumors, false accusations, and attacks on my personal and professional integrity as I took on some of these folks.

Best-selling author Karen Dillon hit the nail right on the head when she said,

EVERY ORGANIZATION HAS ITS SHARE OF POLITICAL DRAMA: Personalities clash. Agendas compete. Turf wars erupt. It can make you crazy if you're trying to keep your head down and get your job done. The problem is, you can't just keep your head down. You need to work productively with your colleagues—even the challenging ones—for the good of your organization and your career. How can you do that without crossing over to the dark side? By acknowledging that power dynamics and unwritten rules exist—and by constructively navigating them. "Politics" needn't be a dirty word. You can succeed at work without being a power grabber or a corporate climber.

Of course, unwanted attention only grew in magnitude when I did become a deputy commissioner, and God forbid I had the gall to take a run at the commissioner's job. I knew that sort of silliness was always there at that level; I just didn't realize how serious it would get with some.

Character Assassination Techniques
Attack the person, showing them to be bad and unworthy. Any of
the "four Ds" below may be used (as well as additional methods):
Discredit them, showing their arguments and decisions
are weak and they are incapable in their work.
Use defamation, damaging the good reputation and name of others.
Demonize them, turning them into bad people that everyone
hates, such that anything they do will be considered bad.
Dehumanize them, treating them as a "thing" and
framing them as non-human with negligible values.

—Unknown, "Character Assassination"

I have said and done some things in my life that I'm not proud of. I have never professed that I am perfect. I'll weather those historical storms if and when they arise. But at times I have been falsely accused of things that were total crap, some involving people I had never met and others that unfairly implicated innocent folks and besmirched their reputations in the process. How sad.

As author Donald T. Phillips describes, Abraham Lincoln was attacked throughout his political career.

As his enemies increased, so did the criticism against him. But Lincoln handled it all with a patience, forbearance, and determination uncommon of most men. He was philosophical about it and in part, fell back on his understanding of people. "Human nature will not change," he said in 1864.

And just think. There was no television, CNN, Facebook, Twitter, or YouTube in the 1800s! Can you imagine how his agenda would have been challenged and how he would have been constantly slaughtered in our current political environment?

Character assassination techniques do not need to be true. "Mud sticks" as they say and an accusation of wrong-doing is enough to sow the seeds of doubt in the minds of others. Witch-hunts, both ancient and modern use such methods. Politicians are famed for their attacks on their political opponents, from sly innuendo to dragging skeletons from hidden closets. Their allies and enemies in the media do this too, and a libelous headline can cause damage that no retraction can erase. With the advent of the web and blogging, the situation is more confused as both propagandists and anti-propagandists make bold assertions that are impossible to verify.

—UNKNOWN, "CHARACTER ASSASSINATION"

So what is the motivation for such attacks?

As with Lincoln, sometimes it is purely jealousy. The leader has a position or status that others wish they had. At other times it is the competition trying to lessen the size of the race. In some cases it is a matter of payback; an individual feels he or she was somehow wronged and is determined to get even.

It is no different from a group of female teenagers being jealous of the prom queen or the captain of the cheerleading team. Or perhaps a group of young males not liking a rich kid or a successful athlete. Petty jealousy and silliness abound and can get quite ugly at times in all walks of life and within all occupations.

What really kills me is the number of people who spend their lives listening to this drivel, then further disseminate it to anyone that will listen.

Having said that, over the course of my career, I myself passed on hurtful rumors that may or may not have been true. In hindsight, I realize that most of them were likely false. I don't feel good about that. True or not, I should have kept them to myself.

Although I feel bad that I passed on the odd silly rumor, the following is a funny story: I once heard something about a coworker that I passed on to another colleague I was close friends with. I made him promise that he wouldn't tell a soul. Weeks later he pulled me aside at work and said, "I don't know if you've heard this or not, and I know I promised whoever told me that I wouldn't tell anyone, but..." and he reiterated the entire story that I had told him in confidence. What a moron! It certainly showed me just how quickly a story can get passed around even twenty-five years ago, without the benefit of the social media and communication tools of today.

At times, colleagues or subordinates are in disagreement with a decision a leader has made or a position he or she has taken on an issue, or in the case of subordinates, anger emerges over a disciplinary matter they have been the center of or a perceived unfairness. Frankly, there are also instances that border on being irrational, where peers or subordinates become obsessed with what they believe to be an injustice involving them personally or professionally. That, of course, is a completely different ball of wax, one that may require risk assessments and intervention, but it does happen.

How do we as leaders react to or address personal attacks? I don't think there is a pat response, as there are too many variables at play.

> *You can't let praise or criticism get to you. It's a*
> *weakness to get caught up in either one.*

> —JOHN WOODEN

The challenge in defending yourself against some silliness is that it furthers the rumor mongering, can take on an unending life of its own, and potentially causes the "other party," if you will, even more undeserved grief.

For example, if a false allegation of sexual impropriety is made against a leader, it potentially hurts two individuals: the leader and his or her alleged partner, if named. Most often in my experience, another participant is named, just to give the story more appeal. Even if the person who fabricated the tale is identified (and that's a stretch), to discipline the person means dragging him or her publicly through a tribunal process. At that point, anyone who hasn't heard the rumor will. Either way, the rumor will re-cycle every year or two and will catch fire as if it were a new story, when it's simply the same old nonsense.

Lincoln had his own approach.

> *Even though he would become weary and discouraged by*
> *all the attacks, when it came right down to it, he normally*
> *would not retaliate against his detractors...*
> *However, on occasion Lincoln would stand up and defend himself*
> *to any and all detractors, especially if the false accusation was*
> *particularly damaging to the public's view of his principles.*

> —DONALD T. PHILLIPS

I guess there are mere annoyances, more troubling times, and then hills worth dying on. Sometimes you simply consider the source, take the high road, and shrug it off as silly, petty jealousy or rivalry. Other instances require a face-to-face discussion with the detractor, which may not go well and could result in a bigger issue for you. Then there are situations that you cannot ignore and may have to take on from an internal-discipline perspective and develop a communications strategy around. And then at the extreme end of the scale, there may be very serious matters, which occur on rarer occasions, that require civil redress or criminal court intervention. When the internal disciplinary or court processes begin, tighten your bootstraps, because it's going to be a much more challenging ride for you and your family. That's your call.

With the proliferation of social media, the possibility of personal attacks coming from a zillion different and unknown sources is alive and well. The damage can be done quickly and anonymously and can be irreversible. We all know that the advent of social media platforms brings us tremendous communication solutions, but unfortunately, with the good also comes the bad. The digital world has created an unlimited number of authors, photographers, and publishers. It has also resulted in an increase in courage on the part of some who would never have the parts to challenge us to our faces. The cloak of anonymity prevails.

Being positive in a negative situation is not naive. It's leadership.

—RALPH MARSTON

Is responding online with tough talk the answer? Perhaps, but I'd suggest thinking hard before clicking the "send" button. The old newspaper-era adage "Don't get into a battle of words with somebody who buys ink by the barrel" is magnified a trillionfold in the social media universe.

When the debate is lost, slander becomes the tool of the loser.

—SOCRATES

Many of the online blog comments I read about myself following an editorial on some news outlet websites are quite humorous. Others are mean; some, downright evil. I try as hard as I can to laugh it off and not lose any sleep over that nonsense, but I admit that the occasional criticism cuts deep.

I read one blog posting to my wife, relating to my stance on responding to First Nations protests. The blogger called me a "closet queer." My wife's reply? No concern. No sympathy or reassurance. Just a simple, "How did they know?" She's a hoot.

In another, a blogger wrote: "He's only fifty-six? He looks seventy." I couldn't help but laugh, but my one daughter wanted to track the writer down.

Lawyer, journalist, educator and author Ellyn Angelotti offers advice in her article "How to Handle Personal Attacks on Social Media." She says,

> There are a number of effective strategies for overcoming the harm caused by a personal attack on social media. And your response can be a democratic one that includes fighting bad speech with more (good) speech.
>
> If someone's attacked you on social media, here are four steps for responding:
>
> 1. Don't panic. Instead, take a deep breath and think about what options exist.
> 2. Figure out if (and how) you want to respond. Consider the motivation of the attacker. Based on this, what's the best approach? What value would come from engaging with the attacker?
> 3. Respond quickly publicly, then take the follow-up conversation offline.
>   In most cases it's good to respond quickly in the same venue where the attack was made by sending a brief, temperate message recognizing you saw the attack. Then, if

appropriate, try to follow up in a more private way, such as a phone call or email. Consider what value would come with taking the conversation offline.

4. Damage control: Determine how to best remedy the harm. Can't I sue for defamation?

In social media, that remedy isn't as effective. A lawsuit isn't quick enough to mitigate harm; the toothpaste is already out of the tube.

Fortunately, those who have been attacked online can now create their own remedies to harm caused by personal attacks. With social media virtually everyone has a publishing platform—and a voice. We can use the power of speech to minimize the harm negative feedback, comments and posts can cause.

When Rick Deering retired from the OPP and became the chief RNC in January 2001, he was one of the first (or perhaps the first ever) police chiefs who was from the Canadian mainland and was not a native Newfoundlander. A couple of their early chiefs had hailed from the Royal Irish on, from which the RNC had earlier modeled itself, but not from one of Canada's other provinces. His selection was welcomed by some members, including some senior officers, but was far from popular or well accepted by others. Some of those detractors felt that they or one of their friends should have been selected, so Rick was fighting an uphill battle with that group.

For those that have never been, Newfoundland is a wonderful province full of tremendous people, mostly very down-to-earth and trusting souls.

The RNC is a proud and very historic police service. One of the oldest police services in Canada, it was the last to be issued firearms in the entire country. The economy there has suffered at times and wasn't strong in 2001 when Rick arrived. The RNC didn't have an adequate budget and, given its far-east location, had been isolated from most of the larger

Canadian police agencies. Changes were required in some areas of the organization. As always, some people welcomed the change, and some people didn't. Rick accomplished a lot to move the RNC forward, including the acquisition of handguns for its members, but was in a no-win position with some senior folks. One inspector who had applied to be the chief and a couple of his or her close colleagues allegedly did their best to undermine him at every turn. Eventually, one of them submitted complaints of harassment. A well-publicized legal process began, and when the silly and false allegations were dismissed, the media gave very little attention to the rebuttal, so many citizens were left hearing only one side of the story. Rick left the RNC, eventually moving back to Ontario. Sadly, these attacks hurt him on both personal and professional levels.

In some cases across Canada, police chiefs have had votes of no confidence brought forward by police associations. A number of chiefs have had a slew of personal and professional attacks made by members, political foes, or media outlets. Disproving these attacks is like fighting a ghost at times, and in many cases, it really doesn't matter: some people don't want to hear the truth.

> *I always cheer up immensely if an attack is particularly*
> *wounding because I think, well, if they attack one personally,*
> *it means they have not a single political argument left.*

> —MARGARET THATCHER

We can never lose sight of the fact that at times, we do err. We make bad decisions. We have flawed logic. We have gotten it wrong and will get it wrong. Hard to fathom, I know. But if we truly want feedback from colleagues and those we lead, we can't consider every criticism a personal attack. We have to listen to the negativity, assess it, learn from it, and move forward.

I had the pleasure of meeting author Aisha M. Johnson at a conference I spoke at in the United States. When speaking of emotional intelligence, she said:

Leaders who exhibit low self-control with regard to criticism are more likely to take the comments of their employees as personal attacks. Therefore, employees may run the risk of facing retaliation when they are merely providing insight and feedback on a specific issue or set of events.

I suppose the bottom line in all of this is that personal attacks will be launched, deserved or not. It comes with the executive-level turf. We have to shrug off the minor stuff and accept it as part of the job, right or wrong. We can mitigate much of that by not falling into traps that give our detractors ammunition to fire at us and by leading effectively on a day-to-day basis. We will build a loyal team of supporters that will head much of it off before it grows legs.

Life is 10% what happens to me and 90% of how I react to it.

—CHARLES R. SWINDOLL

Development and Selection

• • •

*I don't think you can make anyone a leader. I've seen
the Peter principle (promotion to a level beyond one's
competence) occur, and no reasonable amount of training or
development could help those people become good leaders.
To develop a great leader, you need to start with someone who
has the natural ability (work ethic, intelligence, judgment,
people skills), and you need to grow and develop that person
with education, opportunities, and coaching and mentoring.*

—Chief Jim Chu

Has any police department in the civilized world developed a promotional process that the majority of their personnel are satisfied with? I haven't heard of one, if it exists, and I've spoken at length with the current and past presidents of our members association about the issue. Despite their communication with police associations and unions around the world, they can't point to one either.

I am not aware of any police promotional process anywhere that identifies who the best leaders are. As a rule, many police promotional processes test the ability of candidates in terms of their knowledge of legislation, department policy, and management practices and their ability to tell a few lies about what they have done (or perhaps not done) to demonstrate specific competencies. How they treat people, their ability to make decisions, their communication ability in terms of their subordinates and peers, how much their colleagues trust them, whether they'll stand up and be counted for when the chips are down, and whether they'll take credit for the good work of others are in no way tested. The senior officers administering the process may think they know the individuals and their capabilities, but they often know only what the candidate allows them to know. What happens when the senior leaders aren't around can be a different world, but the people that these individuals lead—or will lead if further promoted—may see nothing but a train wreck every time some of these candidates open their mouths.

Résumés, exams, written exercises, oral presentations, in-basket exercises, panel interviews, 360 assessments, personnel-file reviews, or combinations thereof are the norm in most police agencies' promotional processes. Some level of psychological testing has been included intermittently in some services.

Assessment centers can be fairly effective tools but are really just a few days of intense testing using some or all of the methods above. They are also resource intensive and expensive.

Unfortunately—and this also makes me want to self-ignite—personnel files are often full of performance assessments that do not accurately reflect the individual and his or her performance or ability to deal with people.

> *The single biggest way to impact an organization is to focus on leadership development. There is almost no limit to the potential of an organization that recruits good people, raises them up as leaders and continually develops them.*

—JOHN C. MAXWELL, AS QUOTED BY DIANE LANDERS

When I was a brand-new corporal in uniform, I went into the performance review file in the detachment and pulled completed reviews on a few of the best and the worst officers, and some average ones, that other corporals supervised. I was truly shocked. There were very few differences between the comments regarding great officers and those that shouldn't have been allowed to carry a firearm. Wonderful officers didn't stand out when I read the documentation, nor did officers who rarely did anything but cause trouble. How unfair to the good members and how disappointing to the organization that the poor officers weren't being appropriately documented.

> *There's been considerable dialogue in this publication and others that annual employee performance evaluations are useless— unsatisfactory, demoralizing, at best a blunt instrument for a delicate job. I'd argue that employee evaluations are one of the most important but misapplied elements of management. As a long-time corporate manager, I'd say the problem is most often management— not the evaluation tool itself, but the way that tool is used. Why is it in any way objectionable for management to provide comprehensive assessments of how employees have performed over the course of the year? Isn't providing thorough feedback a key function of management? Unfortunately, all too often managers aren't doing their jobs properly, and in such instances the formal evaluation just reflects a broader problem.*
>
> —VICTOR LIPMAN

Unfortunately, during my time in the OPP, little emphasis was placed on previous performance evaluations during promotional processes, although it should have been. Based on the apparent lack of honest feedback in evaluations to that point, that may have actually been a good thing.

Many promotional interviews are competency based. Members appear before a panel and give examples of things they've allegedly done to demonstrate that they understand and practice various competencies. But is any of it true?

I sat on one panel where we interviewed a number of inspectors seeking a promotion to superintendent. Two of them told wonderful stories about being the pivot person in initializing and developing a key investigative unit some years prior. A municipal-police colleague sat on the panel as a guest by invitation and commented later that they both gave good examples but sounded very similar. The reality was they were citing the exact same example of forming the exact same unit, but neither of them had actually done it. I know the then inspector who did do it, and both of those individuals, sergeants at the time, were important but lower level players in a fifty-officer team when it occurred.

Therein lies a danger if the panel doesn't intimately know the history of the organization and the roles various people played. It's much better, in my view, to have written competency examples submitted by the candidates that can be verified accordingly.

On another occasion, just before a panel interview of four candidates for a promotion to superintendent, we were reviewing the résumés that had been submitted by the candidates. One of the résumés was actually my own document with another person's name on it. A year prior, he had competed against me for a position and was told later that his résumé wasn't good and to look at mine as an example to be guided by. I gave it to him when he asked me for it, and there it was in front of me again, with his name on it and the positional history changed to reflect his career. Every other aspect of the résumé regarding abilities, strengths, values, and experiences was mine. Needless to say, he didn't win the day.

But we have to ask ourselves, how valid is any process where key decisions to promote someone or not come down to who writes a good résumé? Or who can spin a tale of lies better than the next guy? If they have to make up examples or embellish them, then they have nothing to say that interests me.

I personally like 360 interviews or assessments so that peers, supervisors, and subordinates can comment anonymously as to leadership ability. They are time consuming and resource intensive as well, but they often tell a valid tale. Sometimes everyone interviewed loves the candidate and gives great examples of how the candidate functions. Other times it's the opposite. In some instances, supervisors love the individual, but all his or her peers and subordinates have nothing good to say. It is seldom the opposite scenario, however.

> *Unfortunately, tools like multi-rater leader assessments, climate assessments, and employee surveys are not commonly used in police organizations. The argument stems from a questionable belief that these "business tools" do not work or translate well to police organizations.*

—ROY E. ALSTON AND GEORGE E. REED

What I have quite seen often is trends in the responses. There may be the odd loyal peer, supervisor, or subordinate who sees the candidate as god-like, but the majority feel the opposite. Conversely, sometimes the odd person thinks the candidate is an idiot, but the trend among others is that he or she is very solid. A more accurate picture is painted.

The responses have to be anonymous, however, or it is all for naught. Some 360 processes allow the candidate to submit two names each of bosses, peers, and subordinates. I don't know about you, but in that situation, I'm not likely to give the names of anyone that I know I have had a conflict with. It's more effective to get a list of all their peers, supervisors, and direct reports and go randomly from there. I guarantee you that if properly done, it is an effective tool.

> *When I studied 82 CEOs who failed, I saw that the most common reason for failure was putting the wrong person in a job and then not dealing with the mismatch. I've seen CEOs take staff people who are in the succession pool because of their brilliance, energy, and business*

acumen, and give them big line jobs to test them. Then the CEOs get busy and lose sight that these inexperienced people are killing the company. In one situation the person put in charge of the largest division took the company into a negative position in less than two years.

—Ram Charan, "An Interview with Ram Charan," by Melinda Merino

Executive teams must be committed to ongoing leadership-development and leadership-selection strategies and should do all they can to support those they lead, at the same time being united to effectively meet the goals and objectives of the organization, through good times and bad. Anything less can bring failure.

There is a saying that God created man in his own image, and I think that this also applies to Leaders too, they want people who are just like themselves in key leadership positions, people who will support their views and make the same type of decisions, in order to maintain the status quo.

—Gordon Tredgold

As I said in other chapters, I watched people who were totally incapable of leading and were powerless to make the simplest of decisions, unless it was to make themselves look good, get promoted again and again. Sadly, as commissioner I approved some such promotions, against my better judgment, but I had to trust the deputy commissioner's decision. The paths of destruction some of these folks left were legendary. As they progressed through ranks and positions that they were unqualified for, they didn't dare promote anyone around them that wasn't similarly void of talent. Nor would they endorse anyone that might give them an honest answer or might know more about their work than they did. What a recipe for disaster.

True leaders want to be surrounded by people who know their jobs, understand organizational history and culture, will give them honest feedback, ideas, suggestions, and will help the team succeed. Loyalty is a must, but not blind loyalty; nothing good can come out from the latter.

We should also want to be supported by real leaders, those that will make the right decisions for the right reasons and will truly support their people, in good times and in bad, to help them develop as employees and into strong leaders themselves.

> *Your competitive advantage in the organisation comes down to growing leaders in every level faster than the competition. The person who sweeps up at the end of the day, an employee in IT, sales, and the one who answers the phone—every single person should start thinking like a leader. And that means no complaining or blaming, innovating, being great in what you do in contributing to the results of the organisation.*

> —Robin Sharma

Some employees, albeit the minority, are completely poisonous individuals. It's challenging enough to manage these people when they aren't in leadership positions. But when they rise to roles that allow them to broadly influence other employees, they can be malignancies. They can ruin people's professional lives, thereby adversely affecting their personal lives, and quite frankly destroy employees.

> *It can be demoralizing when toxic leaders continue to get promoted to levels of increasing responsibility. In a recent coaching course for newly promoted police supervisors, a police sergeant stated, "We all know who the bad leaders are, but the police department sticks that person away in a bureau out of sight where the bad leader can spend all his time studying for the next promotion exam. The bad leader scores high on the promotion exam, gets promoted and is released back on the troops to exact revenge."*

Toxic leaders leave in their wake an environment devoid of purpose,
motivation, and commitment. In short, toxic police leaders deny
police organizations and individual police officers true leadership.
Promoting and moving toxic leaders around the organization might be
an inappropriate organizational response that serves to enable them.

—Roy E. Alston and George E. Reed

I recall the promotion of an NCO into a commissioned-officer position a few years back, a decision of a local police-services board, which is next to impossible to negate. He managed up very well, had no respect from anyone around or below him, was a never a go-to guy even once in his entire career, but yet he "had a good interview." Every time I heard those words, I wanted to scream. But unfortunately that was the process of the day. The fact that in twenty-plus years he had done nothing, including make a good decision, was not a factor. He scored well on the interview, and those solid performers that competed against him didn't score as well even though we all knew they could do the job very well. They were not selected.

I got two phone calls in the five minutes following the announcement. One was a senior manager whom I trust, who said, "You have got to be kidding me. You'll end up yanking him out of there within a year." The second call was from the then police-association president, who said, "You have got to be kidding me. You'll end up yanking him out of there within a year." A snafu at its finest.

Thankfully, the individual didn't totally destroy the place. He had strong NCOs, and they managed to keep the ship on course.

What is the answer? All police services and public and private companies have faced or currently face the same challenges.

I am convinced that the focus on leadership development is in the
wrong place. Most initiatives focus on competencies, skill development
and techniques, which in some ways is like re-arranging the deck

chairs on a sinking ship. Good leaders need to become masters
of themselves before they can be masters of anything else.

—Ray Williams

One complicating factor that we sometimes face in policing, in particular within the OPP, a large deployed police service, is that some great performers and natural leaders do not want to be promoted. They cite reasons such as these:

* "It's not worth the money."
* "I don't want to move."
* "It's not a club that I want to be a member of."

And sadly, many others have tried and failed because of faulty processes in the past and become frustrated. They've made the conscious effort not to put themselves through it again. We have failed some good folks, and ultimately our organizations, by allowing that to happen.

As the world becomes more uncertain with significant
emerging economies, future leaders will need to equip
themselves with a number of leadership competences
and skills to enable them to deliver their vision.
The new Shell Leadership model provides a focus on the leadership
qualities needed for the future. The qualities are defined by four key
attributes starting with "Authenticity" to inspire professionalism
and resilience, "Growth" to ensure leaders capture opportunities to
generate value to the organization, "Collaboration" to build strong
partnerships and "Performance" to deliver extraordinary business
outcomes by investing in people so that teams are fit for the future.

—Shell Corporation

In my view—and I totally blame myself for not fully implementing this in the OPP during my tenure—effective leadership-development processes are key, closely followed by promotional processes that truly identify the best of the best. Thankfully, the OPP is moving the yardsticks ahead very well under its current leadership.

In his *Forbes* magazine article "The #1 Reason Leadership Development Fails," Mike Myatt says,

> Over the years, I've observed just about every type of leadership development program on the planet. And the sad thing is, most of them don't even come close to accomplishing what they were designed to do—build better leaders.
>
> The solution to the leadership training problem is to scrap it in favor of development. Don't train leaders, coach them, mentor them, disciple them, and develop them, but please don't attempt to train them. Training is something leaders dread and will try and avoid, whereas they will embrace and look forward to development. Development is nuanced, contextual, collaborative, fluid, and above all else, actionable.
>
> If what you desire is a robotic, static thinker—train them. If you're seeking innovative, critical thinkers—develop them.

Coaching and mentoring are valid developmental techniques, but it's critical that the coaches and mentors portray the values of the organization and have the credibility and talent to effectively support the development of others, including the patience and communication skills that are paramount.

In fairness to Mike Myatt above, there are good training programs available out there, but many are expensive and require costly travel and accommodation costs. Most of them also tend to focus on management theories and practices as well as emerging issues, change processes, and other important topics, more so than leadership. I know of one example that has been well thought of by all participants that I am aware of: the Rotman School of Management at the University of Toronto. They run a three-week Police Leadership Program that was developed in partnership with the OACP. It covers a plethora of relevant topics to police managers, both uniform and civilian, including leadership. Many senior police executives address the group at various times regarding their views on leadership and personal lessons learned. However, without effective development programs in home agencies, even the best of Rotman's students may fail on the job from a leadership perspective.

I'm sure there are many more, so I would never rule out training, but it cannot be done in isolation of a solid leadership-development program.

Deputy minister Ian Davidson said, "Not all people with natural leadership abilities become leaders, and certainly not great leaders. That takes time, experience, mentoring, and a commitment to learn! Having said that, almost anyone can learn and develop leadership skills if he or she is interested and committed. The greatest leaders are great leaders because of a commitment to lifelong learning. In either case, the common denominator is the human development necessary to become leaders."

Police Associations: "Can't Live with Them..."

• • •

An open and mutually respectful relationship,
with honesty and open communication between the
principals, affords the best prospect for success.

—CHIEF ROBERT F. LUNNEY

IN THE MAJORITY OF CANADIAN police services, save the RCMP and
most (but not all) First Nations police services, the police association is
the bargaining group for the NCOs and civilian personnel. They generally bargain with the municipality or the provincial government (in the
case of both the OPP and the Sûreté du Québec) in terms of salary, pen-
sion, and benefits. Most often during the bargaining process, the chief,
commissioner/director, or designee is an advisor to the employer for the
purposes of working-condition issues and the operational impacts of
relevant bargaining articles related to hours of work (shift scheduling),
overtime allowances, call-back provisions, two-member patrols, and
more. He or she is not the employer so is not the sole decision maker on
these issues.

In most cases, the police chief wants the same result for the membership as the bargaining group (association) does: fair financial compensation, good working conditions, safety, effective leadership, fair processes, and more.

I interviewed former president of the OPPA Jim Christie who said,

> Trust and integrity are the cornerstones essential for positive and productive working relationships. A high trust relationship fosters the freedom to quickly solve problems in an economical manner, both fiscally and emotionally. Trust also involves respecting the other person and their role, even in the midst of conflict. It is important to never lose sight of the common goal, what is best for the police service and the welfare of the entire police association membership. Integrity, both personal and professional, is essential and foundational for both leadership teams, without it trust cannot exist. Regular communication is key because surprise is not your friend; it is actually your enemy.

Although police wages in Canada have risen to the point that policing is an extremely expensive business to be in, and some experts would suggest that Canadian police officers have almost priced themselves out of the market, it's hard to imagine that any police chief would want the employees of that police service to be lower paid than employees in other police departments. That would do nothing for the attraction, retention, or morale of current and prospective employees.

The union must be made alive to the fact that 82-plus percent of the police budget is labor, so there is very little room for discretionary spending. Further, that unsustainable wage increases will likely result in staffing losses (at least by attrition) and fewer opportunities for advancement and special service, as the force is pared down to a basic patrol function in order to exist. At the same time, the pressure is on the chief to make sure sufficient pressure is kept up on boards and councils to fund the force at an acceptable level, to ensure (1)

there is an adequate level of policing to protect the community,
(2) the members are compensated competitively with other forces,
maintaining morale, and (3) there is no reduction in staff or capacity.

—Chief Dan Maluta

The police associations in Canada, particularly the larger ones and their provincial and federal voices, such as the Police Association of Ontario (PAO) and the Canadian Police Association (CPA), carry significant political weight. In fact, they are most often much more influential politically than the various senior officer associations and the provincial and national chiefs of police associations (OACP, CACP, etc.).

There's no doubt that provincial and federal governments will take advice from the provincial and national chiefs of police services on legislative reform issues as well as other public-safety matters, but the chiefs are but a small voice on the provincial and national scales. At times they may be diametrically opposed to their police associations on controversial issues such as suspension of officers without pay. On others, the members and their chiefs may be completely in sync.

Comparatively, however, the member associations swing momentous clout, given their membership numbers and the collateral influence those members can have on their families, friends, and neighbors—voters all. They may be able to influence elections by not endorsing parties or specific candidates—municipally, provincially, or federally—that do not support legislative or policy positions taken by the associations.

Employee organizations and police unions have become politically
active; some unions have political action committees and are
involved in endorsing and lobbying local, state, and national
candidates. In addition, union members have become astute in using
the media to seek support from the public on their positions.

—*IACP News*, "Predicting and Surviving
a No-Confidence Vote"

On a more individual police-service basis, member associations have at times virtually declared war on their police chiefs over real or perceived conflicts. Some chiefs have not survived resulting votes of no confidence; others have. Regardless, these public quarrels often sideline more important public-safety issues as the media circus runs its course, and at the very least they put tremendous stress on the affected police leaders, whether deserved or not.

The *IACP News* article "Predicting and Surviving a No-Confidence Vote" also says,

> A vote of no confidence is an action traditionally put before a parliament by the opposition in the hope of defeating or embarrassing a government. Over the past three decades, police employee organizations and unions have adopted a similar practice to achieve their goals.
>
> The unions have found the no-confidence vote to be one of the most popular, powerful, effective political tools at their disposal, using this means increasingly to apply political pressure to influence employment contracts, wages, and the negotiation process; management policy and decision making by management; and the removal of a police chief from office.
>
> Although a no-confidence vote is a severe test of a chief's leadership, it is an event that the chief can survive.

A number of years back, the chief of a large municipal service in Ontario may well have been subjected to physical surveillance by police-association members in a vain attempt to gather some sort of dirt on him. Totally unsubstantiated allegations were also made against one of his children in an effort to taint his professional image. Sad but true, and a stark reality.

More recently, in another large Ontario service, the conflict between the chief and the association resulted in a number of allegations being made against him for such things as trying to influence officers away from laying charges against a personal acquaintance and other criminal matters. Lengthy independent investigations followed, and the chief was cleared of the allegations, but the situation undoubtedly took its toll on the chief, both professionally and personally. He has since retired.

As such troubling events occur, are real community-safety matters being properly addressed, or do they take a back seat to the controversy? Does the ongoing media coverage negatively impact police leaders' public credibility? Is the harm irreparable? Does the subsequent media play not taint police leaders, and maybe police services across the board, in the eyes of the public? Despite the eventual clearing of the allegations, often the stigma sadly wears on, and the positive findings do not receive the same media airtime as the negative allegations did. The widespread and growing use of social media has increased the ability of associations, individuals, and effectively anyone else to assassinate people's characters exponentially.

Former OPPA president Jim Christie also told me, "There will be times of disagreement that result in tension. During these critical times it is imperative that each party strives to understand the other's point of view, as well as the varying professional and generational perspectives, while staying true to their core values and beliefs. Collaboration does not necessitate both parties agreeing agreeably, a healthy, respectful tension is important for long-term success. Working together toward proactive detection and problem solving should eliminate or minimize the need for third party decisions. Good leadership is equally committed to the task at hand and concern for people."

In the case of Chief Rick Deering, complaints against him several years ago were front-page news for weeks and months, but when he was cleared of the allegations and then launched a civil lawsuit against the conspirators, little media coverage resulted. That left Rick in a bad position: his contract was not renewed, and he had to fight the resulting cross-Canada stigma as he sought other police-chief positions.

These comments are not meant to suggest that police associations are united in resorting to dirty tricks. Far from it. These cases are the exception and not the rule. However, police leaders need to be open to the possibility of such activity as they cross swords with association/union leaders on key issues.

Deputy minister Ian Davidson said,

> Finding mutually beneficial solutions was always my goal. But it is always important to understand that the association by design will have different perspectives on any issue. You cannot take this personally. In fact you must recognize it as a healthy reality for the most part.
>
> This often meant finding compromise when required and expecting concessions when needed. My goal was to be clear, consistent, and fair in trying to represent the public we serve as well as protecting the members of the organization. This requires building trust and getting to know each on a more personal and less clinical level.

The crux of my views on management and association relationships is not about dealing with blatant personal attacks but about developing sound and respectful working relationships for the betterment of the organization as a whole. As leaders, we are generally at the mercy of association leaders in terms of their ethical behavior and personal agendas, and unfortunately, that is often merely a function of random chance. But let's face it: it works both ways. I suggest that the majority of association or union leaders truly want the same for their members as the leadership team wants, and will engage in meaningful dialogue to achieve those mutual goals.

In his paper *Bargaining Units vs. Management: Are Police Unions Necessary?*, Captain Carmen J. Sirolli Sr. states, "In a perfect world, both police managers and police union leaders want to work together to make their community a safer place to live. Unfortunately, we do not live in a perfect world. Police managers and police union leaders regularly work side by side as law enforcement officers but they do not communicate regularly on labor-management issues that arise each day."

Effective communication is key to developing and maintaining trust. Appreciating others' views and political nuances isn't always easy but must be strived for. It's important that it remain a two-way street. Some association leaders can't handle the word "no." Conversely, some leaders consistently think their authority is being challenged and want to dig in and fight to the death over trivial and non-precedent-setting matters.

Commissioner Giuliano Zaccardelli states, "The key is an honest, mutually respectful, and open relationship. Both sides must understand that they have much in common in looking after the interests and well-being of the employees of the organization. However, there also has to be the recognition that the chief or commissioner has an equally important responsibility to ensure the health and survival of the organization and that the will of the citizens and political masters must be considered, as they are the ultimate authority over the police organization."

I have been truly fortunate over my career as a leader in terms of my personal relationship with the OPPA and union leadership. I'd estimate that on 95 percent of the issues, we have been on the same page. At times the OPPA raised valid issues that OPP management needed to address. Individual supervisors or managers may have made a decision that was not fair to an employee or was in total conflict with the collective agreement, or perhaps they did not articulate the reason for a decision particularly well. We could fix those things and move on. At other times, the OPPA raised issues based on the facts as presented to them by a member, and when OPP management delved further into the matter, they found the situation had in fact been handled properly, and the OPPA accepted that. This required conversation, not just e-mails, letters, and text messages but face-to-face (or at least telephone) conversations.

In more-isolated instances, management and the association reach a point where they do not agree on the course of action, and a grievance is filed by the association. Those situations run their course, an arbitrator rules one way or another, and life goes on. In my view, the goal should be to keep those situations—which are taxing in terms of both person-hours and legal costs—to a minimum.

A lot of this can be effectively dealt with in a proactive manner. Regular meetings among senior police and association executive groups just to discuss emerging concerns or direction are a must. One-to-one meetings between the chief and president and genuine "heads-up" dialogue on political issues of concern, such as budget constraints, operational imperatives, and leadership change, are critical as well. Then proper consultation on potential policy changes that may impact processes, uniforms, equipment, or training—whether there is a bargained agreement to do so or not—are paramount to good labor relations.

> *Meet, meet, meet, even when there is nothing to meet about. The relationship needs to be built when times are good to help deal with the turmoil that will come.*

> —SENATOR VERN WHITE

In a suggested test from the National Executive Institute Associates article "The Chief and the Union: Building a Better Relationship," readers are invited to rate themselves regarding the validity of these statements about them and to seek the feedback of others to determine whether their leadership styles are conducive to developing a solid relationship with the police union (association). How would people rate you in terms of whether these statements are true about *you*?

1. Communicates in an open, genuine manner
2. Conducts all transactions with the union in a professional, respectful manner
3. Believes in the basic values of the department
4. Is willing to admit to own mistakes
5. Works consistently to inspire pride in the police department
6. Keeps elected officials abreast of controversial labor-management issues
7. Avoids acting like a big shot or a phony

8. Shows a high degree of personal integrity in dealing with others
9. Gives people the support and encouragement they need
10. Exhibits genuine interest in employees
11. Recognizes the union's right to exist and represent its members
12. Avoids playing favorites
13. Strives to develop an atmosphere of trust and cooperation
14. Encourages bottom-up communication
15. Controls emotions during labor disputes
16. Treats people with respect and dignity regardless of their positions in the department
17. Seeks ways to open avenues of communication with elected and appointed officials
18. Shows care and concern for employees
19. Develops a personal power base in the community
20. Leads by example
21. Speaks out publicly on behalf of employees regarding economic and other workplace concerns
22. Agrees to disagree agreeably
23. Focuses on problems not personalities
24. Resolves union concerns and criticisms internally without engaging the media
25. Acts on personal beliefs as to what is right as opposed to what is politically correct

They are thought-provoking points that we should all strive to make part of our leadership ethos.

Police-association relationships transcend operational boundaries in unusual ways when it comes to policing significant events. When planning for large events that require a significant deployment of personnel and equipment, like a G8 situation, police-service management and association leadership better be engaged in dialogue from day one. Issues will arise daily, and misinformation and rumor-mill challenges will derail the planning process throughout if not proactively addressed. The front-end involvement of the association will undoubtedly help quell much of that.

In the case of our Y2K planning exercise for the New Year's Eve rollover to 2000, the OPP established a team to ensure we were totally prepared from both operational and infrastructure perspectives. On the one hand, we had media predictions of mass critical-infrastructure failures, potential terrorist attacks, armed survivalists digging in for Armageddon, and airliners falling to earth. On the other hand, we had to ensure detachments and communication centers had backup power, a cruiser-fueling strategy was developed, and sufficient police personnel were deployed across the entire province to address whatever actually occurred. Communities were frightened and needed help to prepare as well as confidence in our ability to keep them safe. Our own members' families were understandably concerned about their personal safety and the safety of their loved ones who happened to be OPP personnel, and vice versa. Though the event could have turned out to be as unexciting as Geraldo Rivera's public opening of Al Capone's vault, we couldn't leave a single stone unturned for our communities and for our members.

We decided from the start to invite both of our then bargaining groups, the OPPA and the Ontario Public Service Employees Union (OPSEU), to assign key executive members to our Operational Planning Committee and others to our various working groups. They had input throughout, were aware of why we were doing certain things a certain way, understood our rationale for not doing some specific things, and most importantly, communicated all of that and more to their members. In turn they brought members' concerns to the table and were able to get back to the membership with real-time information in an expedient way. That methodology had a tremendously positive impact on our progress and on our ultimate success.

We took similar approaches in a number of large deployments, including the Vancouver Olympic Games in 2010. In fact, in the case of Vancouver, we allowed OPPA representatives to attend and monitor working and living conditions to ensure our members were being appropriately looked after.

*Distrust often leads to an "us and them mentality," as well as a lack
of respect for the roles that individuals play, placing both organizations
on a continuum somewhere between mild dysfunction and complete
paralysis. Leadership focused on self-preservation is toxic and personal
agendas block goals for "the greater good," often resulting in irreparable
damage. It is imperative for police leadership to focus on the critical
issues of public service, member welfare and financial responsibility.
All roads lead back to integrity and trust. The Association leader
must be satisfied that the service leadership is acting in the best
interests of the public we serve and the members who provide the
service. Any belief that their actions deviate from these principles
and may be straying into the area of self-interest, or the toxic
veil of nepotism or compromise of public or member welfare, can
destroy the faith put in the police leader by the Association.*

—Former OPPA president Jim Christie

Every modern police department has a variety of internal committees
that regularly discuss various organizational matters and try to determine
the best approach or course of action. Sometimes these committees have
decision-making power, and at other times they simply make recommen-
dations to the executive of the police service. Such standing committees
might include clothing and equipment, fleet, employee relations, IT governance, and training. At times, ad hoc committees or working groups are
necessary to address new issues, such as weapon and vehicle selections,
shift scheduling, and more.

Obviously, tragedy will, sadly, strike police services and many private
sector companies over time. When it does, the agency's management team
and the association/union leadership must be in lockstep in actions and in
messaging.

In planning police funerals—something that large police organizations like the OPP and the Toronto Police Service have gotten way too
good at—the police association has always been front and center with the

planning teams. The loss of a member is not a time for political agendas or divisiveness. It is a time for unity and strength. If an element of cooperation, understanding, and, most importantly, trust is not already in place between the association and police-service leaders, it can become a chink in the armor of that collective strength.

During one funeral for an OPP member under my command that was killed in the line of duty, big-*P* politics were hugely at play. An interim premier was in place, an election was looming, and precisely where members of the governing party and the leaders of the opposing parties were assigned to sit in the church became a ridiculous issue. Everyone wanted to be front and center with the grieving family for maximum media exposure. We dealt with it and moved on, always erring on the side of what was best for the family and colleagues of the fallen officer. The smaller-*P* politics between OPP senior management and the OPPA were nonexistent, however. We were completely galvanized and put any unrelated burning issues aside for those several days.

In addition, when highly charged operational challenges occur, like police shootings, perceived or real mishandlings of situations, and those occasional behavioral black eyes that also draw public and media scrutiny, it is difficult for the public to fully understand the line that exists between the police and association leaderships. Messaging can and will differ, and it must. At times, senior police management has to take a higher road in how strongly it defends involved members, of course always erring on the side of allowing the investigative, legal and adjudicative processes to run their course. Firm controls are often placed on a chief regarding what he or she can say about an ongoing investigation, especially one where a member of the public is seriously injured or killed as a result of police action. The association has more flexibility to speak and less control placed on their communications. However, a good relationship between the two entities and an understanding what both will likely say and why will most often prevent a publicly aired conflict and a management versus association appearance. Personalities, egos, and agendas will be put to the test at times, thus the need for the establishment of a respectful and trusting relationship prior to those dark days.

Captain Carmen J. Sirolli Sr. also said,

> According to the authors of *Police Labor-Management Relations* (vol. II, 2006), members of both sides of the bargaining table should learn to communicate, with the following suggestions:
> Have weekly or monthly meetings.
> Invite each other to breakfast.
> Get together to discuss what is going on within the agency over a cup of coffee.
> Start out by talking about small issues that had been going on during the week and what could be done to improve the department.
> Stand by each other on mutual concerns in the community; doing this in an open forum could help develop open communications.

Chief Bill McCormack, who had four children who became police officers, one of whom is the current president of the Toronto Police Association, said the following: "Being in constant communication is a vital need. Be able to have a mutual understanding and a respect. Recognition that both sides are working toward the benefit of the officers. During my service I always said that on joining the police force, I was sworn in as a constable, and I remained a constable throughout."

The troublesome conflict that inevitably occurs between the association and police-service leaders is when the association feels obligated to defend the interests of one or two members when their actions have embarrassed, betrayed, or simply disappointed the entire membership of the police force.

For example, when a member is convicted of an egregious criminal offense, such as sexual assault, theft, fraud, perjury, impaired driving, or God forbid something worse, the association often defends the member against dismissal. Although that member will forever be a liability and most often useless to the police service, as he or she holds a vacancy that a useful employee could fill, the association will argue that he or she can still fill a role in the organization. That boggles my mind, and I will always disagree with the association on such matters. At the same time, some association leaders almost always defend the lazy, the unproductive, and those that continually let their colleagues down. It makes little to no sense to me, but therein lies the proverbial rub. There is no answer to that dilemma, unfortunately.

An article called "Police Labor Relations: Interest-Based Problem-Solving and the Power of Collaboration," from the US Department of Justice *Community Policing Dispatch*, states,

> Not only have few articles been written about police unions, only a few of those published discuss the positive role unions can and do play in working with management to solve problems, implement change, make reforms, and handle crises. It is small wonder that initiatives that attempt to engage both police union leaders and managers in efforts to work together are relatively rare, even though many of the challenges confronting police departments today affect them both.
>
> Issues such as budget cuts, privatization and civilianization, recruitment, health care, and pension benefits, to name a few, affect everyone in the departments. To most effectively address and resolve the challenges facing law enforcement agencies, union and management need to work together.
>
> ...A joint approach to problem solving and planning to address issues of mutual concern, in particular, is more enduring than the more traditional adversarial approach. Moreover, participants were able to see that the success that comes from using a joint process is often magnified by increased trust between union and management and by an increased confidence in their ability to achieve successful outcomes. This trust can also be beneficial when future issues arise.

The bottom line here is this: Police associations and unions are not going to go away, nor should they. They have done wonderful things for policing in terms of working conditions, salaries, and benefits. We truly cannot live without them. They have tremendous political clout that you can use to benefit the organization in a variety of ways. You can work with them or enter into a nonstop adversarial relationship with them that will not be in the best interests of the police service, its people, or ultimately the community being served. That will be nothing but a stressful and draining back-and-forth environment that helps no one. A collaborative relationship takes a concerted effort on the part of both organizational and association leaderships. It requires give and take, the biting of tongues, and a commitment to doing what is right for the right reasons.

If you are trying your best but the association leadership is continually poking a stick in your eye, the membership will see that, and at least in a Canadian police-labor context, I don't believe the broader membership would support such a method of operation. We collectively have good people across the board, save the militant few that have crappy attitudes and we probably shouldn't have hired to begin with. We can't throw the baby out with the bathwater by making decisions that harm the overwhelming majority of our employees who are good folks to get back at a few bad apples.

I realize that I am speaking only of police bargaining groups here, given my experience, but I'm sure there are numerous parallels between these examples and the relationship issues between private company and government-entity executives and their unions or bargaining groups.

Regardless of vocation, as a leader, you can do only your part to make the relationship beneficial, but it is well worth the effort.

Two-way communication that incorporates both actively listening to your executives and inspiring them to work together with you is vital. I seek to find ways to not only achieve our goals but also help them achieve theirs. Sometimes when those goals seem to be at cross-purposes, the ability to trust one another and to communicate well will help each have a respectful understanding of when it is necessary to disagree but find common ground to move the organization as a whole toward a workable agreement. It is important for chiefs to not only know and understand their role and perspective but also for the association to see them as willing to listen to what is important to the association members so that they are more willing to work with chiefs rather than against.

—CHIEF LAURIE HAYMAN

Media: Problem
or Solution?

• • •

*Police and Media Relations has been a concern for both the police and
media for decades. How to bridge that gap has puzzled brilliant minds in
both professions. For law enforcement, the policy has always been to give
as little information as possible. The media is believed to be the enemy
who is always looking to destroy the credibility of officers. The media
feels that law enforcement is always hiding information. Media feel that
they are the ears of the public and it is their duty to "tell it like it is."*

—LARRY JONES

MANY POLICE LEADERS—MEN AND WOMEN who have seen the worst society has to offer, confronted gunman, dealt with youthful victims of hor-
rific crimes, and led the charge to deal with massive and often dangerous
challenges—would much rather face an armed and deranged serial killer
than a smart reporter with a camera and a microphone.

We traditionally haven't placed enough focus on effectively dealing
with the media. We train our members extensively to use firearms, but
generally we don't give them any media training until they reach a certain
rank or position. I don't mean to trivialize the use of deadly force, but
as police executives, we probably cringe more often—and pay out more

money in lawsuits—over inappropriate comments made in the media than we do over the inappropriate use of firearms.

I truly think that many officers are afraid of getting grilled on a difficult situation. Others are fearful that they'll be asked about something they are unprepared for. Many just don't like certain reporters or media outlets, or perhaps they abhor all media, and others simply have that age-old fear of public speaking.

Some police leaders have been offended by specific reporters or media outlets, rightly or wrongly, and have then declared that they will never do interviews with those folks again. I understand their thinking to some degree, but I'd much prefer to work through those issues as they arise and reach a common ground moving forward rather than have specific news outlets or reporters planning my or the police services' demise. Having said that, try as I may, I know that there's one reporter out there who has fantasies about me hanging naked over a crocodile pit. All we can do as leaders is try our best.

The media operate under the guiding principle that the public has a right to know, and they are generally correct. However, that right does not extend to information that may jeopardize an investigation, identify an informant or a victim, Freedom of Information legislation, or harm the integrity of any judicial proceedings. At other times we are asked by next of kin of deceased persons not to identify them in the press for personal reasons. We and the media also have to abide by the rules contained in legislation such as the Freedom of Information and Privacy Act and the Youth Criminal Justice Act, which detail specific information that none of us can legally release in most circumstances.

The media should also report in an accurate and unbiased way. Sometimes we are frustrated when we read articles or editorials that we feel are antipolice or inaccurate. That will never change, unfortunately, but by doing our best to provide accurate information to the media, reporting inaccuracies will occur less often, as will any biases that may exist. If we don't tell them anything or if we mislead them, they will dig to find enough information to pass on and may end up printing or airing information that is not true. That is never a good thing.

Chief Gerald W. Garner has written numerous books on police leadership and the challenges therein. He states,

Contrary to the opinions of some, law-enforcement leaders and journalists actually can work together effectively. But police leaders and journalists looking to nourish mutually beneficial working relationships first have some baggage to overcome. In the "bad old days," many reporters tended to see cops as often brutal, frequently lazy, and not very bright. Police bosses were seen as evasive, if not outright liars. They were viewed as cynical and secretive.

For their part, police viewed journalists as bleeding hearts who were predisposed to believe a crook over a cop. Reporters were seen as self-appointed police experts who knew nothing about real police work or the dangers cops faced. Some law-enforcement officers saw reporters as hating all authority figures. In that atmosphere, it is hardly surprising that law-enforcement leaders and reporters viewed each other as enemies. In that environment, misbehavior on both sides was hardly a rarity.

In reality, police and reporters have a lot in common. Both law-enforcement agencies and the media are highly visible, powerful institutions. Both professions attract ambitious, strong-minded employees who possess a strong sense of justice and a desire to help others. Both professions are frequently criticized by the public they serve and are highly sensitive to that criticism. The professionals of both can be highly defensive and feel that they are poorly understood by their critics. Both professions are sometimes secretive about their operations and their methods for gathering information. Professionals in both endeavors see themselves as vital to the public welfare.

When I was the director of the OPP CIB many years ago, a veteran journalist from northern Ontario called me to set up a meeting in North Bay.

This guy was the salt of the earth, highly respected by media colleagues and the public. He'd take an occasional light shot at us when we had it coming, but he was always a strong supporter of the police.

He outlined a situation weeks prior where a man had murdered his wife in a small community and then set the house on fire. Uniformed OPP members, tactical officers, canine units, detectives, and our helicopter had descended on the town. Roads were blocked off, and it was obvious to anyone with a molecule of brain matter that something big and ugly was going on. Our media-relations officer's response to his query as to what the heck was happening was "No comment." When I delved into it further, the poor officer had been directed by a CIB detective inspector who was en route to the scene, "Don't give the press anything."

The point of the veteran reporter was simple: He said that when we give the media nothing in a situation where something significant has obviously occurred, they'll find something to report on. They'll talk to neighbors, local community leaders, or kids walking by with their dogs, and they *will* report something. The largely inaccurate information that they will release may then create false public perceptions and unfairly prejudice any resulting judicial process.

That was clearly a situation where the media-relations officer or an NCO could have easily scripted a few key messages to address any public-safety concerns and appease the media in the short term, and more details could have then been provided when the tense situation had ended. That error was not the fault of the poor officer at the scene but in the blind order to "say nothing." As a result, we made several changes to our protocols to prevent similar situations from occurring in future.

Chief Clive Weighill said, "My greatest setback came when I was attempting to argue a certain position in the media when there was no need. On many occasions, it is better to take the criticism, acknowledge it, and move on. I've learned the more you keep an issue alive, the more people jump into a negative discourse, which in turn keeps it in the public arena longer."

Ari Fleischer, who was press secretary to then president George W. Bush, addressed the FBI National Executive Institute in 2012 regarding police-media relations. He said, "Define your message positively. Write the headline that you'd like to see in the paper following the interview, then don't give an answer that creates a different headline."

There are many occasions when we need the media's cooperation in communicating important information to the public. Warnings of area predators, requests for witnesses, missing-person information, community dangers, significant police events, identifying human remains, locating wanted persons or suspects, and so on are all examples of items that need to be communicated to the public in a timely way. We can't ask that of the media and then stonewall them on information they are seeking from us if we have no defensible legal, moral, or operational reason for doing so.

We also need to market our people and our agencies. In the competitive policing environment we presently find ourselves in, and at a time when rising police costs are top of mind with elected officials, it's important that we do all we can to ensure the public sees and hears of the things our police services do so well. Significant arrests, drug sweeps, finding lost people, and saving lives are all things that the larger media outlets will print or air. In the smaller media markets, many of the occurrences that our people successfully handle every day are worth publishing by the local papers and airing by the local radio and TV stations.

The taxpayers we serve and the community leaders that additionally hold our purse strings need and deserve to know what we're doing, why, and how. In addition, a big part of effectively communicating our successes is to assure them that we're out there and keeping them safe.

Larry Jones also said,

Studies have been concluded that suggest that improved media relations could positively influence the effectiveness of law enforcement agencies.

The new philosophy can only result in positives for law enforcement. Agencies can still restrict crucial information while appeasing media outlets. The need for the media to start a "witch hunt" would be greatly diminished if information was readily accessible to them. The anti-police sentiment could be overwhelmed by accurate and timely information given by police.

Enhanced media relations could assist law enforcement to achieve its primary mission which is the reduction in crime. The media can paint a picture of a department that is honest and professional or one that is corrupt and not trustworthy. The public obtains its impression of police through media outlets. If they only hear positives they will gain a trust and confidence with the local agency. There is probably no way to gage the impact of positive community relations on the reduction of crime, but it is proven that unhappy citizens will not cooperate.

It was discovered that a positive relationship gained public confidence and led the public to accept budgetary requests. It cited honesty, candor and access as key elements needed to secure public approval (Karchmer, 2002).

When the premier of Ontario called a press conference at the provincial legislature in July 2010, the media gathered, anxiously awaiting the announcement as to who would be replacing Commissioner Julian Fantino. They were all gathered in the main hallway outside the Media Gallery, and a door opened. Out walked Premier Dalton McGuinty, Minister Rick Bartolucci, and little ole me.

My daughter Stephanie, who also works for the Ontario Public Service, was standing among the reporters and heard one say, "There's the premier, there's the minister…but who's that other guy?" Despite the fact that I was a deputy commissioner with thirty-two years of service, the media group did not know me. They all knew Julian Fantino, but they didn't know the kid from the Sault.

The media loved and hated Julian. He'd always give them the sound bite that would grab headlines, but sometimes they wouldn't like his message. I'm not being critical of him at all, but to the media, the OPP was all about Julian Fantino at that time. Even when he was away and one of the deputies was sitting in, when the media called on an issue and learned he was out of the country but that a deputy commissioner was prepared to speak to the matter, the reporter would often say, "I'll wait for Julian." Once again, no slight to Julian, but the media should know the deputy commissioners and deputy chiefs very well. If they don't, then the deputies need to do what they can to get some profile. Not to further their careers but to laud their people and at times to pass on critical information to the public. If at some point they will be trying to reassure the public on a critical matter, they better earn some public trust and some scar tissue along the way.

Chief Gerald W. Garner also said, "Police leaders should also realize that it is not all about them. They should maintain a sense of modesty when dealing with reporters. They should know that their media contacts are seeking the insight and information they possess; the media are not out to make them famous. They should understand that when they are gone, the media will lavish equal attention on their replacements." That message should equally apply to executives in any vocation.

It's not rocket science to develop key messaging and stick to it in preparation for an interview. You have to think dirty and assume that the reporters will too. Consider the audience, the concerns that certain facets of the listeners/readers will have, and address them up front when feasible, as well as what they really want to know in terms of reassuring them and their confidence in the police. "We have the situation stabilized. There's no further threat to public safety. We will fully investigate the incident." These are all things the public wants to hear from its police service.

At times there are perceptions of police mishandling of a situation, and let's face it: sometimes the perceptions reflect reality. We can't be afraid to assure the public that we will get to the bottom of it and will deal with any disciplinary issues or operational shortcomings. Follow-up from there will be key. You can say, "We will debrief the operation as we always do, and we will examine our policies and training and make changes accordingly." Or in other cases, "We will conduct a full investigation into what occurred and take appropriate action from there."

Bear in mind that you will be asked down the road what your review or investigation revealed and what action was taken. Your credibility will be on the line when that time comes.

Risk-adverse legal counsel will often try to talk you out of saying anything that may indicate liability. We pay them to conduct the risk analysis and provide that direction. But there are times when you know full well that your folks erred and that you will be writing a check; the only question is how many zeroes will be on it. Do not avoid at any cost admitting mistakes and apologizing to individuals of families that suffered or were somehow disadvantaged by that error. You don't have to throw your people under the bus, but admitting organizationally that you are truly sorry that something occurred and you'll do your best to make sure that it never happens again will undoubtedly restore stakeholder confidence in your organization.

Obviously, the above situations often do not see the chief as the spokesperson, but there are times that he or she should be. That right time and place for the leader of the organization to be front and center is for you to decide. But without a doubt there are times that the public and your own people will want to see the "big guy," and so they should.

During my part-time employment as the CTV television network's public-safety analyst since retiring from policing, I have seen the media outlet's side through a different lens. There are certainly times where saying a bit more and having the comment come from a senior police leader quells public and media concern on the legitimacy (or lack thereof) of a brewing serious issue. Stonewalling or having some poor media-relations constable provide uninformed comments often leads to a lack of trust unnecessarily.

We live in a multimedia world, and if we want to maximize our communication ability, we must use a multimedia approach. More people probably follow social media networks now than watch major news networks. Capitalize on that, but don't forget the local paper, the local news station, or the major outlets at the same time. Hit them all in an effort to ensure that very few community members will miss hearing and reading your message.

Most police agencies are now communicating the good and the bad through social media the moment something happens. Soliciting the public's help in solving a crime or finding someone can be done in mere seconds. Traffic congestion, various threats to public safety—boom, the messages are out there. No print or telecast deadlines, plain and simple. In addition, significant issues that require a coordinated communication strategy should almost always include a social media element.

In 2012 and 2013 Canada faced a wave of protests by First Nations people dubbed the "Idle No More" movement, the vast majority of which were very peaceful. However, they taxed police resources and led to much frustration in some affected non–First Nations community members. The media coverage became very judgmental of the apparent nonaggressive action of the police, including the OPP—which oversaw the majority of the protests—and of me personally.

The chief of the Sarnia Police Service was under attack for not arresting some protestors that closed a railway spur. The OPP did not immediately jump in and arrest the protestors, who blocked a national rail line in eastern Ontario. Nor did they immediately arrest those protesting on a number of highways across Ontario and beyond. Although we fully appreciated the concerns of motorists who were unfairly held up or rail passengers that had to disembark and travel by bus, we also knew that we were at a critical juncture with these growing protests.

Hard-line protestors were taking over the agenda. What had started as a grassroots protest by some First Nations women in western Canada was taking on a life of its own as more-militant protestors—who were hoping for a fight—jumped on the backs of the well-meaning community members, and all hell was on the verge of breaking loose across the nation. The peaceful agenda of many was being hijacked by the radical few.

Allowing protestors to conduct peaceful protests and working through those events without a show of force carried the day. If violence had erupted between protestors and those opposed to being inconvenienced, arrests would have been made. In some past situations that were similar, when negotiations failed, carefully planned out arrests were made—but in a way that maximized public and officer safety.

Had such operations occurred in this instance, people who were caught in the middle, including elderly First Nations people, woman, and children, may well have been hurt in the process as agitators fought with police. Those arrested and some officers would have undoubtedly been hurt. Sympathetic protests would have occurred across Canada with increasing volatility. Major highways and trade routes would be shut down for days, weeks, and months. The cost to the taxpayers of Canada would have been insurmountable. The events in Oka, Quebec, and Ipperwash, Ontario, and the resulting Ipperwash inquiry taught us valuable lessons on the ramifications of aggressive police action. Lives were lost, some were forever ruined, and many were negatively altered for all eternity.

A railway sought and obtained a court injunction, forcing us to remove the protestors near Tyendinaga. We didn't immediately act, as we needed to amass sufficient resources and develop plans for a substantial arrest as well as to defend ourselves from the hundreds of protestors, some armed, who we knew would immediately follow. At the same time, our provincial liaison team was engaged in dialogue with the protestors, who we knew would leave the tracks voluntarily before we could put together the plans and teams to enforce the injunction. They subsequently did leave the tracks within a few hours of our receiving the court injunction, without any use of force on our part. I was relieved—as were police leaders across Canada—as we all knew that if this one went bad, we were all in trouble. Like it or not, that was the reality of the situation.

Of course, understandably, the public did not comprehend all of that. I can sympathize with their feelings and the resulting media negativity. We couldn't publicly provide our strategy or all of the intelligence information that we knew. Even the justice who signed the order slammed us publicly. It was a no-winner all around.

I jumped into the media fray. Not because I was going to be the savior but because our people were being criticized nonstop. They and their families needed to see their boss defend them, and the public needed to hear the reality of the situation from the leader of the OPP, as opposed to the unknowing naysayers out there. I joined live radio shows and addressed concerns, did television and newspaper interviews nonstop. I even called a live Toronto radio show where a former Ontario premier was criticizing our members and me personally for our stance. This former premier, whom I happen to like, was a key member of the government in power the day we marched down the road in Ipperwash in 1995 and killed a native protestor. Our approach that day didn't work out so well for anyone. Apparently, we all need a strong reality check on occasion.

The key messages were well crafted, open, and completely honest. I acknowledged the legitimate public concern but defended our position and that of Chief Phil Nelson of the Sarnia Police Service. I explained that it wasn't a case of us "not doing our job," as some had reported and many had felt, but was actually us "doing our job": protecting the peace, life, and property through negotiation. My statement on that was firm: "I'd rather be criticized for ending these protests peacefully and not getting anyone hurt than for taking action that got members of the public or police officers hurt or killed."

I constantly stated that although we were legally bound to execute the order of the court, we could use our discretion to take action when we felt it was safe to do so and when properly resourced and had operational plans sufficiently developed. I also reminded people of the many times we had made arrests and laid criminal charges in similar events across Ontario and how we were quite prepared to do that again at the appropriate time and place. I emphasized that nobody was hurt in those instances; they were thoroughly investigated, and charges laid as appropriate.

We recorded a video of me saying all of that and more for internal OPP consumption. One of our deputy commissioners, Scott Tod, watched the video and suggested we put it on YouTube so that even more of the public would see my message and that I was saying the same thing internally as I had been saying externally. We did just that. Thousands of people watched it; many changed their views; others didn't. The fact that we had turned to YouTube became the story, and media outlets across Canada actually communicated our key messages by constantly showing the video or printing my comments therein. The tide turned completely. Some respected law professors and others wrote articles and letters defending our position regarding peaceful resolution.

The Vancouver Police faced a firestorm of Canadian and US media criticism following their perceived lack of planning and response to violent rioting in the streets after a key NHL hockey game there. Chief Jim Chu did an excellent job in handling the aftermath. He told me,

> In policing, there will be great times and bad times. The Vancouver Police basked in the afterglow of the 2010 Winter Olympics. It was easy to sit back, smile, and soak up the plaudits.
>
> But my greatest success was not the Olympics. Just sixteen months after the Olympics, Vancouver experienced a hockey riot. I had to step forward to meet the critics head on, to defend the Vancouver Police Department's planning and response the night of the riot, and to assure my own people, who were under attack as an organization, that we did the right thing. I had to speak many times to the news media and explain and defend our actions as the public face of the VPD. I had to appear confident and in control to the public. During a forty-five-minute press conference the morning after the riot, a reporter asked me, "What do you think about the calls for your resignation?" My answer (delivered in a serious tone) was, "That's not the first time I have heard that call." The reporters laughed at the answer. But my senior officers that were there liked that line, and it showed that I was handling the heat and that the pressure wasn't getting to me. Showing fear and pessimism would have undermined our organizational resiliency to make it through those tough times.

Over my career as a police executive, I have travelled the province in various capacities in an attempt to get to know the media, let them get to know me, and help them better know the regional and detachment commanders, the local community-services officers, and other staff who regularly deal with the media. Many faces come and go on both sides of the equation, and it is important that we know each other and understand each other's needs on a face-to-face basis. This has been a very successful way to clear the air on previous misunderstandings and ongoing challenges and to establish or enhance trusting relationships between the media and us.

I've been fortunate to have developed some allies in the media over the years. They still ask the tough questions on critical issues and challenge me if they don't agree, but I understand that. They know that they can ask my opinion on an ongoing issue and I'll always be honest, off the record, or I'll tell them that it's a matter that I don't want to get into and why. They respect that. Of course, I fully understand the concept that nothing is really "off the record," and I run the risk of being burned anytime. Thankfully, that hasn't happened yet. But some of these relationships are twenty years old and based on decades of trust. I can also pick their brains on issues, so at times they are advisors and barometers for me. The relationships and levels of mutual trust have benefitted us all.

> *When the media ask George W. Bush a question,*
> *he answers, "Can I use a lifeline?"*
>
> —ROBIN WILLIAMS

Our community-services officers (CSOs) or public-information officers (PIOs) are trained to efficiently release information to the public through the media. They know what they can say, what they can't say, and the most effective way to do it. In addition, our communication-center sergeants and our shift supervisors have all received additional training to better deal with media issues.

However, there isn't always a fully trained media-relations person on site as things happen out there. In the case of the OPP and our massive geography, the media can get to a scene before us, and quite often before we can shuffle a sergeant across the landscape.

Our standard messaging to our people on the ground is this:

Don't be afraid of the media. If approached by them at a scene, remember that they have a job to do, as do you, so be professional. If they're not in any danger, let them take their pictures or video footage. They know what is appropriate for them to show later and will edit accordingly. If they want an interview, steer them to the CSO or a sergeant on scene at a large occurrence or have them call into the com center. If a sergeant or CSO is not immediately available, have them contacted by radio or phone.

In the meantime, don't be afraid to confirm that something has happened; that is almost always obvious to the media, or you wouldn't be standing there, nor would they. However, you should never speculate on what the occurrence might be or lie to them. For example, it's better to say, "We are investigating a death" rather than speculate it is a homicide or a suicide. Don't give out any personal information either. We never identify victims or suspects. We also don't identify deceased persons unless the next of kin have been advised, so it is a must to leave those questions to the CSO or sergeant.

If you are working on an investigation in your detachment area, keep the media as up to date as you can. They'll often bend over backward to help you find out more information or identify a suspect. Letting them know a new court date or the results of a court appearance they didn't cover will go a long way toward helping you develop your own credibility as a police officer, as well as the media's full support. Once again, if entering into gray areas when fielding questions from the media about your investigation, seek advice from your CSO rather than releasing information that may hurt you later in court.

The bottom line is if you try your best when dealing with the media and end up making an honest mistake while doing so, so be it. We all make honest mistakes every day. The quicker you can report the problem up, the quicker some element of damage control can be done.

Mistakes get made. We deal with them and move on. I'd prefer to have the odd mistake made by a well-intended officer than be accused of being uncooperative or stonewalling the media.

It has been my goal to change the old way of thinking from "Don't tell the media anything unless you have to, and then tell them only enough to make them go away" to a more modern approach of "Tell them all you can," with the proviso that if there is something we can't tell them for legislative, personal information, or operational reasons, we'll explain that to them.

The media have an important role in society as they keep many, including the police, accountable to the public they serve. Modern society remains stronger as a result. Love them or hate them, that's their role. The police have their role as well, and the two entities should work hand in glove as much as feasible.

Effective media relations will always be an important part of what we do as professional police services and as police leaders. We should do all that we can to keep police-media relationships strong.

The media are an extremely powerful force. Current NYPD deputy commissioner and former CBS journalist John Miller, who was also once an FBI employee, said something in one of his lectures that I had the privilege to attend. His words were to the effect that when it comes to fame, money, and power, the media has the ability to get you all three or help you lose all three.

I suggest that we never forget his very relevant comment.

> *The media's the most powerful entity on earth. They have the*
> *power to make the innocent guilty and to make the guilty innocent,*
> *and that's power. Because they control the minds of the masses.*

> —MALCOLM X

What Are Our People Saying about Leadership?

• • •

*Leaders: Some excel, some totally fail, some
never do either. They simply survive.*

—Unknown

I'M SURE THAT IF WE queried all of our personnel to see what they would really like to have on their work-life wish list, most would say "more money." I know that at times during my life it would have been on top of the heap for me! But the reality is that the people we lead are truly deeper than that.

An article by Geoffrey James intrigued me for that very reason. It shows that employees more often describe their wants as intangible items, not things that would augment their physical wealth or personal status.

Making big money is often less important to employees than satisfying these basic needs.

Contrary to popular belief, employees value many things more than the amount of money they're being paid. If they're treated right, employees will not only work for less, they'll be happier and more productive as they do so.

Based upon hundreds of conversations I've had about bosses and jobs, here's what employees really want:

To feel proud.

When asked what they do for a living, employees want to boast rather than apologize.

To be treated fairly.

Employees hate favoritism. They expect the perks and promotions to go to the people who work hard, not the people who kiss butt.

To respect the boss.

Employees want to believe in that their boss is a leader who is worthy of their loyalty.

To be heard out.

Employees don't expect the boss to always take their advice, but if the boss won't hear them out they (rightly) assume the boss doesn't care about them.

To be coached not micromanaged.

What employees don't want is to have the boss looking over their shoulder all the time.

To feel less stress.

Bosses must plan carefully, anticipate problems and set realistic goals, so that they don't accidentally and unnecessarily add stress to employees' lives.

To beat the competition.

Finally, never underestimate the power of teamwork, especially when teamwork means grinding the other team into the dust. Employees don't want to be team players; they want to play on the winning team.

Fascinating stuff! The majority of their wants are truly related to things that organizational leaders can provide or at least strongly influence.

The miracles of modern technology and the social media environment in which we now operate present never-ending challenges for law enforcement and for us as leaders, but also, thankfully, a tremendous number of solutions and benefits.

One of the benefits for me has been the ability to better communicate messages internally and externally, and that includes the ability to obtain feedback on a variety of critical issues. With the good comes the bad, unfortunately, as two-way communication enables people to tell us things we may not like or want to hear, but that comes with the turf.

Against the advice of some, I started a "Commissioner's Blog" on our internal intranet page two years ago. There is always a question or theme du jour that I may be seeking specific input on, but I've communicated regularly that I am open to any thoughts, ideas, feedback, or suggestions on any topic, anytime. That opens a tremendously wide door, but it has been a huge success story.

In March 2013, I put the following in a new blog entry:

2013-03-01
Leadership Is a Two-Way Street
I'm currently writing a book on police leadership, entitled "Never Stop on a Hill." It is a nonprofit venture, so if it does sell, any profits will go to the Law Enforcement Torch Run for Special Olympics. I enjoy doing it, and hopefully it will benefit current and future police leaders and therefore make the police services in which they serve better organizations.

As part of my work, I surveyed a number of current and retired police chiefs across Canada and asked them a series of questions and got their feedback.

For two reasons, I want to ask all of you the same questions. Firstly, I want to hear what you have to say and see what's important in terms of leadership to all those aspiring to be promoted and all supervisors, managers, and commissioned officers. Secondly, I'd like to relate your feedback in my book for the eventual readers to consider.

I will use some of the quotes and at the very least some statistical data from your feedback, but will not name any submitters in the book.

So here we go!

We've all been employees working under someone's direction. Without naming names, think about the best supervisor or manager you ever had. What quality or qualities did he or she have that made him or her a good leader? How did that impact you?

Without naming names, now think about the worst boss you ever had. What was it that he or she did that made him or her so bad? How did that effect you as an employee?

Thanks! I look forward to your feedback!

The blog entry had over twelve thousand visits in five months. It was the main topic for a month; then it became an archived post that employees can, and certainly do, continue to visit and respond to. There were almost six thousand visits during that first month, which was record setting and clearly showed me that this is a topic of great interest to the organization.

Here's but a mere sampling of the responses:

* He was always there jumping in to help with arrests, paperwork, etc. He had a great sense of humor; he never ignored requests from anyone and always gave credit where credit was due. He always had our respect and gave it in return. In this profession, when we generally hear nothing but complaints and whining, a kind word of appreciation goes a long way toward improving moral. He was always encouraging and gave great advice. I wish I could put his name here. I'm sure many others feel the same way about him. I'm in a supervisory position now, and I have tried to emulate him.
* No one wants a leader/supervisor that is untrustworthy and just looking out for him/herself. In too many cases, supervisors are

looking for the "next bump" for financial reasons. This is NOT the reason to try and lead someone.

* Too often I've seen and heard bosses brush off great ideas, ignore employees (myself included), go out of their way to make some officer's life miserable, and not give a little praise when it would have made a big difference. These bosses were micromanaging, untrustworthy, uncaring, butt kissing and downright ignorant about their employees and their own positions.

* Leaders need to be chosen because they want to lead, not because they want a pay raise and the prestige of rank. Having said that, just because someone wants to be a leader and has passed a test and interview doesn't mean he/she SHOULD be a leader.

* I have been a very proud member of this organization for twenty-three years and have seen many supervisors come and go. It has been my experience that those that lead by example are the better ones. A supervisor you can trust to keep things to themselves when you ask. That understands that you have a life beyond the OPP. That listens and considers your opinions.

* I have been very fortunate to work on platoons with responsible members who conducted themselves with pride and respect for all those around them. They conducted themselves as the adults they are. This made the supervisors' job pretty simple; they were there to answer questions and clarify when we were unsure but did not need to micromanage, because they knew we were quite capable of doing our jobs.

* I have worked in the same office as a micromanaging-style supervisor, and that platoon seems very unhappy. The comment I most often hear is that they feel like they are being treated as children. We ARE adults after all and should be able to take responsibility for our own actions. I think that if you give the officers that responsibility, they will take up the challenge and act accordingly; however, treat them like a child, and they will act as such.

* I am a former military officer and enjoyed the experiences of leadership many years ago, but what passes for police "leadership" holds little interest for me. I guess part of the problem is that there seems to be little or nothing in the promotional process that seeks to identify actual leaders or leadership qualities.

* The majority of police supervisors I have experienced, and I have worked in four jurisdictions now, are primarily concerned with advancing their own careers. Not all, of course, but many.

* Here's a message for supervisors: Do you want to know the simplest way to inspire your people? Just give them a word of encouragement once in a while. Tell them if they do a good job. Yes, we're professionals, and no, we don't need a head pat every day, but from time to time, seek out the opportunity to recognize your people's work. I think you'll find the examples are ample. Funny, because it costs absolutely nothing, can pay an enormous dividend, and yet seems to be parted with about as frequently as hoarded gold.

* I frankly expect leaders to put their guys' welfare above their own (a lot to ask in this day and age, I know). Otherwise I expect competence, trust in our abilities, and that any lower-level supervisor will get their hands dirty once in a while (that part shouldn't need explaining).

* OPP supervisors must keep their personal agendas and organizational-ladder aspirations in check while extracting the best performance from an employee's abilities under his/her care.

* The key word in this discussion is LEADERSHIP. There is a huge difference between a supervisor or manager and a leader. Anyone can be given the title of supervisor or manager and be given that task. A leader is someone who earns the status of leader. A leader is someone who people will follow and perform for because they want to, not because they have been told to.

* His team would have done anything for the man. The reasons were simple. He never asked anyone to do something that he wouldn't

do himself. He always gave credit where credit was due. He never put his aspirations ahead of his team. He allowed people to perform in the areas that they were best suited to. He never expected anyone to put the job before their family, but when they did so willingly, he made sure they were rewarded for it. He trusted and allowed his people to make decisions. If you screwed up, he would boot your backside, but he never held a mistake over anyone's head. He gave every member of the team opportunities to develop and experience variety. I could go on and on, but he simply made it fun to come to work and made it fun to work hard.

* I have had two sergeants who were dishonest, untrustworthy micromanagers who were only interested in making themselves look good and looking after their buddies. They took great pride in writing someone up for a minor issue. They did not give everyone equal career-development opportunities and found countless ways to beat down certain members of the team. This included some of the highest producers. They did not allow the team members to make decisions on their own, and if the member did make a decision, they would be second-guessed.

These two sergeants completely divided the team and sucked the life out of some very hardworking constables. While working under these people, I personally lost interest in coming to work. It became a chore. In spite of this, I maintained a high workload, but more than once, it was suggested that I should take time off due to the stress.

* The best leader I've had the opportunity to work for was smart, kind, insightful, honest, trustworthy, open. He could be counted on to praise you when you did well and hold you accountable when you did not. And when he held you accountable, it was more an instructional opportunity than a punishment. I actually enjoyed what he dubbed "fireside chats" when I failed to meet his expectations...and let me tell you—I worked VERY hard to meet his expectations. He was also open to input on how he did his job! He

cared how we perceived his efforts and took any comments as an opportunity for him to learn and improve.

* There have been many who talk the talk but do not walk the walk. Too many who are just looking for the next promotion and are not willing to rock the boat and do the work that must be done. It takes courage and selflessness to be a great leader, not the ability to check off boxes in a plan and tell the board what a wonderful person you are!

* An excellent human being who made work a lot of fun, and his commitment was contagious.

* I believe there is confusion between the two concepts of leadership and management. Too many OPP managers think they are leading when they are not, and too many leaders are simply just managing. While there are many positions in our organization that are attained in the rank structure (positional power), there are many more people that attain leadership at any level (personal power) because of their experiences and personalities. This can be a positive or negative.

* The best boss I have had in the OPP is my current sergeant. The quality that he has that I admire is the ability to form a cohesive platoon that works well together no matter who happens to be on our platoon. There just never seem to be any personnel problems. He is an authentic person who steps in when he feels the officers need guidance but otherwise lets officers go about their days.

  He is honest, almost painfully so sometimes, but you come to like that quality, if you know what I mean. You can trust him. People that are supervised by this person are uniformly productive and happy. He can also be very funny. This has impacted me in that I look forward to coming to work and am comfortable and want to do well.

* The worst boss I have had in the OPP was the person who was a micromanager in the extreme. You couldn't do anything without getting criticized. He played favorites. He would complain about

you behind your back to people you respected. Personnel problems followed this person at every level. Frequent conflict with multiple officers, good officers, under the guise of mistakes they had made that he felt needed correction.

* What do I look for in a good leader? Charisma, knowledge, self-sacrifice, integrity, professionalism, honesty, courage, recognizing the hard work of our members. Certainly a good leader, as stated above by another poster, has to place the needs of his men and women above his/her own. A good leader is not afraid to make decisions, especially those that won't make him/her popular. As long as those decisions are made for the greater good. I have twenty-nine years of service and have seen quite a few leaders and managers in my time. Unfortunately, I haven't seen many leaders who possessed all those traits.

What makes a leader a bad one? How about dishonesty, not caring for your troops, delegating all of your work, always taking the Fridays off, speaking down on your people, swearing at your members, always reminding us that you are the boss, talking the talk but not walking the walk, not holding people accountable, not leading by example—I could go off on a tangent here.

Being a supervisor myself for twelve years now, I came to realize quite early when I was promoted that it wasn't a popularity contest. I didn't get promoted to be popular but to lead, to help junior officers expand their knowledge and skills up to a level that I knew they could achieve. Over the years, I have grown very fond of my boys and girls on my platoon. They are simply superb officers and superb human beings. I always tell my wife that when I retire, which is very soon, I will certainly miss them very much."

* I am a twenty-seven-year member of the OPP and have certainly seen the style of our leadership change over the course of my career. My first detachment commander was universally detested by all who worked for him, and when he was nearing retirement,

the senior officers in the detachment always talked about holding his retirement party in a phone booth because no one would ever dream of attending! I have to say, being brand new to that detachment and busy learning how to become a good officer, I had very little direct dealings with the detachment commander but saw much of the aftermath and effect on the supervisors and staff trying to deal with his demands—if nothing else, from that detachment commander, I learned that consistency was a very beneficial characteristic in a leader, and his lack of compassion highlighted the negative effects of always beating down the troops. This man was at least a consistent dictator, if nothing else. Once you understood his approach, you were able to determine your own best approach in successfully working in that environment and meeting the expectations and requirements of that detachment commander. Leadership style—dictatorship! I learned from that experience that two important leadership traits are consistency and compassion. This issue of consistency became very relevant as I moved on to my second detachment.

True leaders project calm in the midst of chaos. They make decisions based on sound reasoning, provide clear, concise direction, and calm the fears of those they are leading. They make you believe that everything will be OK, and lead you safely to the other side. Consistency is key. Once you have worked for one of these leaders, in the midst of a major incident (such as rioting in Caledonia, the aftermath of a multiple homicide, or an officer-involved fatality), you'll know exactly what true leadership is. You'll believe in them—and you'll follow them to the end of the earth.

The best supervisor I ever had was the one that built up my confidence by telling me to trust in my gut and act. Confidence, in my opinion, is highly important in this line of work. It's not to say this supervisor never discussed my actions, but the person would approach it in such a way to offer advice.

The worst supervisor I had was the one that micromanaged. After each call the supervisor asked what I did and why I did it. With that supervisor I quickly started to lose confidence and question what I was doing every step of the way and worry over every minor decision I was making. It took the enjoyment out of coming to work. Rather than wake up excited to go to work, I started to regard it as putting in time. It created an officer that would rather not stop that vehicle for fear of the questions my supervisor would ask.

❄ In serving with both the military and the OPP, I have worked for many leaders. Some better than others. I'll leave it at that. The ones that really stand out were those who displayed one of the most important leadership qualities in my opinion. Courage! The courage to embrace change, the courage to hold others accountable, and the courage to do the right thing even when it is not the popular thing to do. And an area where I have seen a lot of leaders fall flat on their faces: the courage to hold themselves accountable when things do not go as desired with their teams. Wisdom is also good, but that comes with time. The only way one becomes old and wise is to first be young and stupid.

❄ Best manager I ever had just retired this month. Upon his leaving, he shared his three critical success factors:

1. Remember your humanity—get to genuinely know the people you work with and for—and care about them.
2. Remember your priorities—work/life balance, and he led by example.
3. Remember why you started in this profession.

❄ Worst experience with a manager who was a good person but terrible communicator. They did not know how to provide constructive criticism and had a low emotional intelligence quotient (EQ).

* Supervisors and leaders are two different entities. A leader is someone who can generate positive attitudes, motivate his/her workers, and engage their employees. I once told a leader who was going into a position, where he was not too sure if he was going to be able to succeed in an area that he, at the time, had no knowledge of, to "treat people like people, and they will work with you and work for you." Sounds so simple, but it is so true.

* Unfair treatment of staff causes morale problems, makes and contributes to a poisoned work environment, and causes dissention between members. Human nature dictates us to react unfavorably to being treated "differently" or "unfairly." When I work with great leaders, I feel that I am included as part of a team, I feel great about my work, I feel I am much more productive, and I am very proud about the work I accomplish and also the organization I work for. When I work with supervisors who are not leaders, I feel the exact opposite, and it makes me feel somewhat unwanted and very much unappreciated.

* The best leader I had was the detective inspector I worked for while working on a number of homicides in the crime unit. This person was knowledgeable, calm, respectful of everyone's opinion, humorous, and driven to solve the case. As a constable, I always felt comfortable expressing my ideas regardless of rank.

* I have worked for very good leaders, and the commonality is the respect and approachability they portray. Good leadership is almost intangible—it is a mix of intelligence, charisma, confidence, fairness, and empathy. If we can find a way to develop officers that possess these traits, then perhaps we are on the right track.

* For me, true leadership boils down to trust. I want to trust the answers offered will be the right ones. I want to trust my mistakes won't be addressed with that self-righteous indignation that makes my hands shake and my temples throb. I want to trust that all my hard work and experience will be recognized and fit into the

equation. I want to trust that when I leave the room, I won't be the one criticized and second-guessed the way that we have all seen happen in the constables' room too often. I have grudgingly come to expect that from my peers, but when a supervisor is involved, it's pure poison.

* The leader is the one I trust and so the one whose opinion of me matters. The one whom I want to impress. The one who will have my loyalty and my honest effort wherever and whenever it's asked for, whether I'm keen about the task or not.

* Good leaders are ALL the employees who remember the oath they took when they joined, realize that they work for and are paid by the citizens of Ontario, treat their coworkers and their clients with the utmost dignity and respect, have the courage to acknowledge their own limitations and seek only positions they truly have skills for, have the highest integrity on and off duty, and are loyal for the right reasons.

* I've worked for great sergeants who led by example and commanded respect; it made going to work a pleasure, and I learned a lot from them. That kind of leadership is what forms young officers into great police officers, and it inspires them to become leaders also.

  I've also worked for people who have rank but no leadership skills whatsoever—we've all seen them walking around thinking they've earned or deserve respect because of their ranks when in reality everyone looks at them shaking their heads, wondering how they ever got promoted. The sad thing is that I've seen these people continue to move up the ranks for political reasons or because they were yes-men, someone who won't think on their own but go with the flow and never question anything. That is not a leader; it's a follower who's now in charge of leading—a recipe for disaster.

* You knew going into any situation that he would give you the information he had, lead you in, and be the last one out, protecting

your retreat as best he could so you were free to make your own decisions. He would interfere only if he felt we were going so far offside we could not recover by ourselves. This provided us with confidence, self-respect, and experience we would never have had any other way.

* I am in my thirty-seventh year of policing—over twenty-four of them municipally and the last twelve-plus with the OPP. I have been fortunate to work for some wonderful leaders. Each had their own style and personality, but the common dominator with each is that they would lead from the front—they would have your back not only in in a street brawl but in a public complaint or an internal issue. My own performance was motivated in no small part from not wanting to let them down.

* At times, he would show up after a call had been dealt with and throw questions at you such as, how did that go? How did you feel you handled that? Do you think you could have handled it differently? Is there anything else you could have done? And so forth. These questions on some occasions were annoying, but when you sat back and reflected, he was actually teaching and providing you with guidance and options. In essence, he cared. He cared about how you learned from your experiences; he cared in knowing about you; he cared about his officers and worked hard at it. He loved telling us stories about back in the day and sharing. He has long since retired, but he definitely made an impact, and I have yet to meet another mentor such as him.

* I believe a number of folks have made great points as to the attributes of what makes a good leader, and you reiterated it—it's people skills that make the difference between the task monger and an exceptional leader, in my view.

* Throughout my career I have found that there has been only one NCO that I admired and wanted to style myself after. This was my first corporal who himself had previous military experience, and when I worked for him, he had twenty-five years with the OPP.

What made him an excellent NCO was that he never expected men under his command to do what he himself could not. He led by example and always had encouraging words for the work performed. If you messed up, he was there to see what could be done to minimize or correct the error.

＊ I do not recall a worst NCO, but I have had a lot of mediocre ones. I have seen individuals who have been promoted who do not have interpersonal skill sets that are needed to inspire and assist those under their direction. Too many times I have seen NCOs that are afraid to make decisions that may impact their chances to move on.

If you are going to lead men, and especially into battle, make decisions firmly and with conviction. Even if your decisions are wrong, men will follow you and believe you will get them out of trouble. With leaders that have their men's faith, obstacles are overcome. There is nothing worse than NCOs and officers who waffle; this makes men panic and mistrust leadership and, as a result, perish.

This was hugely interesting and telling feedback from a very large uniformed- and civilian-member audience. It tells a tale of the importance of people skills to those we lead. It is a litany of what works, what fails, what really counts, what doesn't, and what is truly meaningful to a broad base of employees. All of us can learn from those thoughts and experiences, both good and bad.

I believe that it is quite demonstrative of what people in all of our police services are thinking and saying about leadership, as well as within most private and public sector organizations in the developed world. You could easily take the policing context, ranks and tiles out of the feedback and the points made would equally apply to leadership successes and failings in any organization.

In order to be a leader a man must have followers. And to have followers, a man must have their confidence. Hence the supreme quality for a leader is unquestionably integrity. Without it, no real success is possible, no matter whether it is on a sections gang, a football field, in an army, or in an office. If a man's associates find him guilty of phoniness, if they find that he lacks forthright integrity, he will fail. His teachings and actions must square with each other. The first great need, therefore, is integrity and high purpose.

—Dwight D. Eisenhower

The Leaders on Leadership

• • •

It is better to lead from behind and to put others in front, especially when you celebrate victory when nice things occur. You take the front line when there is danger. Then people will appreciate your leadership.

—Nelson Mandela

I'VE SELECTED ONE QUOTE FROM each of the current and retired police leaders that I interviewed that I felt was indicative of their particular leadership styles. Enjoy!

Chief Bill Blair:

> I don't want to be the great man that made every decision himself but instead the man that assembled and led a great deal of extraordinary leaders.
> Any success I've had is because I've led a strong team.

Chief Jim Chu:

> A successful leader has successful followers.
> My favorite is a quote that originated with Warren Buffet. When you look to hire/promote someone, look for intelligence, initiative, and integrity. But of all of these three, look for integrity first.

Because if that person doesn't have integrity, you'd better hope he or she doesn't have intelligence and initiative.

Ian Davidson, deputy minister:

There is no greater privilege or opportunity in life than to lead. And leaders who have the privilege of holding office, rank, or title have an obligation to leverage that gift to create a better future for us all. As leaders we can cast our shadow into the future by leaving an organization prepared to succeed in our absence.

Chief Rick Deering:

In my view, there is no singular quality that defines great leaders. Great leaders have an in-depth knowledge and appreciation of their respective cultures and those that form them. They are able to assess situations on an individual basis and take the most prudent course of action, keeping in mind the value of their decisions to both the greater good and the individual(s) involved.

Most importantly, they are able to make the right decision, even when they know it will not be popular and may place them in personal jeopardy with their political masters.

Chief Frank Elsner:

Not just leadership but good, moral, ethical leadership is vital to a PS. It sets the direction and standard for the members to emulate and follow. It creates an environment where people do the right things for the right reasons whether the leader is present or not. Our people do much of their work without supervision; we need to trust them to do that. So the leader needs to instill in them the values, ethos, and vision of the organization so they are the norm, with or without the leader present.

Chief Jennifer Evans:

Ethical leadership within a police organization is critical to its success. Leadership defines the rules, sets the example and the direction of the police service. Without proper leadership, a police service will lose sight of its obligations to the community. Transparency and ethical actions help to ensure public trust.

The Honorable Julian Fantino:

Leadership is best defined as the convergence of an abundance of technical skills and the expertise and common sense that enables the leader to inspire and motivate his or her subordinates to excel in all that they do in the performance of a common goal.

Chief Leanne Fitch:

Leadership is an honor and a responsibility to be taken seriously. There are positive leaders and negative leaders. In the absence of good, compassionate, strong, moral leadership, followers will follow anyone, in almost any direction, that will give them a sense of mission, belonging or purpose, or value. Good leadership is a tremendous opportunity to influence others in ways that improve social conditions and contribute to the well-being of others. Good, compassionate, strong, and moral leadership will see people follow in order to fulfill a greater mission in life. Leadership must be nurtured at every level and does not belong to a sacred few.

Chief Kimberley Greenwood:

Leadership is more than leading, coaching, and mentoring followers; it involves leading leaders. It is important to assist those leaders you are mentoring to invest in developing potential leaders themselves. I have had the good fortune to work with great leaders, great partners, and great colleagues, both past and present. They have challenged me, mentored me, and motivated me. They inspired me to learn more, do more, and become more. They taught me the importance of professionalism and respect. I am indebted to so many, and I will "pay it forward."

Chief Laurie Hayman:

Good leadership is vital to the success of organizations that require people to work together. In policing, the outputs of our work are differently measured, diverse, and at times high risk. Leadership is essential to not only accomplish organizational and goals and meet the needs of the people we serve but also mitigate the risks to those people and the organization.

I'm grateful for having had many different leadership roles in policing, each one providing many opportunities for success. There are many times when I have felt very proud of the men and women with whom I have served and for whom I have had a tremendous responsibility. Seeing those officers come together with and for each other as a team, working hard to serve the public and achieving their own personal and professional goals, is extremely rewarding.

Chief Barry King:

Leadership may be a gift some are born with, but it takes a high degree of understanding, confidence, insight, passion, self-assessment, and personal dedication for it to self-actualize. We are seeing, more and more, a number of great police leaders emerging in recent years. I believe this is the result of higher levels of education and a personal commitment to results-oriented community policing.

Chief Rod Knecht:

The tone is always set at the top. Particularly in policing, employees want to know where the organization is going, both short and long term, so they can see how they fit into the future of the organization and whether they want to be a part of that vision and that future. Most everyone that joins the profession wants to do good, help others, and place service before self and has a very clear personal belief as to what justice looks like. It is essential that the leaders reflect those beliefs in everything they say, but more importantly in what they do.

The leader in a police organization holds a position of extraordinary power, more so than in the private sector. It is a position of extraordinary trust. Because policing is about the people, both internally and externally, a poor leader can harm the organization long beyond his or her tenure. Conversely, a great leader can positively influence that organization long beyond his or her tenure and often carry it through bad leadership—at least for a period of time.

Chief Robert F. Lunney:

The role of the leader is to inspire people to achieve a higher purpose and to perform at a higher level. Envisioning goals, affirming values, motivating, explaining, representing, and serving as a symbol are all part of the chief's role, but the chief must also foster the process of organizational renewal. A leader who demonstrates moral courage—one who is steady, reliable, and fair—will consistently attract loyalty and trust.

Chief Dan Maluta:

Great leadership is the hard-sought and rarely attained quality that causes organizations to thrive, businesses to prosper, governments to rule justly, and all of humankind to benefit. It is vital to the success of a police service, no different than to a successful business, collective, or government, because it creates a culture of integrity that resonates through the whole organization.

Chief Edgar MacLeod:

Leadership is championing a vision and creating a pathway to change. Inspired police leaders have a unique ability to inspire others to share in this vision and work collaboratively toward the realization of this shared vision.

Chief William McCormack:

Leadership is about people having a passion and a desire to work for you and with you because they want to, not because they have to.

Deputy Minister Dale McFee:

Community safety is bigger than policing; if we truly are going to reach our potential, then we must engage our partners. "Alone we go fast, together we go far," and this is a marathon and not a sprint. We do not need any more problem identifiers. There are more than enough already. We need problem solvers; we need people who are willing to take the first step and not those that have paralysis through analysis. In simple terms, people complain because when they stop, they have to take responsibility, and that can be hard work!

Commissioner Thomas B. O'Grady:

It has been said that the public is generally oblivious to good policing; rather, it is the absence of it that draws public attention and concern.

By comparison, an efficient and effectively functioning organization is the result of good leadership, a fact that usually goes unnoticed. Only when the organization begins to malfunction does the subject of good leadership, or the lack thereof, become a subject of public debate.

Commissioner Bob Paulson

Leadership, adversity, and success are all inextricably linked. Good leaders take their people through adversity to success. Where the adverse conditions are complex or concealed and hard to get at, they courageously hunt it down, simplify things, and bring their people to success. Where there is no adversity, they protect success by preparing their people for when it comes.

Chief Paul Shrive:

A great leader passes the "mirror test" every day. You must be able to look at your reflection each and every day of your command and be able to honestly state that you are doing the right things for the right reasons. None of your problems will be easy. The easy ones don't end up on your desk. You will find your life as a commander easier if you have a strong moral compass and a natural ability to find fairness in all of your actions.

Chief Clive Weighill:

Optimism is the most important quality in a leader! There are many issues facing a police service every day. It is very easy to point fingers at others, push back to the criticism, and become demoralized. It is imperative to keep a positive attitude and not pass the negativity to the rank and file. There is nothing more damaging to an organization's psyche than a leader constantly appearing negative, fighting with his or her police board or the media. It casts a cloud of discontent throughout the organization, makes people inside think they don't have the support of the public.

Senator Vern White:

I believe that leaders need to focus on doing their jobs rather than keeping them. If they do, they will exhibit the very leadership their members demand and expect.

Commissioner Giuliano Zaccardelli:

The ability to clearly articulate a vision or direction for an organization or group of people, obtain their commitment to work toward the achievement of that vision, and then allow them to own and achieve the vision.

And last but certainly not least, Commissioner Chris Lewis:

Leaders build trust through their actions and words. They inspire and support others to be the very best that they can be, as they work together to achieve results that are in the best interests of the people they serve.

My quote above stood as my personal and organizational vision on leadership during my tenure and is contained in the 2013 OPP document entitled *Leadership in the OPP*.

We Can Never Forget
Our Veterans

• • •

We stand proudly on the shoulders of those officers that came before us.

—Julian Fantino, associate minister

Back when I was in our Eastern Region in the early 2000s, a retired colleague called me at the office and was very upset. He had just learned that the wife of another retiree whom he had worked with decades prior had passed away following a lengthy fight with cancer. He said, "If that had been Jim that passed, I would have heard the news through someone and would have attended the funeral. But because it was his wife, I didn't hear a thing. I didn't even know that she was sick." I felt awful. Then he asked me about a few old friends and when they had retired, where they were living, and more. I realized that he was really out of the loop on a variety of issues, and that seemed sad to me.

I then spoke to our OPP Veterans' Association (OPPVA) rep in a nearby town and found out that a number of our vets didn't yet have e-mail so weren't receiving messages from them. He also told me that the OPPVA didn't receive a lot of updates from the force, except members' death notices. Well, we quickly changed that piece and ensured that in our region, they were learning of retirement functions and the passing of members' spouses and children, as well as illnesses. I let the other regional commanders around the province know and left it to them to do whatever they felt was right in their areas. The flow of information to our vets certainly improved to some degree.

Then in October 2008, I attended the funeral for OPP Constable Steve Swrjeski (retired) in Killaloe. He was a great guy, a fixture in the community for his twenty-eight-year career and over the many years since his retirement.

I saw a large number of serving and retired members at the funeral, both uniform and civilian, from the OPP and other police services. As I met with the many in attendance, it struck me yet again that our retired members play a significant role in our communities long after they retire from active service. They were all wearing jackets and ties, stepping forward to do all they could to help with the ceremony, with the reception, and for the family. It was truly heartwarming to see. Some of the retirees were not in great health themselves but wouldn't have missed that funeral if their lives depended on it.

I met frequently with the OPPVA Board of Directors and brought them up to speed on various issues, our people, and any changes within the OPP. They wanted to know what was happening because they truly cared about the organization, the police profession, and the OPP family as a whole. Through their system of connections, they regularly tried to keep each other apprised as to the status of all retired and serving members and their families.

They continue to do it through e-mail, at OPPVA branch meetings, and through a network of coffee shop meetings across the province. There's no rank among them anymore. They don't care who was what rank; they are all just brothers and sisters with a common bond: policing and the OPP. I know that this same activity occurs across Ontario within all the fine police services that this province is blessed with.

I also attended their annual general meetings to speak to them and their spouses and partners on OPP and policing happenings. It always amazed me and gave me a great sense of pride that they truly wanted to know how we were now structured and why, who was where, and the challenges we faced in policing and as an organization. They were the veteran officers that I looked up to as a young officer. They were men and women who helped mold me into the police officer and leader that I became. They were the people that I snapped to attention for and always called "sir" or "ma'am" or by their rank. But then they sat there proudly, dressed in business attire (in an era where we couldn't get serving members making close to $100,000 a year to wear their hats when they got out of the car), and they called me "Commissioner" and "sir." That's still hard for me to fathom to this day.

This is the OPPVA's mission statement:

> The Ontario Provincial Police Veterans' Association shall strive to maintain its link and support of its past by committing to promote the social, economic and physical welfare of its members. This achievement is attained by instilling fellowship, continuing relationships, renewing friendships and remaining active, thus rekindling a sense of pride and purpose for the organization.

When Julian Fantino was our commissioner, he and I were visiting our Northwest Region when we became aware of an elderly OPP vet that lived in Thunder Bay and was quite ill. I suggested we stop by and visit him, and Julian said, "Let's go!" without hesitation. Julian always cares about police-service history and culture and those members who went before us. It's quite fitting that he is currently the minister for veterans' affairs in our federal government. We contacted the veteran's daughter and planned a visit. It was a day that neither of us will ever forget.

S. Sgt. Len Chambers (retired) was skinny as a rail but proudly sat wearing a jacket and tie, knowing that the commissioner and a deputy commissioner were coming to visit. It was a big day for him! He had all sorts of memorabilia laid out for us to see, some of which were items that he probably should have turned in when he retired years prior, long before I even joined the force. He also had news clippings about Julian's appointment to the OPP commissioner position. He obviously maintained his interest in the police force that he'd proudly served.

His story was so fascinating. I could have listened to him all day. Len was wounded in battle in World War II and shipped back to Toronto on a medical discharge. But he was young and healed up pretty quickly so went looking for work. A friend told him about a job that he thought was a security-officer position, and Len soon found himself a member of the OPP in a small detachment in southwestern Ontario. He ended up in Hearst in the 1950s, working alone without a radio. When he had to take the train to respond to crimes even further north, he'd tell his wife that if she didn't hear from him within four days, "You'd better call headquarters to send me some help." He didn't put bullets in his gun. He said he'd take a beating if he had to, but didn't want them to get his gun and kill him.

The most interesting part of the visit was the notes he showed us from an investigation he did in his early days into a bank robbery and double murder in Langton, Ontario, in 1950. After the brazen robbery, the killer was chased by two local men, who were then killed in a hail of machine gunfire. When the convicted killer, Herbert McAuliffe, was hanged in Simcoe, Ontario, Len attended as a witness. His daughter was horrified when she read a news article in which her dad was interviewed and, when asked how he felt to watch the hanging, he said words to the effect that it didn't bother him in the slightest, and in fact after the event, he went home, had supper, and "slept like a baby."

His handwritten notes were very detailed and quite extensive. He had drawn great sketches of the scene and of the victims, showing the location of every bullet hole in their bodies. This was a man that had very little training and minimal education, but sixty years later, his notes were every bit as thorough as those of a modern-day, highly trained police professional. Visiting him will go down as one of the highlights of my career.

Weeks later we were advised of Len's passing. Neither of us will ever forget him.

I often wonder whether people who serve in private sector organizations remain committed to their companies and colleagues and as a part of the organization's "family" when they retire as they most often do in policing. I highly doubt that they do. I can't imagine that the aging retired members of those companies are visited in their final days by company leaders who never even knew them.

Our retirees are dedicated ambassadors for all police services within the many communities where they live. They are always remembered for having served in a police service and are natural community leaders as a result. Many sit on local councils or police-service boards, and some are or have been provincial and federal MPs. Many are community volunteers in various capacities. They continue to advocate for policing and the police service that they served in, wherever they go and with whomever they are speaking.

They are a great barometer in terms of how police are perceived in the community and perhaps how things could be done better. Our retired members can always be counted on to step forward during the good times and during crises within their communities, when many others would flee. They are still running into events and controversial discussions, when others are running out or shying away. They are a wonderful and professional resource that will always be there for the community and for our police services.

It's important for us to remember that there are retirees out there who have been around for the past fifty or sixty years of our history and more. We didn't become the great organizations that we are just because we arrived on the scene. Although we certainly all greatly contribute to the keeping the policing tradition strong, our organizational foundations were built through the hard work of many men and women before us. If they hadn't toiled under less than favorable conditions for many years prior to us, our police services would not be the organizations they are today. Many of them were key to developing wonderful relationships with our communities and the trust and respect of the community members that we now benefit from.

This quote from SearchQuotes.com by an unknown author was apparently written about military vets, but it applies equally to those retired from any emergency service: "Veterans are experienced persons who are experts in a particular subject or field. Veterans deserve a lot of respect and salutation because they have excelled in a particular subject more than their younger generation. Their adventures and experiences are very valuable so that we can learn a lot from lessons from them and avoid many mistakes. Veterans are also soldiers who have made great sacrifice for their country in the war front. If not for them, we will not be able to live in peace in our country."

As leaders in policing or any vocation, we should never forget the retired members within the communities in which we live and work. Please do your best to keep them posted on happenings in your services. Drop in and visit them, and encourage your members to do the same. Invite them to your events. Stop by and join their coffee meetings, and let them know who you are. Establish communication links to keep them apprised on issues and events within your police force. They often view you as their leaders, despite the fact that many retired long before your appointment to lead the currently serving personnel.

I forwarded the OPPVA president a copy of every nonoperational OPP-wide communique that I sent out so that they could learn what I was doing and why and hear of noteworthy matters occurring across the OPP. He'd then distribute it to thousands of veteran members, both uniform and civilian, by e-mail. It was not a daunting task for me to send it, and they appreciated it greatly. I found it so fulfilling an effort when I subsequently travelled the province and our veterans would comment to me on some issue that I had included in those communiques. One veteran told me, "It's gone a long way to reconnect us with the brass of the OPP and make us feel like we still belong."

We established an OPP Veterans' Day in 2012. It is now held annually across Ontario on June 6, which is the day that the OPPVA was formed many years ago. We encouraged our detachment, bureau, and regional commanders to have local events whereby the vets could drop in for a visit, touch base, and have a coffee with our people. In some areas, that has become a barbeque lunch and more. We hosted a similar event at our

General Headquarters in Orillia, with some light refreshments and brief comments. I'm hopeful that this worthwhile day of celebration and acknowledgement of our veterans will continue for all eternity. It's the least we can do.

I attended a bridge-dedication ceremony in an Ontario community, wherein a local bridge was dedicated to a fallen OPP officer who had died in the line of duty many decades prior. The deceased member's son and grandchildren participated in an emotional memorial for the man the son barely knew, since he had been a mere infant when his father was killed. He told me that his mother received a fraction of his father's meager salary for only one year following his death and had a visit from a local OPP NCO once a year for many years, and then the family fell off the OPP page. That story made me feel very sad. It wasn't a criticism of the OPP; it was simply a stark reality of those times. I told the son and the many present that the OPP of fifty years ago is not the OPP of today. We are a different police organization. We will not forget our fallen members and their loved ones, who will always be an important part of the OPP family. The same should and will apply to our veteran members.

We should never overlook the fact that we will all be veterans of our beloved police services or organizations someday. We'll also want to feel like we too still belong.

> *When a RCMP Veteran passes away – their old*
> *colleagues pause for a moment to reflect on the good*
> *times they had and the memories they created.*

—VANCOUVER RCMP VETERANS' WEBSITE

FINAL THOUGHTS

• • •

I CERTAINLY HAVE NOT BEEN shy in extolling the criticality of effective leadership in the police services of today, but if you feel that my musings apply only to the police-department world, you have missed a valuable point. Leadership is a transferable skill that is imperative for all organizations—large and small, public and private sector.

If you look back at the many quotes I have provided, although many relate specifically to policing given that I interviewed only Canadian police chiefs past and present, far more come from authors, academia, political and military leaders, and the private sector. What is so interesting to me is that they are largely united on the majority of principles of true leadership and that all agree that leadership is key to organizational success. Combine all of that with the OPP employee blog comments that represent the thoughts and feelings of thousands of OPP personnel, both uniformed and civilian. It paints an incredible picture of the good and bad of leadership. It speaks immensely of the importance of people skills and very little of technical ability or job knowledge.

Here's my sixty-second sound bite about good leadership:

It is all about people, not things. Communication is key to connecting with people and building mutual trust. Although some leadership skills are intrinsic, they can be learned and improved upon. The scar tissue acquired through trying, succeeding, and failing is invaluable in leadership development. Always do what is right and for the right reasons. Do something. Make a decision. Be accountable and take the fall if it goes bad, but pass on the credit to others when it goes well. Being fair and ethical and acting with integrity will set a positive example and will lead to trust. Relationship building up, down, across, internally and externally, will help you succeed. Personal attacks come with the turf, so get ready. Give people the freedom to use their heads, to try and fail, but support them along the way. Seek their input. The media and the labor groups are not the enemy, so manage them well. Remain positive, optimistic, and resilient. Remember the good leaders who made you want to be the best you could be. Do what they did. Remember the bad leaders as perfectly good bad examples. Don't do that stuff. Be the positive example yourself at work and at play. *It takes great leaders to develop great leaders.*

That was sixty seconds—bang on. (I know you'll time it...)

Now for one minute about bad leaders:

Ineffective leaders are closed-minded, negative souls. They think they are the only ones who really know how to do anything right. They care about nobody but whom they see in the mirror. They think people are simply a means to their own personal success. They don't know management from leadership or leadership from sheep shit. They'll take credit and pass blame. They push rather than pull as they set the wrong example. They can't name their direct reports. They don't know their people so won't see changes in them that are worthy of action. They support no one but themselves. They only manage up well. They say "me, my, and I" in every sentence. They run from every hill. They play favorites. Coaching and mentoring are only for football players, in their minds. They create silos. They actually think they know what's going on. They've never had an original thought. They discourage good work and encourage unproductive and unprofessional behavior. Nobody trusts them. They make employees want to quit, go home, and cry themselves to sleep. *Bad leaders beget bad leaders.*

Remind you of anyone?

Who do you want to be: the good or the bad leader? What do you want the leaders in your organization above, beside, or below you to be? What do you do day in and day out to model the leadership qualities and behaviors that you expect out of others? I am confident that my thoughts and information have all been thought provoking in that regard, at minimum.

American poet and civil rights activist Maya Angelou historically said, "People will forget what you said. People will forget what you did. But people will never forget how you made them feel."

I couldn't have said it better myself. Now go forth and lead.

AFTERWORD

• • •

IN JULY 2013, MY DAUGHTER Melissa and I were jogging in my hometown of Sault Sainte Marie. We had a wonderful run around the city, through beautiful Bellevue Park and along the Saint Marys River waterfront. All are places that have great meaning to me from when I was both a child and an adult. Then we came to the start of a steep hill at the bottom of Pine Street.

Melissa gave me that all-knowing grin, and we were off, racing up the hill. When we got to the highest point together, my then-fifty-six-year old lungs felt as if they were about to spontaneously combust, so I stopped to either catch my breath or die on the sidewalk. Melissa pointed to the road ahead, which wasn't steep at all but was a gentle, long, and steady incline. She laughingly said, "Hey, Dad, never stop on a hill."

I replied, "My book isn't called *Never Stop on an Incline*, honey. I'm dying here." We had a good laugh together. It was a precious moment I will never forget.

Three weeks later, she showed me her first tattoo. In free-form handwriting facing in a forward direction on the side of her right foot, the following words are now inscribed: "Never Stop on a Hill."

REFERENCES

• • •

Adams, Susan: "The Best Leaders Care about Their Status More than Their Power,"July31,2012,http://www.forbes.com/sites/susanadams/2012/07/31/the-best-leaders-care-more-about-their-status-not-their-power/

Alston, Roy E. and Reed, George E.: "Toxic Police Leadership," 2013, http://www.lawofficer.com/article/leadership/toxic-police-leadership

Amazon: Preview of *Leading at the Edge: Leadership Lessons from the Extraordinary Saga of Shackleton's Antarctic Expedition*, https://www.amazon.ca/Leading-Edge-Leadership-Extraordinary-Shackletons/dp/0814431941

Ambler, George: "5 Habits of Effective Executives," March 17, 2013, http://www.georgeambler.com/5-habits-of-effective-executives/

Anderson, Amy Rees: "Success Will Come and Go, but Integrity Is Forever," November28,2012,http://www.forbes.com/sites/amyanderson/2012/11/28/success-will-come-and-go-but-integrity-is-forever/

Anderson, Erika: "Are Leaders Born or Made?," November 21, 2012, http://www.forbes.com/sites/erikaandersen/2012/11/21/are-leaders-born-or-made/

Andrews, Robert: "Eight Tips to Help You Deal with Bad Leadership," June 13, 2013, http://www.theleadershiphub.com/blogs/eight-tips-help-you-deal-bad-leadership

Angelotti, Ellyn: "How to Handle Attacks on Social Media," August 20, 2013, http://www.poynter.org/how-tos/digital-strategies/219452/how-to-handle-personal-attacks-on-social-media/

Badaracco, Joseph: "Communication Can't Always Follow the Top Down," undated, http://en.thinkexist.com/quotation/communication_can-t_always_follow_the_top-down/150957.html,

Baldoni, John: "Advice: Manage Better by Leading Well," March 20, 2013, http://www.forbes.com/sites/johnbaldoni/2013/03/20/advice-manage-better-by-leading-well/

Belker, L. B.: "Leading Thoughts," undated, http://www.leadershipnow.com/communicationquotes.html, undated

Bennis, Warren: "A Corporate Fear of Too Much Truth," February 17, 2002, http://www.nytimes.com/2002/02/17/opinion/a-corporate-fear-of-too-much-truth.html

Biro, Meghan M.: "Leadership Is about Emotion," December 15, 2013, http://www.forbes.com/sites/meghanbiro/2013/12/15/leadership-is-about-emotion

Blanchard, Ken: *Critical Leadership Skills: Key Traits That Can Make or Break Today's Leaders*, undated, http://www.kenblanchard.com/img/pub/pdf_critical_leadership_skills.pdf

Bock, Wally: "Three Star Leadership—Are Leaders Born or Made?," 2011, http://www.threestarleadership.com/articles/bornormade.htm

Bonokoski, Mark: "'I'm Not Afraid to Admit That I Cried' Letter by OPP Deputy Commissioner Chris Lewis after Const. Vu Pham's Death," April 10, 2010, *Toronto Sun*

Byrnes, Jonathan: *The Essence of Leadership,* 2005, http://web.mit.edu/ jlbyrnes/www/pdfs/The%20Essence%20of%20Leadership%20 HBSWK%209-05.pdf

Carrison, Dan and Walsh, Rod: "Why Marines Never Use the 'M Word,'" 2013, the CEO Refresher, http://www.refresher.com/adcrwthemword. html

Changing Minds: "Character Assassination," accessed August 12, 2013, http://changingminds.org/techniques/propaganda/character_ assassination.htm

Clark, Dorie: "How to Transform Difficult Relationships," November 27, 2013, http://www.forbes.com/sites/dorieclark/2013/11/27/how-to-transform-difficult-relationships/

Clark, Dorie: "Why Great Leaders Make Bad Managers—and That's OK," January 10, 2013, http://www.forbes.com/sites/dorieclark/2013/01/10/ why-great-leaders-make-bad-managers-and-thats-ok/

Community Policing Dispatch: "Police Labor Relations: Interest-Based Problem-Solving and the Power of Collaboration," September 2009, http://cops.usdoj.gov/html/dispatch/September_2009/labor_rela-tions.htm

Conley, Randy: "Three Words to Power Up Your Relationships," March 28, 2013, http://leaderchat.org/2013/03/28/three-words-to-power-up-your-relationships/

Constantino, J.: "How Do You Build Trust," March 22, 2011, http://businessmarketingsuccess.com/2011/03/22/how-do-you-build-trust

Courtney, Henry A.: "Thoughts on the Business of Life," undated, http://thoughts.forbes.com/thoughts/ego-henry-a-courtney-the-bigger-a

Covey, Stephen M. R.: *The Speed of Trust*, Free Press, 2006

Dale Carnegie Training: *Dale Carnegie's Golden Book*, 2011, http://c.ymcdn.com/sites/www.nshmba.org/resource/resmgr/2014Kickoff/Dale_Carnegie_Golden_Book-Se.pdf

Davenport, Tom: "The Big Lesson from Twelve Good Decisions," October 28, 2013, http://blogs.hbr.org/2013/10/the-big-lesson-from-twelve-good-decisions/

David, Susan and Congleton, Christina: "Emotional Agility," *Harvard Business Review*, November 8, 2013, http://hbr.org/2013/11/emotional-agility/ar/1

Deutschendorf, Harvey: "5 Ways to Spot an Emotionally Intelligent Leader," November 6, 2013, http://www.business2community.com/author/harvey-deutschendorf

Dillon, Karen: "HBR Guide to Office Politics," December 9, 2014, Harvard Business Review

Drucker, Peter: "Business and Organization Leadership Development," 2013, https://depts.washington.edu/leaders1/our-favorite-leadership-quotes/

Drucker, Peter: *Effective Executives*, 2006, Harper Business Essentials

Eikenberry, Kevin: "Seven Ways the Best Leaders Set an Example by Going First," August 22, 2011, http://blog.kevineikenberry.com/leadership/seven-ways-the-best-leaders-set-an-example-by-going-first/

Eliot, George: Good Reads, undated, http://www.goodreads.com/quotes/search?utf8=%E2%9C%93&q=Keep+true%2C+never+be+ashamed+of+doing+right%3B+decide+on+what+you+think+is+right+and+stick+to+it&commit=Search

Evans, Richard: *Management of the RCMP Disciplinary Process 2009–2010 Annual Report*, 2010, http://www.rcmp-grc.gc.ca/pubs/adj/ann-09-10/index-eng.htm

Exforsys Inc.: "How to Set an Example for Your Followers," July 22, 2006, http://www.exforsys.com/career-center/leadership-skills/how-to-set-an-example-for-your-followers.html

Farber, Steve: "Extreme Leadership," 2013, http://www.stevefarber.com/extreme-leadership/

Fink, Nicole: "The High Cost of Low Morale: How to Address Low Morale in the Workplace through Servant Leadership," March 20, 2014, *Leading Edge*, www.roberts.edu/Academics/AcademicDivisions/BusinessManagement/msl

Froschheiser, Lee: "Communication: The Most Important Key to Leadership Success," undated, http://www.reliableplant.com/Read/12675/communication-most-important-key-to-leadership-success

Fuller, Ed: "Treasure Your Relationships: They Are the Currency of Any Culture," January 17, 2014, http://www.forbes.com/sites/edfuller/2014/01/17/treasure-your-relationships-theyre-the-currency-of-any-culture/

Gardner, Howard E.: *Leading Minds: An Anatomy of Leadership*, 1996, Basic Books

Garner, Gerald W.: "Surviving the Circus: How Effective Leaders Work Well with the Media," March 2009, *Police Chief*, vol. 77, no. 3

Geneen, Harold S.: "Harold S. Geneen Quotes," undated, http://www. brainyquote.com/quotes/authors/h/harold_s_geneen.html

Gibbins, Roger: "Public Sector Resiliency; Striking the Balance," 2013, *Public Sector Management*, vol. 24, no. 2

Gillespie, Judith: "A Speech by Deputy Chief Constable of the PSNI Judith Gillespie," October 22, 2013, http://www.britishirish.org/speech-by-deputy-chief-constable-of-the-psni-judith-gillespie/

Gino, Francesca: "How Anxiety Can Lead Your Decisions Astray," October 29, 2013, http://blogs.hbr.org/2013/10/how-anxiety-can-lead-your-decisions-astray/

Gitomer, Jeffrey: "Good Reads," undated, http://www.goodreads.com/quotes/search?commit=Search&page=3&q=resilient&utf8=%E2%9C%93

Giuliani, Rudolph W.: *Leadership*, 2002, Miramax Books

Gower, Stephen: "What Do They See When They See You Coming?," 2014, http://www.stephengower.com/about/

Halsey, William F.: "Forbes Quotes Thoughts On The Business Of Life," undated, http://www.forbes.com/quotes/9820/

Harrison, T.: "Change Morale Improve Productivity," 2007, http://www. isa.org/InTechTemplate.cfm?Section=Career_Front1&template=/ ContentManagement/ContentDisplay.cfm&ContentID=61426

Hillier, Rick: *Leadership*, 2010, Harper Collins

Hope, John Middleton: *Challenges in Contemporary Police Leadership*, February 2007, International Police Executive Symposium, Working Paper no. 3, http://drr.lib.athabascau.ca/files/crjs/490/CRJS490Unit7JMH. pdf

Hubbard, Elbert: "A Message to Garcia," 1899, https://courses.csail.mit. edu/6.803/pdf/hubbard1899.pdf

Iacocca, Lee: *Where Have All the Leaders Gone?*, 2008, Scribner

International Association of Chiefs of Police, IACP: "News—Predicting and Surviving a No-Confidence Vote," July 2013, http://www. policechiefmagazine.org/magazine/index.cfm?fuseaction=display_ arch&article_id=1695&issue_id=122008

International Association of Chiefs of Police, IACP: "Model Policy on Standards of Conduct," Undated, http://www.theiacp.org/Model-Policy-on-Standards-of-Conduct

James, Geoffrey: "6 Habits of Extraordinary Bosses," 2013, http://www. inc.com/geoffrey-james/6-habits-of-extraordinary-bosses.html

James, Geoffrey: "10 Things Employees Want More Than a Raise," October 7, 2013, http://www.inc.com/geoffrey-james/10-things-employees-want-more-than-a-raise.html?goback=%2Egde_4501708_ member_5793713165820768260#%21

Johnson, Aisha M.: *The Impact of Managerial Emotional Intelligence Perceptions on the Occupational Well-Being of Employees in a Police Department*, November 2011, dissertation, Walden University

Johnson, Marguerite Ann: "Daily Quote,", undated, http://www.dailyquote.eu/maya_angelou/2

Jones, Larry: *Police and Media Relations: How to Bridge the Gap*, undated, http://www.fdle.state.fl.us/Content/getdoc/9a5940ba-6100-45e3-86a2-092f72480769/jones-larry-final-paper-(1).aspx

Josephson, Michael: "12 Ethical Principles for Business Executives," December 12, 2010, http://josephsoninstitute.org/business/blog/2010/12/12-ethical-principles-for-business-executives/

Kanter, Rosabeth Moss: "Cultivate a Culture of Confidence," *Harvard Business Review*, April 1, 2011, http://hbr.org/product/cultivate-a-culture-of-confidence/an/F1104E-PDF-ENG

Kanter, Rosabeth Moss: "Great Leaders Know When to Forgive," *Harvard Business Review*, February 26, 2013, http://blogs.hbr.org/2013/02/great-leaders-know-when-to/

Kanter, Rosabeth Moss: "Ten Reasons People Resist Change," *Harvard Business Review*, September 25, 2012, http://blogs.hbr.org/2012/09/ten-reasons-people-resist-chang/

Keating, Steve: "The Difference between Managing and Leading," 2013, http://stevekeating.me/2013/11/08/the-difference-between-managing-and-leading/?goback=%2Egde_4501708_member_5806780244975181828#%2

Keyser, John: "14 Tips for Developing 'Leadership Presence,'" January 8, 2014, http://www.theglasshammer.com/news/2014/01/08/14-tips-

for-developing-leadership-presence/?goback=%2Egde_4501708_
member_5827459087717117953#%21

Kotter, John: "Management Is (Still) Not Leadership," 2013, http://blogs.
hbr.org/2013/01/management-is-still-not-leadership/

Krause, Thomas R. and Hidley, John: "Accountability as a Best Practice,"
August 10, 2013, http://www.bstsolutions.com/gb/resources/knowl-
edge-resource/accountability-as-a-best-practice

Krogerus, Mikael and Tschappeler, Roman: *The Decision Book—Fifty Models for Strategic Thinking*, 2008, Profile Books

Landau, Heinz: "Knowing Your Employees," September 14, 2012, http://
www.thecareguys.com/2012/09/14/knowing-your-employees/

Landers, Diane: "12 Steps to Leadership Success," March 2012, http://
www.cenews.com/article/8750/12-steps-to-leadership-success

LinkedIn: "What Amazing Leaders Do Differently," August 19, 2013,
http://www.linkedin.com/today/post/article/20130819115750-
7374576-7-things-amazing-leaders-do-differently

Lipman, Victor: "3 Simple Questions to Help Ensure Effective Employee Evaluations," February 12, 2013, http://www.forbes.com/
sites/victorlipman/2013/12/02/3-simple-questions-to-help-insure-
effective-employee-evaluations/?goback=%2Egde_4501708_mem-
ber_5814021361563099138#%21

Lipman, Victor: "Suggestions for Managing Someone You Don't (Truth
Be Told) Really Like," March 12, 2013, http://www.forbes.com/sites/
victorlipman/2013/12/03/suggestions-on-managing-someone-truth-
be-told-you-dont-really-like/

Lopis, Glenn: "7 Reasons Employees Don't Trust Their Leaders," December 9, 2013, http://www.forbes.com/sites/glennllopis/2013/12/09/7-reasons-employees-dont-trust-their-leaders/#

Lorenz, Mary: "The One Thing Every Great Leader Must Do?," February 22, 2011, http://thehiringsite.careerbuilder.ca.php53-21.ord1-1.websitetestlink.com/2011/02/22/the-one-thing-every-great-leader-must-do/

MacArthur, Douglas: "Douglas MacArthur Quotes", undated, http://www.goodreads.com/quotes/359193-a-true-leader-has-the-confidence-to-stand-alone-the

Madwed, Sidney: "The Quotations Page", undated, http://www.quotationspage.com/search.php3?homesearch=madwed&page=2

Maguire, Stephen and Dyke, Lorraine: *CACP Professionalism in Policing Research Project*, 2012, http://www.cacp.ca/media/library/download/1242/Survey_Results.pdf

Malcolm X: "Malcolm X Quotes", undated, http://www.goodreads.com/quotes/74430-the-media-s-the-most-powerful-entity-on-earth-they-have

Manciagli, Dana: *4 biggest challenges facing business leaders today*, The Business Journals, April 13, 2016, http://www.bizjournals.com/bizjournals/bio/16631/Dana+Manciagli+

Marston, Cam: *Motivating the "What's in It for Me?" Workforce*, 2010, http://www.fsbmedia.com/article_display.php?article_id=250

Marston, Ralph: "Inspirational Sayings and Quotes," undated http://www.starstuffs.com/inspirational_sayings/ralph_marston.htm

Maxwell, John C.: *Ultimate Leadership: 21 Irrefutable Laws, Developing the Leader within You*, 2007, Thomas Nelson Inc.

May, Rob: "How to Be a Good Leader: Be Fair," February 3, 2007, http://www.businesspundit.com/how-to-be-a-good-leader-be-fair/

McCarthy, Dan: "10 Reasons Why Managers Are Clueless about Leadership," December 2013, http://www.greatleadershipbydan.com/2013/12/10-reasons-why-managers-are-clueless.html?goback=%2Egde_4501708_member_5823139792002506755#%21

McCormack, Lee: "Striking the Innovation Bargain," *Canadian Government Executive*, May 2012, http://www.canadiangovernmentexecutive.ca/management/risk/item/329-striking-the-innovation-bargain.html

McKeown, Les: "4 Signs You Will Fail as a Leader, Inc.," January 28, 2013, http://www.inc.com/les-mckeown/4-signs-youre-a-weak-leader-.html

McKeown, Les: "The 20 Most Powerful Words in Business," July 15, 2013, http://www.inc.com/les-mckeown/the-most-powerful-20-words-in-business.html

Merino, Melinda: "You Can't Be a Wimp—Make the Tough Calls: An Interview with Ram Charan," November 2013, http://hbr.org/2013/11/you-cant-be-a-wimp-make-the-tough-calls/ar/1

Mills-Scofield, Deborah: "Four Lessons from the Best Bosses I Ever Had," September 2012, http://blogs.hbr.org/2012/09/four-lessons-from-the-best-bo/?goback=%2Egmp_4501708#%21

Murnighan, J. Keith: *Do Nothing! How to Stop Overmanaging and Become a Great Leader*, 2012, Penguin Group

Myatt, Mike: "Businesses don't fail, leaders do", January 12, 2012, http://www.forbes.com/sites/mikemyatt/2012/01/12/businesses-dont-fail-leaders-do/#2c78f3416b91

Myatt, Mike: "The 1 Reason Leadership Development Fails," December 19, 2012, http://www.forbes.com/sites/mikemyatt/2012/12/19/the-1-reason-leadership-development-fails/

Myatt, Mike: "Why You're Not a Leader," January 23, 2013, http://www.forbes.com/sites/mikemyatt/2013/01/23/why-youre-not-a-leader/

National Executive Institute Associates: *The Chief and the Union: Building a Better Relationship*, June 1999, http://www.neiassociates.org/storage/ChiefUnion-BuildingBetterRelationship-labor.pdf

Nohria, Nitin: "Nitin Nhria Quotes", undated, http://en.thinkexist.com/quotation/communication_is_the_real_work_of_leadership/147111.html

O'Toole, James: ""Leader"...an Earned Title – Not Given", Octopber 11, 2012, https://seekingexcellence.wordpress.com/2012/10/11/leader-an-earned-title-not-given/

Ontario Provincial Police Veterans' Association: "Mission Statement,", undated, http://www.oppva.ca

AmazonPerkins, Dennis N. T.: *Leading at the Edge: Leadership Lessons from the Extraordinary Saga of Shackleton's Antarctic Expedition* (second edition), 2013, http://syncreticsgroup.com/leading-at-the-edge/

Pershing, John J.: "Quotes about Motivation", undated, http://govleaders.org/quotes.htm

Phillips, Donald T.: *Lincoln on Leadership*, 1993, Business Plus

Powell, Colin: *A Leadership Primer*, undated, http://www.blaisdell.com/powell/

Psychology Today: "All about Resilience," accessed September 5, 2013, http://www.psychologytoday.com/basics/resilience

Rocky Balboa, Metro-Goldwyn-Mayer (MGM), Revolution Studios, 2006, Columbia Pictures

Rohn, Jim: "The four building blocks of good communication," June 12, 2016, http://www.success.com/article/rohn-the-4-building-blocks-of-good-communication

Rotary International: "Guiding Principles", undated, https://www.rotary.org/myrotary/en/learning-reference/about-rotary/guiding-principles

Ruhl, Dick: "Resilience in Challenging Times—4 Tips for Staying in the Game," March 30, 2013, http://leaderchat.org/2013/03/30/resilience-in-challenging-times-4-tips-for-staying-in-the-game

Ruskin, John: "Greats Books Online—Quotations," undated, http://www.bartleby.com/348/704.html

Saint Cyr, Christopher: "Two Things Leaders Care About," October 29, 2013, http://christopherstcyr.wordpress.com/2013/10/29/two-things-leaders-care-about/

Sandburg, Carl: "Carl Sandburg Quotes", undated, http://www.brainyquote.com/quotes/quotes/c/carlsandbu281336.html#1ulabgYkJYTUuruG.99

Sarkis, Stephanie: "Here, There, and Everywhere: Time Management and Organization Skills from an ADD Expert," February 24, 2011, http://www.psychologytoday.com/blog/here-there-and-everywhere/201102/36-quotes-leadership

Sarkis, Stephanie: "A Good Boss Is a Good Leader, Quotes" May 14, 2011, http://www.psychologytoday.com/blog/here-there-and-everywhere/201105/good-boss-is-good-leader-quotes

Schachter, Harvey: "The Hands-off Approach to Leadership," *Globe and Mail*, August 14, 2012, http://www.theglobeandmail.com/report-on-business/careers/the-hands-off-approach-to-leadership/article4480738/

Schachter, Harvey: "The Leader's Bookshelf," *Canadian Government Executive*, 2013, http://www.canadiangovernmentexecutive.ca/component/k2/item/8-why-people-fail.html

Sharma, Robin: "The Leadership Hub Daily," March 15, 2013, http://www.theleadershiphub.com/

Shawn: "The Quest for Resilience," *Cross Border Journal*, June 27, 2006, http://www.xborderjournal.com/

Shell Corporation: "Shell's Leadership Develops the Best People to Secure Global Future Energy," 2012, http://www.shell.com/kwt/aboutshell/media-centre/news-and-media-releases/2012/global-future-energy.html

Simmons, Michael: "If You Want to Go Fast, Go Alone. If You Want to Go Far, Go Together," May 22, 2013, http://www.forbes.com/sites/michaelsimmons/2013/07/22/power-of-relational-thinking/2/

Sirolli, Carmen: *Bargaining Units Vs. Management: Are Police Unions Necessary?*, February 2008, http://www.fdle.state.fl.us/cms/FCJEI/Programs1/SLP/Documents/Full-Text/sirolli-carmen-final-paper.aspx

Sohn, Paul: "Interview with David Burkus: The Myths of Creativity," November 20, 2013, http://paulsohn.org/interview-with-david-burkus-the-myths-of-creativity/

Squire, Des: "Catch the High Tide to Productivity," June 2014, http://www.hrfuture.net/on-the-cover/catch-the-high-tide-to-productivity.php?Itemid=33

Starkey, Bob: "Be a Leader—12 Habits plus One," May 23, 2011, http://hoopthoughts.blogspot.ca/2011/05/bill-walsh-be-leader-12-habits-plus-one.html

Stewart, Potter: "Potter Stewart Quotes", undated, http://www.brainyquote.com/quotes/quotes/p/potterstew390058.html#e0DSpzkBl1YMTbEm.99

Stover, Teresa: "The Awakening by Max Igan," December 6, 2012, http://softnvid.wordpress.com/2012/12/06/

Swindoll, Charles R.: "Quote by Charles R. Swindoll", undated, http://www.quotery.com/life-is-10-what-happens-to-me-and-90-how/

Taggart, Jim: "The Leader Sets the Tone," July 1, 2013, http://www.theleadershiphub.com/blogs/leader-sets-tone

Thorsborne, Margaret: *Integrity: The Seven Heavenly Virtues of Leadership*, 2003, Australian Institute of Management, McGraw-Hill

Tracy, Brian: "Positive Quotes," undated, http://www.positivelypositive.com/quotes/successful-people-are-always-looking-for-opportunities-to-help-others-unsuccessful-people-are-always-asking-whats-in-it-for-me/

Tredgold, Gordon: "If You Want to Know Who to Blame Then Get a Mirror," September 4, 2012, http://www.leadership-principles.com/2012/09/04/if-you-want-to-know-whom-to-blame-then-get-a-mirror/

Tredgold, Gordon: "The Impact of Bad Bosses," June 10, 2013, http://www.theleadershiphub.com/blogs/impact-bad-bosses

Tredgold, Gordon: "Politics and Leadership, the Uncomfortable Mix," August 18, 2013, http://www.theleadershiphub.com/blogs/politics-and-leadership-uncomfortable-mix

Tredgold, Gordon: "You Can Fool Others, but You Can't Lie to Yourself," September 21, 2013, http://www.theleadershiphub.com/blogs/you-can-fool-others-you-cant-lie-yourself

Tripathi, Pankaj: "Interview: OPP Commissioner Chris D. Lewis," September 25, 2012, *TopSpot, Tomorrow's OPS Today*, vol. 6, no. 2

University of Maryland: "Setting the Example," December 31, 2013, http://www.sas.umd.edu/~jlemich/leadership/example.html

US Department of Justice Community Policing Dispatch: "Police Labor Relations: Interest-Based Problem-Solving and the Power of Collaboration," September 2009, http://cops.usdoj.gov/html/dispatch/September_2009/index.htm

Vancouver RCMP Veterans: "Gone but Not Forgotten," September 25, 2016, http://www.rcmpveteransvancouver.com/sept-25-30-gone-but-not-forgotten/

Viesturs, Ed: "No Shortcuts to the Top—Challenging the World's 14 Highest Peaks", 2007, W.W. Norton & Co.

Welch, Jack: "Top Leadership Tips," August 20, 2008, http://www.freshbusinessthinking.com/top-leadership-tips/

Welch, Jim: "The real reasons why employees leave", April 29, 2008, http://www.computerdealernews.com/news/the-real-reasons-why-employees-leave/14269

Palazzolo, Piera: "Why Engaged Employees Can Make or Break Your Business," August, 18, 2014, https://www.linkedin.com/pulse/20140818144624-4830871-why-engaged-employees-can-make-or-break-your-business

Williams, Ray: "Why Leadership Development Fails to Produce Good Leaders," 2013, http://business.financialpost.com/executive/why-leadership-development-fails-to-produce-good-leaders

Williams, Robin: "George W Quotes", undated, http://www.brainyquote.com/quotes/keywords/george_w.html

Wilson, Alan M.: *Policing Ireland's Twisted History*, 2011, iUniverse

Wooden, John: Quotes Alarm, September 5, 2016, https://twitter.com/quotesalarm/status/772902258497429504

Zenger, Jack: "Ethics in Leadership: The 8 Rules to Prevent Misuse of Corporate Power," June 20, 2012, http://www.forbes.com/sites/

jackzenger/2012/06/20/ethics-in-leadership-the-8-rules-to-protect-corporate-power/

Zorbas, Nikk: "Living with Integrity," March 4, 2013, *Mesquite Local News*, http://mesquitelocalnews.com/

ABOUT THE AUTHOR

• • •

CHRIS D. LEWIS, COMMISSIONER (RET.), Ontario Provincial Police, was born and raised in Sault Ste. Marie, Ontario, Canada. He began to keenly observe leadership while playing high school sports, then during three years of working on commercial ships on the Great Lakes, Lewis was inspired by the leadership ability of the ships' commanders.

He then began his police career as a constable in the Ontario Provincial Police, Canada's second-largest police force in 1978 and was named commissioner 32 years later.

Lewis served throughout Ontario in numerous challenging operational and command roles, including as the director of criminal intelligence for

Ontario's Ministry of the Solicitor General and on secondment with the Royal Canadian Mounted Police.

Commissioner Lewis retired in 2014 and joined CTV as a public safety analyst. His commentary is regularly featured on Bell Media television and radio programs.

Lewis lives with his wife, Angie Howe, near Barrie, Ontario. Angie currently serves as a Chief Superintendent in the OPP. They have two grown daughters.

CPSIA information can be obtained
at www.ICGtesting.com
Printed in the USA
LVOW10s0014120917
548294LV00014B/2017/P

9 781535 154468